**TERRY SUTTON**

# GIVE ME THE CHILD
## BRIAN ELKS

WHEN I was a cub reporter more than 50 years ago I remember my senior colleagues speaking in hushed tones about the death of a "local hero".

His name was Jack Elks and he was secretary and agent of the National Union of Mineworkers in Kent, in the days when there were four collieries in the area.

People spoke with respect about Jack Elks. Some considered him a dangerous left-winger. But others knew he fought hard for those who toiled 3,000 feet under the green fields of Kent.

Jack died in 1950 in Buckland Hospital and is buried at St James' cemetery. Scores of mourners walked behind 56 bandsmen as the cortege moved from the NUM offices in Maison Dieu Road to the cemetery.

Now his grandson Brian Elks, 67, who was born in Temple Ewell and lives in Oxfordshire, has written a heart-tugging story about Jack Elks. Warts and all.

His book, Give me the Child (£10), details the slog Jack had to educate himself as an 11-year-old pit boy in Bloxwich, Staffordshire (where he was born in 1885) and how he came to East Kent to work at the doomed Shakespeare Colliery.

The yarn spares no punches as the author paints a pretty grim picture about the way Jack treated his wife and family while he climbed the ladder of trade union authority.

But maybe that's how many men behaved in those days when jobs were scarce and poverty reigned.

The author – whose father worked at Snowdown – comments in his prologue about his "forbidding" grandfather: "More's the pity he could not show affection himself. If he ever knew love or truly loved anyone we shall never know."

Author Brian Elks weaves an extremely interesting and accurate story path through the ups and downs of the Kent coalfield. He acknowledges much of the information came from the columns of the Dover Express.

The book is written in partly fiction style, but well laced with fact, and is a must for anyone with an interest in the Kent coalfield.

For those who think they are hard done by in this world today, a read of this book might convince them how lucky they are.

And that's thanks to trade unionists like John "Jack" Elks. A canny trade unionist who won battles through education and not through brawn.

● Give Me The Child (ISBN 0 9540236-1-7) can be obtained from the author at 12 Cheshire Road, Thame, Oxfordshire OX9 3LQ.

# GIVE ME THE CHILD

By

Brian Elks

An Early Story of the Kent Coalfield

First published in 2002 by Brian A F Elks
12 Cheshire Road
Thame, Oxon
OX9 3LQ
United Kingdom
Tel: 01844 – 214361

ISBN  0 9540236-1-7

Cover design by Peter Aylward, 18 Cheshire Road, Thame, Oxon

Printed and bound by Antony Rowe Ltd
Bumper's Farm, Chippenham
Wiltshire  SN14 6LH
United Kingdom

This story relates to events both in and surrounding the life of John 'Jack' Elks, born in Bloxwich, Staffordshire in 1885. It is written for his children's children and those to follow, for as long as they care to remember and to understand the way it was, yesteryear.

Ignatius Loyola was the founder of the Jesuits and was born in 1491. After his death he was made a saint. His Jesuit army, the soldiers of Jesus, was feared and respected for its single-mindedness, dedication and devotion to duty. He knew that the years of childhood were the formative ones. Those early years that shaped character and allegiances and would last a lifetime. Ideas, aspirations and inspirations would be indelibly printed deep in the mind, impossible to erase.

'Give me the child, until seven,' he would say, 'and I will give you the man.'

Parents show a child the way, so by example lead
Minds guide and shape so as a shepherd heed
To encouragement and hope, love and measured care
Children are your gift to life do not stint or pare
Sow harmony, fair discipline the essence of good bands
Direct and hold all young life precious in your hands
Parents should remember this throughout a childhood span
'Give me the child – and I'll give you the man.'

Author's Acknowledgements

The Dover Express, 1914 to 1950

The records of the Kent Miners Association held in
the County Archives, Kent County Council, Maidstone

The records and history of the Miners Federation
of Great Britain and NUM, 1889 to 1947

My memories of growing up in a mining community:-

A world of people bonded together by hardship and
common danger;
people who stood shoulder to shoulder;
the sharing of sorrows and joys;
the sociability of the working men's club;
and last but not least, those men and women of the mining
community of Kent, who, late in life, made me welcome,
shared their memories and advised me where to look.

Brian A F Elks, Oct 2001

Other books by the author:

Light a Candle
My Heart and I

## THE KENT COALFIELD

About 1850 a coalfield was established near Calais in France. It was thought the seams might run across to southern England. An abortive drilling at Battle in Sussex closed off further action. Just after 1880 an attempt was made to create a channel tunnel. When this was stopped for military reasons the equipment was put to use to drill for coal and about 1890 a seam was found. The resulting Shakespeare Colliery, at Dover, was a failure but drillings elsewhere proved more favourable. Snowdown Colliery was the first mine which went into production on the 19th November 1912 and within two months over 800 tons of coal were being produced each week. The Tilmanstone Colliery had started earlier but mining problems and lack of finance prevented proper output until late 1914. In 1919 the first coal was raised at Chislet. For many years the costs of mining exceeded the value of the coal produced and both Snowdown and Tilmanstone came close to closing. Production at Betteshanger started in 1927. Because of severe housing shortages the owners were forced to build new homes at Elvington, Woolage, Aylesham, Mill Hill by Deal, Betteshanger and Hersden.

From the beginning, until well after 1950 when this book ends, there was continuing talk of expansion and new pits. Recessions, competition and production difficulties prevented this from happening. By 1990 not only had the mines closed but also almost every trace of their existence had gone, despite the fact that reserves were estimated at nearly 2000 million tons of coal. In its heyday it provided jobs for over 7,000 men plus all the ancillary support that must have been needed. In the process of closure the old mining communities were decimated and tossed aside in the name of progress.

# Contents

Prologue

Chapter 1     The Anvil of Life

Chapter 2     Jack the Lad

Chapter 3     The Canal Tavern

Chapter 4     The Garden of England

Chapter 5     Honest Jack from Kent

Chapter 6     The Years of Struggle

Chapter 7     The War Years and After

Epilogue

## PROLOGUE

When John, 'Jack', Elks eventually found his niche in life he gave his energy, wit and devotion in support of that which he knew best. The miners. Hard working men of the coal pits that he had grown up with, worked, roistered and played with – in particular, the miners of Kent. Those men were often thought of as lowly, ignorant men, fit for nothing else and paid a pittance often, to do a dangerous and dirty job; despised by their so called 'betters'. In their defence he worked a twelve hour day, six days a week with almost no recorded holidays, for over 30 years. He also gained what he wished for, power. Power for himself, maybe, but also for those he represented. He knew enough of poor pay, poverty and bad conditions first hand, so he became a socialist and an early supporter of the Labour Party. But that socialism arose from a deep conviction that social justice is not freely given but must come from political action.

When he died, many ordinary folk expressed deep gratitude for what he had done and spoke out their affection for him. More's the pity he could not show affection himself. If he ever knew love or truly loved anyone we shall never know. Were he to have done so, his life would have been better for it. Three bands led his funeral and hundreds of working men showed their respect by travelling dozens of miles, as well as losing a day's pay, to stand in silence at his graveside. I can still remember that day when, as a boy of fifteen, I saw grown men weep. At the time I wondered why? After all, he was only my grandfather and a rather forbidding one at that! Having researched his life and written this story I can understand. Now I know. It was love.

Only four months after the funeral I left home to join the army. The 'pit' was not going to be my life! Not today, not tomorrow, not ever! But the desire for social justice, ingrained from early childhood, has never left me.

# Chapter 1

## THE ANVIL OF LIFE

## 1890

The children in the street had taunted Jeremiah as he had left home to walk to the colliery. In fact they seemed to like tormenting him and laughed out loud if he stumbled or cursed them. But it was soon over, they lost interest at the end of the street. Later in the day darkness was closing in as Jeremiah walked slowly back to the small cottage in the row of huddled homes on the edge of Bloxwich. His crippled leg and twisted arm made for slow progress and the cold air penetrated his thin, threadbare clothes. In his good hand he held a small bag containing about four pounds of coal fragments, the result of hours of work picking over the spoil heap by the colliery. Competition from children and other men had made his task harder, only the kindness of a passing haulier in letting a few pieces of coal fall from a tub had made his time worthwhile. There had been a time when he could have competed with the best of them but the collapse of a tunnel roof had put paid to that, thereafter he could only earn a few shillings a week working at menial jobs such as a watchman and so on. Now even that was beyond him. He shivered in the cold and wished he had a coat but that had gone to the pawnshop along with the rest of his possessions as he and Mary had eked out a precarious existence. His cheap fob watch had gone first, then the furniture, and then the beds as they struggled to survive. The heart rebelled but his brain told him it was the end of the road. They would endure somehow but the hope had gone, to be replaced by despair.

As he reached the door and let himself in, Mary, his wife came to meet him.

"I was so worried about you - you have been so long!"

He gave her the small bag and embraced her. Mary was only fifty but was aged and withered, her hair grey and her face pinched. Not that he saw that, he remembered the dark-haired, laughing, bright-eyed girl he had courted and the day he had asked her to marry him and she said "What took you so long!" To him she was still twenty and he had never, could never have wanted anyone else. Mary placed the coal in the grate and lit the wood, very carefully. As the wood flared she tore up the box that had held the matches and fed it to the flames. That was her last match. "There, that will go now." She gently blew on the flames, her lips pursed.

There was a half-inch of candle on the mantel over the grate. Mary went to light the candle but thought better of it.

"I'll save the candle for later, when it gets properly dark. Sit yourself down now. I have a pinch of tea to make a cup for you."

Jeremiah eased himself down on the stool, the only furniture they had left.

"Yes," said Mary, "you ease your leg while I get the kettle on the fire." That done she pulled her shawl around her shoulders and sat down on the floor beside him. Jeremiah could hardly bear the words but he had to say them.

"This is the last night we will be together my love, I have let you down. When we leave tomorrow it will be the worst day of my life." She put her head on his knee and gazed at the fire. "I am so ashamed to bring you to-to-to this." His voice faltered as he spoke.

Mary's voice was very low as she answered. "It's God's will. There would have been a comfort had the children lived. How I would have loved a grandchild." They had been blessed with six children and not one had lived beyond the age of five. Jeremiah stroked her hair, knowing how the memory of the children made her heart ache. He wished he could remember them but time had erased the memory of their faces.

Mary stirred. "There's a piece of bread, Jeremiah, you must be hungry."

"I couldn't eat it, it will be too hard for my teeth."

"I will put some hot water on it. You must eat. We have a long walk tomorrow."

Tomorrow it was the workhouse or starve, they would have to live in separate parts of the house, he with the men and she with the women. They would meet only for a few hours on a Sunday. Within those walls they would live and die but not together.

They sat in silence for a while each trying to find words of comfort. The only sound came from the fire as it crackled into life throwing flickering shadows around the kitchen. Jeremiah's voice trembled as he spoke.

"The bailiff will be here in the morning, Mary. Then we must go. I could bear it if we were to be together - I had thought of the open road but we are too old for that."

"We have had many good years, Husband. Soon another family will be here and there will be laughter in this house again."

"But not more love, Mary, there will never be more love."

She squeezed his hand. "Shush you now - you will make me cry."

They were both awake when the loud bang sounded on the front door. Already Jeremiah had shaved in cold water and Mary had cleared the grate and packed their few possessions in a bag. She went to the door. The Bailiff put his cudgel under his arm and thrust a piece of paper at her.

"Unless you pay the back rent of nine shillings you will leave now - also there's two shillings for my fee!"

Jeremiah limped to the door. "We have no money."

"Then get out!" The Bailiff strode into the cottage and

looked around. "Is this all you've got?" Picking up the stool and kettle he stared hard at Mary. "These are mine." He grabbed Mary's hand. "Where's yer ring?"

Her wedding ring was the only thing Mary possessed and knowing what was to come she had sewn it in her bodice the night before. She could not part with that.

"Pawned."

Mary took Jeremiah by the arm and they stepped out into the street. As she did so the Bailiff took the bag from her. "You won't need that. It'll be the workhouse garb for you. You know where it is?"

Jeremiah nodded. A seven-mile walk lay in front of them.

While this was going on a large crowd of children assembled and started jeering and shouting. Jack saw his chance and pulled the hair of several girls, making them scream. Then the children started dancing around and chanting and Jack was one of the ringleaders in all this. What great fun! "Paupers, paupers, going to the workhouse! Paupers, paupers, going to the workhouse!"

Then as Jeremiah and Mary walked away the chant changed. "Cripple, cripple, the old man's a cripple! Hipple, pipple, the old fool's a cripple!"

This day the taunts followed them for two streets until their tormentors lost interest. At that moment, one of the girls whose hair had been pulled gave a hard kick. "I hate you Jack Elks, you're a pig!" Jack turned to give battle. His Ma had told him, "Don't come home crying, stick up for yourself - or you'll get my hand as well."

## 1895

Lizzie had been born Elizabeth but the only day she had been called anything other than Lizzie had been on her wedding day and then only once. She had just fetched the coalscuttle from the yard and banked up the range fire, noting in the process that they were nearly out of fuel. That added to her bad temper. Her back ached from the constant work. Only that morning she had carried a twenty-pound sack of flour home from the grocer and the muscles in her arms still felt knotted.  She had been up at five, as usual, to prepare Bill's breakfast after lighting the range fire.  Then there was his snap-tin and tea-can to do, ready to see him off at six.

This had been followed by the making of dough for baking later in the day, just in time to get the kids up for school, breakfasted and dressed.  When they had gone there had been the baking, shopping and a tub of washing.  Most of the washing was still draped around the kitchen range in a vain endeavour to get it dry before the evening when she must do the ironing.  All this was interrupted by the children home from school for dinner and now, with so much to do they were due home again shortly.  Why do they need to go to school, she thought, when they could be helping here?  That damn fool husband of hers; drat you Bill Elks for insisting they all go to school.  A fat lot of good it would do them!  What good was school when they would go down the pit or to the pottery or the leather works?  Lots of kids missed school; she knew at least eight sent to work instead of school.  Her frustration increased as she thought of the eight pence a week to pay the school fees for the four boys.  The oldest girl, Emma was working as a domestic servant at sixpence a day.  Out from seven in the morning until seven at night.  She had been of great help to her before but now the pitiful small wage was of more use to the family than a helping hand.

As Elizabeth put the scuttle down the pain in her stomach made her pause and bile rose in her throat.  All this to do and pregnant yet again.  Damn Bill again.  When Bill proposed she had jumped at the chance.  "Lucky to get a man," her father, Levi Martin, had said, "a sour faced beggar like you!"  After years of servitude and drudgery nothing could get worse was her opinion.  So she had accepted and one life of drudgery had been exchanged for another and the smile lines on her face were missing.  As the stomach pains receded she noticed the kitchen floor needed cleaning; wearily she fetched a bucket and brush.  Today was

Friday and her temper did not improve even at the thought that it would soon be Sunday when, with Bill off work and no school for the kids, she would have a slightly easier day. Though she didn't know it, it had been nearly twenty years since she had smiled.

The day had started badly for Jack. First he had got into trouble with his Ma for being tardy about getting out of bed. Then he had not been paying attention when the Class Register was called and he failed to respond promptly. The other children had giggled and Mr. Aspen, the teacher, had not been amused. He was a strong believer in firm discipline. There were eighty boys and girls in the single classroom, with the small children at one end under the eyes of a side teacher and the older children under the vigilant eye of Mr. Aspen at the other. "Come here immediately, Elks." So in front of the whole school Jack had bent over and received a double thrash of the cane across his backside. He had no pants on under the thin trousers and it hurt. He desperately wanted to rub his buttocks to relieve the pain but dare not move. Mr. Aspen, cane still in hand, stared at him coldly. Not a single sound or noise emanated from any of the assembled children.

"What were you dreaming about, Elks?"

"Don't know, Sir."

"Don't add dumb insolence to your bad manners!"

The cane swished menacingly so Jack decided to come clean. "About leaving school, Sir."

"Yes, you'll be free to leave soon. There'll be no dreaming then! You'll not get paid for dreaming. If you get a job there will be no dreaming! Hard work, boy, not dreaming! Do not fill your head with dreams!"

Jack worked hard at his punishment for the rest of the day, penning out the words in his copybook in his best copperplate writing. He wrote the sentence out many times.

*Emancipation does not make man. Emulate your betters and above all learn good manners.*

Jack couldn't understand most of it, so the message was rather lost on him.

Come four thirty Jack and his brothers Len, Ernie and Billy walked home from school together, pleased to be released for the weekend. Rain had just started to patter down but that didn't dampen their spirits as they chased and kicked a tin can along the road. They would have loved to stop in the street to play but they were under strict instructions to go straight home. Ma was waiting for them and woe betides them if they disobeyed. Jack reached the kitchen door first and raised the latch; he opened the door cautiously. Ma was on her knees scrubbing the floor and she looked even more sour faced and angry than usual. Hearing the noise she looked round; the scrubbing brush hit the floor with a bang. She growled it out, "Don't come in till the floor's dry!"

Jack momentarily relaxed and went to close the door.

"Wait there, all of you! Jack, there's tuppence there." She pointed to the dresser. "Take that and get two buckets of coal from Atkinsons' yard."

Jack groaned to himself, it was a long walk to the yard.

"And while you're out get some segs put in Len's boots."

Jack picked up the two pennies and put them in his pocket as Ma arched her back and eased her shoulders, glaring at Jack meanwhile.

"What you do at school today?"

"Copy writing, Ma."

Ma sniffed. "Umph! - Fat lot of good that'll do yer."

Jack knew she did not approve of schooling, she had said so often enough. As she had made plain, she could see no point in it.

"You should be out earning a wage - be more use!"

All four boys kept quiet knowing better than to speak. Ma waved a reddened hand at them and then brushed a wisp of hair from her face. "Bin lis'ning to your father again - eh?" She waved them away and returned to her scrubbing. "Off you go then - and straight back, mind you. When you're back fill the bath with water ready for your father so he can have a wash when he gets home."

They all edged out of the doorway and into the yard. They could hear her, still talking.

"Waste of time sending kids to school till they're eleven. And damn Bill for filling their heads with nonsense - no good will come of it!"

Jack and Len picked up the buckets and the four of them left the yard just as the heavy rain started. Within a hundred yards they were soaked. Not that they minded, they were away from Ma's sharp tongue for half an hour.

The Black Country was living up to its name, everywhere grey or black, except for rusting metal. Thick cloud blotted out the sun. In the colliery yard steam billowed from the engine house and drifted over the blackened ground. Miners emerging from the cage ran towards the pay office to avoid the rain as much as possible, their hobnailed boots throwing up gouts of dirty black water from the many puddles. The moleskin trousers they wore were so grimed that the raindrops couldn't penetrate and simply bounced off.

William Elks was oblivious to all this, for the moment he was safe in the office. The office was cold and damp but at least he was out of the rain. Bloxwich at its worst, he had considered minutes ago. The heavy rain pelting on the metal roof blotted out the noises in the yard. The single window was grimed, it had never been cleaned and now condensation was building up, reducing the light even further. William's view of the yard was becoming more obscured by the minute. Not that it mattered now as he had completed the day's tally roll. His job was to log everything that went into and out of the mine. The office desk was high with a sloping top to aid writing and was crudely made from battered and worn wood. Long ago, William had pushed it nearer the window to maximise the light. In front of the desk

William sat perched on a high stool, his elbows on the desktop and the end of his pen pursed in his lower lip. He was deep in thought. The big round clock on the back wall showed twenty past five and was ticking the seconds away. His right foot rested on the desk rail; the other leg with its peg-leg attachment just hung down. Getting up on the high stool was difficult but after years of practice he could manage it without falling over. In much the same way he no longer needed a crutch to walk, though a walking stick was useful on stairs.

William's mind was on the coming local election and in particular the committee meeting he would attend that evening. The minutes of the last meeting were securely fastened in his coat pocket. Much as he would have loved to take them out and read them that was far too dangerous. If the Colliery Manager or Overman were to see him it could well mean the sack. They frowned on any political involvement by a staff man. Oh, if only we had a reforming man like Joe Chamberlain on the council, he thought, we could do wonders just like in Birmingham. Not like the damn landowners we have. The latest rumours on the election front were troubling. It appeared that another candidate had suddenly emerged at the last minute. But who the hell was he? Where did he come from? It wouldn't be another Tory, of that he was certain. William just knew it meant trouble but the answers would have to wait till the evening meeting.

He chewed his pen top in exasperation. They had been so sure they could get their man elected this year. At the last election they had lost, then found that dozens of their natural supporters had failed to register; so over the last few years they had worked incessantly to make sure every potential supporter was on the roll. It seemed all they had to do was to roust them all out on polling day. At least now the opposition couldn't spend money on free drink and divert people away from the poll-stations and into the public houses. In theory, he considered, we should cakewalk this one. We've just got to get the Tories out and get some better schools, roads and services. The cottage hospital was a disgrace.

He touched his peg-leg at the thought and shuddered at the remembered pain. What's more they had thrown him out after four days to fend for himself. Four days after an amputation! Before that he been earning top wages but a rock fall had ended his career as a miner. Rotten luck too because it was after that he had met Elizabeth. She must have been desperate to take up with a crippled man; little did he know what a sharp tongue she had! Still you made your bed and lay on it, he reflected. Lucky for him, as a boy, his father could afford the fees for elementary school and he had developed a fair hand for writing and had been particularly good at sums. He had been duly grateful to be offered the clerk's job at the colliery because it was better than picking out slag on the screens as the coal was sorted. Especially in a slump, he had been lucky to find work. Mind you, he had been hurt inside to be offered a miserable twenty-one shillings per week but at least it was steady, so he put a brave face on it and appeared outwardly grateful. He quickly learned that the owners were miserable bastards, always complaining about wages and costs while they lived in mansions out in the country. Lord Enstone, the owner, had visited once and what a flap and nonsense there had been that day; then he only stayed a few minutes.

His reverie was abruptly interrupted as the door banged open and the colliery manager entered the office, dripping with rain. He looked angry, very angry, decided William.

"Bloody ungrateful troublemakers are at it again - complaining about dust! What they're complaining about I'm damned if I know. You can't dig coal without dust and that never hurt anyone!" Joseph Hardcastle shook his bowler hat vigorously, glaring at William all the time, then put it on a peg. William maintained a judicious silence, knowing he was not required to respond. A finger jabbed at him.

"You heard owt, Elks?"

William shook his head. When Mr. Hardcastle was in this mood it was best to be discreet. William knew that complaints

18

had been made to the Overman in charge of the shift. However, prior to that, as he did his daily count at the weighing machine he had noted the mounting volume of dust coming up from the mine in the transport tubs, before they were tipped onto the screens for sorting. He was told and could see, that the tubs coming up the shaft were full of dust. At every place the coal was shovelled, transported, tipped and sorted it was breaking up. The coal dust was useless, it couldn't be sold and the men didn't get paid for producing it. Mr. Hardcastle was not mollified by William's silence.

"Damn men must think we're made of money. We can't afford to have extra men to damp down the face and the roadways. If I hear any more of this nonsense there's going to be some sackings! Plenty of men at the gate each morning begging for work."

William was disturbed because he knew the dust was potentially explosive but also it got inside a man and might kill him slowly. There were no old men underground, he couldn't think of a man over forty working below but there were plenty on top working on the screens and picking slag, coughing their lives away. William knew that Mr. Hardcastle was aware of all this, as he was. The manager pulled out his fob watch and checked it against the office clock, then after carefully putting it away got out his pipe and tobacco. William knew what was coming next so he swung down from his stool, the tally roll in his hand.

"We could double the amount of water we're sending down with the returning tubs. I could tell the traffic foreman for you." William suggested.

"Yes, yes." Mr. Hardcastle was getting testy. "You got the week's figures for me, Elks?"

"Aye, all ready Mr. Hardcastle."

"How many tons today?"

"Two hundred and eighty tons."

Mr. Hardcastle sucked his teeth and scooped some tobacco into his pipe. "Good god, man. That makes only a thousand six hundred tons for the week! It's that damn union checkweigher isn't it! Doesn't know his job."

William and the union appointed checkweigher, weighed, counted and agreed all coal produced to ensure a fair calculation of the men's wages. Hardcastle always blamed the checkweigher whether production was up or down. William thought of saying that the checkweigher was more likely to over rather than underweigh. Certain it would do no good he kept quiet. The pipe waved at William again. "You sure of this, you're sure these figures are right?"

William reddened at the inference. "It's all correct Mr. Hardcastle, and double-checked. I all'us check me-sen."

William handed over the tally rolls, which were accepted without thanks, so he pulled his cap firmly down on his head.

"If you don't need me anymore, Mr. Hardcastle, I'll be on my way. Get my pay and be off home."

Outside the rain was still pelting down and he was thinking it would be a long wet walk home, then he stooped over and picked up his tea-can and snap-tin. Mr. Hardcastle lit his pipe and took a few gratifying puffs.

"Right, Elks. Before you go let the Overman know I want to see him." William nodded.

"Right now, mind you, not in half an hours time."

"Goodnight, Mr. Hardcastle." William got out while the going was good. There was no reply so he stepped out into the rain. Luckily the Overman, the man in charge of the shift, was on his way in so William was saved a journey. He pulled up his collar but it didn't help much. The Pay Office had a large overhanging porch where the men could queue. As William reached cover a collier was leaving. He was black from head to foot. William knew him, as he knew all the men at the pit.

"Hello Jim, off home now?"

Jim smiled and nodded. "Hello Bill, lovely weather for ducks, innit?" His mouth showed bright red, framing gleaming white teeth, against the blackness of his face.

William smiled back. "You won't need a bath tonight when you get home, not with this damn rain!" He stepped up and under cover gratefully, glad to be out of the rain again for a while, then he stomped along to the office hatch window and peered in. Herbert Morse, the pay clerk, was at the back of the office, picking up a ledger. "Hello Bert, it's me, Bill." Bert didn't look up.

"I know it's you Bill. I could hear your peg-leg all the way along the landing. Come on in."

One of the few privileges of being a clerk, thought William, was being allowed in the pay office. He let himself in while Herbert returned to his stool by the hatch. "Here's your money, Bill. You're the last today - sign here."

William pocketed the cash and signed his name. Herbert picked up two old chipped tin mugs. "How about a warm cup of tea?"

William had not had a warm drink since seven that morning. Each working day was the same, cold snap and cold tea brought from home. The snap-tin held four slices of bread secure from dust and was strong enough to defy destruction even at the coalface.

"Thank you Bert. That would be most welcome." So the Friday afternoon ritual was played out. Herbert was lucky, only the manager and the pay-office were allowed a stove for a fire. William sipped his tea with pleasure for a while, before speaking. "You heard about the dust, Bert?"

Herbert nodded and glanced out of the hatch to make sure they were alone. "All clear, Bill."

"Hardcastle is hopping mad. Who's speaking up?"

Despite the fact that they were alone William had kept his voice low.

"All the men are concerned, Bill, but it's Tom Prentice and his gang who are the leaders. They're stirring up the others and protesting to the Overman. Talking of making it a union matter."

William took his time with another swig of tea.

"Well, we've got trouble, Bert. Hardcastle's got his tits in the wringer. Tonnage is badly down and he thinks we might have to close. He's been called to see Enstone in the last week."

Herbert raised his eyebrows. "You sure he's not fooling you, Bill? I'm not sure I trust him."

"No, Bert - not this time. You don't have to be a genius to work out how much coal we're producing and what the wages bill is."

They sipped their tea in silent contemplation for a while.

"I dunno about you, Bert, but I don't fancy the bloody workhouse!"

Herbert rubbed his chin and thought about it. "Won't be easy, Bill. That Prentice is a right hothead."

"Have a word with him this weekend. He lives near you doesn't he?" Herbert nodded and William continued, "Say we've got to get production up, tell him to get the shift to wear wet face cloths. Hardcastle has agreed to increase the amount of water sent down."

Herbert looked very dubious, so William went on. "Use your loaf, Bert. Tell his wife as well. She'll not want to be without wages! I've heard she scares him shitless. She's a big cow! We were at school together and she frightened the life out of me, I can tell you, even then!"

They both had a good laugh at that and finished their tea. William stared out of the hatch.

"The rain is easing, Bert. I'd best be on my way."

All the way home to Wallington Heath, William was deep in thought.

About seven o'clock that evening, William slipped into the Election Committee room, his peg-leg making the stone floor ring. Behind him was Jack. Jack hadn't wanted to be there but had been promised a pennyworth of chips at the end of the evening if he helped with the poster campaign. William turned and pulled him inside and pointed. "Sit down there quiet, son.

And say nowt!"

He looked around the table as he sat down. "My lad Jack is going to help me with the posters after the meeting." Jack edged in and sat in the corner trying to be as quiet as possible. Three committee men were already seated at the table, pipes lit, pungent smoke filling the air. "I've got the minutes of the last meeting so if the Chair is ready I'll check all the action points." As he said it he got out his notes and set them on the table in front of him.

Alf Rose, chairman, solemnly nodded assent, his pipe bobbing up and down. "Proceed, Mr. Secretary."

William outlined all the salient points and noted where action had been taken.

"Did you collect the new posters, Henry?"

The small man on the left sat up in his chair and pointed to the pile of papers in the corner of the room.

"They're all there - and here's the bill."

Chairman Rose removed his pipe and slowly looked around the table; he loved a bit of respect. Pompous sod, thought William, but wisely kept his thoughts to himself. "I think we can get on with the main purpose of this meeting. The chair calls on Mr. Botley."

Fred Botley sat up, obviously feeling important and coughed to clear his throat. Fred worked as a doorman at the town hall and it was his job to keep them up to date with any worthwhile details that came to his notice. Fred loved a bit of gossip and was ideal for the task.

"There's a third candidate been put forward, a chap called Matlock."

There was indignant tut-tutting around the table and the chairman had to call for order.

"What's he standing as, that's the important thing?"

"Liberal." said Fred.

There were more indignant exclamations around the table. The chairman banged the table. "Order gentlemen please. Mr. Secretary, is that legal?"

William looked up from his papers. "Afraid so, Mr. Chairman. Anyone on the roll can put forward if they pay the fee and have a few supporters to sign the application."

Henry was outraged. "How can he call himself a Liberal? Our man is the official Liberal-Labour candidate."

Alf Rose shook his head in sorrow. "The bastard will split our vote, won't he? You sure he's paid his deposit, Fred?"

Fred shrugged. "Must'a done. They've accepted his papers I'm told, and the list 'as gone to the printers!"

Alf looked sternly around the table. "Does anyone know who this Matlock is?"

"Aye, I know him," said William, "he's a foreman at Parsons Pottery. He's no political man. He's been put up to it."

Alf Rose sucked fiercely at his pipe. "'Tis deliberate then. What's your assessment, Mr. Secretary?"

"On our reckoning we were about one hundred and twenty ahead but since the failure of the potash works we've about fifteen on parish relief so they can't vote. As long as we work hard to get 'em to the polling stations we should win. But you're right, this will cause confusion and we could lose."

William could tell from all their faces that they knew they were facing defeat. They had been out-manoeuvred. Henry sounded real sad.

"I really thought we could do it this time and get those bloody Tories off the council."

William shuffled his papers into order. "We'll lose unless we fight. It's that damn Tory Parsons at the bottom of this - he's paid Matlock to stand. We'll just have to fight dirty. This is not for the minutes, Mr. Chairman, so I propose we declare the meeting over and get down to tactics."

Alf Rose formally declared the meeting over.

Half an hour later William and Jack were out in the town. William carrying the posters and Jack carrying the paste pot and brush.

"Right Jack, this is the best we can do for a start. We want three posters in every street. Every time you see a poster that's not ours, paste ours over it."

On they went posting and pasting. When they found a Matlock poster, William made sure Jack could recognise it.

"Can you remember that, Jack?" On they went, with William getting more annoyed. "Tomorrow evening you're to go round the town and cover up all the Matlock posters you can find. Take Len, Ernie and some of your mates. Not Billy, he's too small."

Jack looked a bit apprehensive. "Yes Pa, but what if we get caught?"

"Just be careful - make sure you organise look-outs. I'll have new posters for you tomorrow."

"Do we get paid, Pa?"

William raised his eyebrows. "I'll take you all to the magic lantern show on Sunday." Jack looked pleased. On they went posting and pasting.

"Why are you the secretary, Pa?"

"Well son, it's like this. I'm the only one who can read and write properly. That's why. The written word is power, son. That way I can control what's going on. Don't you forget that!"

"I won't, Pa."

"Learn to use your brain. There's always a way through a problem if you use your loaf. You've got to think ca-canny."

"I'll try, Pa."

"I think you had better join the library."

"I will, Pa. I'm going to be a secretary one day, just like you."

"Do that son, and you'll get on."

Right up to polling day the posters appeared. "VOTE MATLOCK, YOUR OFFICIAL TORY CANDIDATE".

# Chapter 2

## JACK THE LAD

## 1896

William's day had been long and hard when he arrived home at six in the evening. The recent dampness in the air seemed to have made his peg-leg ache with rheumatic like pain and he sat down to his dinner with some relief. He had looked to Elizabeth for any sign of a welcome home but it was not to be. As she set his dinner down in front of him he considered that the milk might go sour from her look. The children were out playing in the yard and he could hear the sound of the skipping rope twirling and the chant of girls as they amused themselves, their heels clicking on the flagstones.

> *'Vote! Vote! Vote for Jessie Walters*
> *In comes Alice at the door,*
> *For Alice Tilling is the woman,*
> *And she likes a batter pudding,*
> *So we won't vote for Jessie anymore.'*

Elizabeth silently returned to her seat beside the range, where the kettle was coming to the boil, sat down and resumed her sewing. It was the first rest she had had all day; she didn't show it but she was grateful that baby Bertie was asleep in his cot in the corner of the room. She screwed up her face at the thought that he would be awake and need feeding soon and her breasts were sore. William noticed the grimace but said nothing. Then he heard the skipping girls mantra change to a new jingle.

*"Eight hours work,*
*Eight hours play,*
*Eight hours sleep,*
*And eight bob a day."*

William was secretly pleased at the thought that the children might be developing political ideas. The memory of the heavy Liberal losses in the '95 elections still rankled with him. At the colliery things were relatively quiet but the price of coal was still poor and Hardcastle was as grumpy as ever. William spent as much time as possible in the yard. As production levels had gone up with the opening of a new drift he could genuinely claim there was more tally work to do. He mulled over his conversation with the checkweighman, surprised at being asked for advice, it always being supposed that he was Hardcastle's man.

"I understand you're a man of learning, Bill. I need a bit of advice."

William had been guarded in his response. "I'll help if I can."

"Alf Rose said to have a word with you."

William did not want to admit to any political connection so he looked around to make sure no one could overhear.

"Aye, I've met Alf a few times - had a drink with him."

Dick Webb, the checkweigher, was the chairman of the union lodge. "There'll be owt said by me, Bill."

Dick took his silence to be agreement. "It's about that Bert Slatcher. You remember, the lad who was crushed when the tubs came off the rails. It's maybe that he will never be able to work again and he's got a wife and five children. We've been to Hardcastle about compensation and he told us to bugger off. Said it must'a bin the lad's own fault, that miners must accept that sort of thing."

William considered it for a moment. "It'll be tough, Dick.

Slatcher will have to sue, always assuming he's got any money. You sure Hardcastle can't blame the 'hurriers'."

The hurriers were the men who tended the coal tubs moving backwards and forwards to the coalface.

"No, it wasn't them. A rail had come loose. What we need, Bill, is an agent. Someone to look after our interests, represent us. We need an educated man of letters." He looked with a questioning stare, his eyebrows raised. "Aye, we need a good man, as soon as we can afford one."

"Well, Dick, I can't help you direct but if you're sure it wasn't the 'hurriers' then I suggest you speak to Dingle and Bradley in the main street, get statements from any witnesses of course but you'll need to be prepared to support Slatcher from union funds. Just don't forget, it's you, not Hardcastle that has to prove negligence."

"Thanks, Bill. I won't forget this!"

Thoughts of the conversation eddied around his mind as he contemplated the possibilities. The union was certainly growing, the constant disputes saw to that and William knew, from his job and experience, of the myriad problems of wage rates and poor working conditions. Also the 'Mineworkers Federation' was getting better organised. Yes, he thought, I fancy myself as the local agent. I'll cultivate Dick Webb. Who knows what may come of this.

As he finished his dinner he pushed his plate away.

"I'll have that cup of tea now, Lizzie. I need our Jack."

Elizabeth sniffed, took the plate and went to the door. "Jack, come here, your Pa wants yer!"

Jack, who had been waiting on tenterhooks, came in immediately. "Yes, Pa?"

"Sit down here." William pointed to a chair at the table. Jack had finished school that day and, beneath the table, he kept his fingers crossed.

"Have you got your Labour Certificate, son?"

With great pride Jack produced the small slip of paper, evidence that he had reached grade five of the school examinations. His passport to a new world of work, he had reached the limits of the school primary level of attainment. "Yes, Pa, here it is." He put it on the table.

"Well done, son! Well done!" William looked pleased. "I've good news for you, Jack. I had a word with Mr. Hardcastle and he's said you can start the day after tomorrow as a day-boy on the screens. You'll get nine pence a day for the first month, then it'll go up to ten pence a day if you work hard. What do you think of that?"

Feeling very grown up, Jack was enthusiastic. "Fine, Pa."

"Tomorrow you get some strong trousers, snap-tin and can." He put a half crown on the table. Jack's eyes boggled, he had never seen so much money.

"Now let's get things straight, lad. There'll be no slacking with your learning. You'll buckle down, reading and writing 'til I'm satisfied. You know the old saying?" Jack shook his head.

"God helps those who help themselves!"

"I've heard that, Pa. I promise, I want to be someone."

William was pleased with his determination, tousled his hair and smiled.

"Every week mind you, down the library. Start reading the newspapers as well. You're going to be my right hand man."

Jack needed no urging really. Already he knew it was devil take the hindmost. Not for him the lifetime as a miner. He had seen, without pity, the worn out old men and the cripples. William brought him out of his reverie.

"Sorry it's the mine, lad, but work is so short at the moment."

"I don't mind, Pa."

Elizabeth has listened in silence while this was going on. More work for me, she thought bitterly but dare not say so in front of William. Her voice was sharp when she spoke.

"There's something you forgot, Bill!"

William looked at her enquiringly.

29

"He's to give me his pay packet, unopened, each week. He'll get nine pence for hisself." She glared at them defiantly as she spoke. "And Emma will have to stay home to help!"

Jack was angry to be treated like a child; he was a man now. William was more conciliatory.

"I think, Lizzie, it should be a shilling as he's got to get paper and pen to keep learning."

"Be better to put food in our bellies!"

"I'll brook no argument on this, Lizzie," sullenly she returned to her sewing as William looked severe, "I'm the master in this house!"

Jack agreed, a man must be master in his own house. He could conceive of no other way.

"There's another thing, son. You'll meet Dick Webb. He's the union leader. He'll speak to you about the union, you'll tell him you want to join. It'll cost you a penny a week but it'll be worth it. We've to cast a few sprats to catch a mackerel. There's two men who are important to us at the moment. If Hardcastle or Dick Webb say jump, the only thing you say is 'How high, Sir!'. Get that!"

Jack nodded. "Yes, Pa."

Elizabeth looked up from her sewing. "An' one thing, Jack, there's wimmin on the screens. You keep away from them, you hear me. There'll be no love-birds around here." For a moment Jack thought she was going to smile but the smile never happened. Jack had no idea what she was talking about; he knew the facts of life. It was the love bit he didn't understand

Two days later Jack started on the screens. Dirty monotonous work, helping to empty coal tubs onto vibrating screens to separate the coal by size and sitting endlessly beside the belt removing dross and slag. Then pushing refilled tubs to the assembly line for transporting to the barges on the canal. Most of the time they were in the open in all weathers, drenched when it rained, sweating when it was hot. As his hands hardened his mind and heart hardened too. He must get away from this mine; there must be a better way. In the evenings he studied till he slept, often falling asleep with a book in his hand. The more he learnt the more he realised he didn't know and this drove him harder. Still his mother jeered at him when his father was out.

"Wasting yer time lad, no good'll come of it!"

## 1897

When Jack was twelve the Overman sent for him. Jack was pleased to be away from the screens for a while.

"You're Bill Elks's son, aren't you?"

"Yes, Sir."

"I've had good reports 'bout you. You're a hard worker I'm told."

"Thank you, Sir."

"You're twelve now. There's a vacancy down below helping on transport, working with the ponies. You want it?"

Jack had known this was coming as William had spoken to him the day before and briefed him what to say.

"I'm obliged, Sir. I promise I will work hard. Could you tell what me what my wage will be?"

The Overman got out his notebook and entered the details. "One shilling and thruppence a day. Go and get a token from the lamp shed and get a helmet from the store. That'll cost you two shillings to be deducted from your first week's pay. Be here at six in the morning. You'll be on alternate day and evening shift. Report to Percy Ibson, the traffic foreman."

"Thank you, Sir."

"You get all that?"

"Yes, Sir."

"Well, don't stand there gormless. Get on with your work."

Jack went, suitably impressed - he had spoken with one of God's anointed.

Jack thought his Ma would be pleased when he told her and he was disappointed when she responded. All she could think of was the extra work, baths after shift work, dinners at awkward hours, getting up earlier and getting to bed later. Matters could only get worse as Ernie, Lennie and Billy grew up and started work. Ernie was due to start soon. God I'm tired now, she thought. She gave Jack a stern look. "There'll be no extra pocket money. Even if you had it you'd only waste it on damn books."

"The books are free, Ma. It's a free library."

"There's nowt free in this world!," she snapped at him, "still perhaps you'll be able to read a book to the ponies. And don't you cheek me, either, or you'll get the back of my hand."

Jack retreated into silence but was undeterred. He was going to be a somebody. Elizabeth interrupted his thoughts, "While I'm getting the tea ready you can take Bertie out for a breath of air." Ma had an old bassinet, shaped like a coalscuttle on wheels that she had bought second hand years ago. Jack was mortified. A man didn't push a baby. Oh, the shame of it!

"I can't do that, Ma!"

"No," thought Elizabeth, "all you damn men can do is fill the damn things." So with a scowl she let it pass. As she was thinking, "How I hate men." Jack was thinking of how he hated women.

Next morning he was up at five, ready for the hour-long walk to the mine. His Ma had got up to make his breakfast but the whole transaction had been done in stony silence. She hadn't even thanked him when he fetched coal from the yard, without being asked. Surrounded by darkness he made his way to the pit and drew his lamp, then waited in the queue for the cage. The hewers and other face workers went first as they had the furthest to go at the pit-bottom. Jack and the transport gang were last. The dropping cage caused momentary fear as he went down for the first time. In the confusion the traffic foreman, Percy lbson, collared him and pushed him along to the underground stables.

"Right, lad, I've plenty to organise so you get in there. See

those empty tubs there? Fill 'em up as fast as you can."
"Yes, Mr. lbson." Percy looked at him in the faltering light of
his lamp and could see confusion on Jack's face.

"You know what horse-shit is lad, don't you? Well, find a
shovel and fill those tubs with it. I'll be back in an hour and I
want those stables so clean you could eat your dinner off 'em."

The smell of horses and manure was nauseating and Jack
wanted to be sick. He thought longingly of the open air on the
screens above.

Percy started to move off. "Don't stand there like a pillar of
salt, lad! Move yourself! Count yourself lucky, you're joining
the heroes." Jack looked even more puzzled. "Hercules, lad,
Hercules! One of the seven labours of Hercules. But you're
being paid for it!"

Percy disappeared into the gloom, laughing at his oft-repeated
joke, leaving Jack disoriented, confused and feeling sick. After a
week it got better but Ernie, Lennie and Billy kept holding their
noses whenever he walked in the house.

## 1901

Jack had been at the pit for just over five years now and
familiarity had calmed his nerves whilst in the cage and down in
the depths of the mine. He could find his way around even in the
dark and had done most of the various underground jobs bar one.
The elite workers, the top wage earners, were the coal hewers and
gangs at the coalface. Jack wanted to be a hewer. Over the years
he had grown to almost full height and his body was muscled and
firm from constant labour. Being on the coalface meant top
wages. "Thirty shillings a week," he thought, "I could live like a
king on that." But first he would have to work as a filler. Jack
knew that selection depended on the Overman so whenever the
Overman was around he made sure he was seen to be working
even harder. Jack was also scrupulous about safety too so that
other men trusted him. The Overman might put him on the face

but he needed to be accepted into a gang and that was trickier. There was no way a single man could work the face alone because of the piece work rates. A gang was more efficient at getting the tubs in, ripping out the coal and loading. That was the way to top rates and the jingle of money in the pocket. He had made a point of speaking directly to the Overman and respectfully asked for an opportunity. Reminding him that he always worked hard and had never been in the book for bad behaviour. The Overman kept a book and in it went details of all the daily events. Men working, changes to work rates, disciplinary matters, fines and so forth. Once you were in the book there was no escape. No promises, the Overman had said but I'll keep it in mind. There might be a vacancy in the number two gang shortly. Jack knew what that meant. Someone was having difficulty keeping up with the work rate and would be offered a lighter job. Offer not being quite that, it would be a case of "take it, or leave it!" Jack didn't give a damn. He had the learning, now he wanted the money.

About a month after speaking to the Overman, Jack was allocated to a gang. At the end of his shift he waited for the gang to come up in the cage as he had been instructed. The gang leader, Tom Walsh, blackened from head to foot, looked him up and down.

"Overman sez you can join us? You're Jack, Bill the clerk's son. Right?" Jack nodded in agreement.

"'Ow do we know you're not a bloody nark, eh?"

Jack coloured. "I've been a union member for five years. And my Pa's not like that!"

"Don't get yer back up, lad! We've heard he's a good man otherwise we wouldn't be talking to yer."

Another hewer butted in. "Why do yer want to join us?"

Jack was getting a bit upset. "Cos I want to earn some decent bloody wages, that's why!" He almost shouted the words.

Suddenly all the black faces in front of him were smiling.

"My, we've got a feisty one here, lads. Looks strong enough, doesn't he? Think he'll do us?" Tom Walsh looked around the gang, but there was no dissension. "Good lad, join us sharp at six, we're first down. Bring a shovel." As Jack turned away, Tom called after him. "I'll be in the Bolton Arms in Pearce Street this evening - you can buy me a pint."

Jack had not been in a public house before except to fetch an odd pint for his father at the local "Bottle and Jug" bar.

"You'd better go," advised William, "otherwise he'll be offended." Somewhat reluctantly Jack went, spending his entire book and paper allowance in one go "I shouldn't say owt about learning and such, Jack," William had warned him. That evening Jack was introduced to a whole new world of beer and tobacco. He was the only man at the bar without a pipe and resolved to get one; and the beer, well, that first pint was nectar. When he returned, Ma was waiting.

"There's beer on your breath!" Ma was shocked, if not mortally wounded, and with an acid tongue lashed him about the perils of drink.

It was snap-time at the coalface and the whole gang stopped and sat around in a group to eat and have a drink. In the middle of the banter one of the men called across to Jack.

"You got a girl, Jack? Tell us all about her."

There was quiet as Jack shifted uncomfortably at the direct question; he hadn't got a girl.

"Come on Jack, no secrets here. Tell us all about her!"

Pride stopped Jack from telling the truth. "I'm going out with Alice Dunn."

"Cor! I bet she's a hot one, eh, Jack?"

"She's a very nice girl," said Jack, "she's a housemaid." There was raucous laughter all round.

"Oh, dear me Jack! The nice ones are no bloody good!"

"No, what you need is a hot piece, Jack, get your flag flying!"

"Have you got inside her bloomers yet, Jack?"

Jack was squirming with embarrassment.

"What you need, Jack, is a bit of stuff that doesn't mind black hands on her bottom!  Come on lad, tell us, when did you last have yer oats?"

Jack had never had a proper girl.  He thought if they were going to josh him like this every day he had better get one quickly.

"Nothing like a nice bit of cunny, lad!"

"I do believe our Jacks' a virgin!"

Jack squirmed even more as the gang fell about laughing. Throughout the break Jack was the centre of attention and much lurid advice, blushing furiously beneath the cover of coal on his face.

On his first full week's pay-day after joining the gang Jack collected his pay packet and ripped it open, gazing in appreciation at the silver coins in his hand.  Eighteen shillings, eighteen lovely shillings!  It was the first time he had earned more than twelve shillings.  When he got home, he paused at the door, pulled his shoulders back and marched in.  Ernie and Len were already home.  Ma was pouring more hot water in the tin-bath.  There was no greeting.  Jack marched over to the table and counted out five half crowns on the table.

"What you think you're doing, Jack?"  Ma's face hardened as she spoke.

"There's my keep, twelve and sixpence.  I think that's fair."

"You know my rules, where's your pay packet?"

Jack braced himself and looked her in the eye.

"It's my pay packet - not yours.  Twelve and six is fair. There's plenty pay less."

"Then get out of my house!  I make the rules here."

Jack was not for beating.  "Tek it or leave it.  And it's not your house.  You'll not treat me like a whipped boy."

She scooped the half crowns into her apron pocket.

"I'll speak to your father about this!"

Jack knew he had won but couldn't resist putting the boot in.

"I shall want my dinner as soon as I'm bathed." He was finished with being pushed about by women.


# 1902

Evening was failing as Jack led Rose from the country lane onto the bracken-covered bank. They had met at four in the afternoon for a country walk. Rose was a good girl really, getting on for eighteen, slim, dark-haired and pretty. Rose was also deeply in love. She stirred to Jack's kisses and caresses and dreamed of being a married woman. As they lay in the bracken she had offered no resistance when Jack unbuttoned the top of her dress and fondled her breasts, whilst at the same time he kissed her with open mouth and probing tongue. This had become normal during their courting over the last few weeks. Rose was a maid at the large house about a mile from Wallington Heath and every Tuesday afternoon, when Jack's shift permitted, they met. The rest of the time she was on duty. She dreamed of the day when she could leave and have a home of her own. With all her heart she loved Jack. He was not really tall but in her eyes he was the most handsome man she knew, with his grey eyes, dark wavy hair and smooth even features. His face was pale and unblemished, unlike the local farm labourers with their tanned weather beaten faces, dirty boots and clothes. Jack was a bit of a toff in his cap and suit. All the girls she worked with were envious of her. She didn't know that Jack was courting three girls simultaneously, taking full advantage of their hours of work and time off arrangements. She, unwittingly, was his Tuesday girl. Jack held her firmly and whispered sweet words in her ear.

"You're the loveliest girl in all the world." His hand played on her heartstrings. "Your skin is so smooth and inviting - I can't resist you, Rose."

"You do love me, Jack? You really do love me, don't you?"

His hand never stopped stroking.

"Course I love you, Rose - I'll always love you."

"Oh, I do love you, Jack. I do - I do - I. Will you marry me, Jack? I do so love you."

The accomplished lies poured from his lips.

"You're the only one for me, Rose - I never been with a woman before - I'm your slave for life my sweet lovely."

Later they lay back on the bracken, Rose held Jack tight, her hand on his chest. The words came out in a whisper. "I've never been with a man before. Jack - you're the first one - I never want another."

Mechanically Jack stroked her hair. He was already looking forward to Thursday when he was to meet Rachel. Rose persisted. "You do believe me Jack, don't you?"

Jack did not really want to speak but he wanted to keep her sweet and compliant.

"You know I do, Rose."

Rose tried to be persuasive. "I do wish you'd give up boxing, Jack, I'm so afraid you'll get hurt." She touched the small bruise by his eyebrow.

Jack boxed with the other lads at the 'Bloxwich Junior Sporting Club'. He was very strong in the arm and shoulder and he loved the conflict and exhilaration of winning. What he didn't like was being manipulated. His free time was his own, his freedom fiercely protected.

"I'll give up when I'm good and ready and not before."

Rose pouted. "When we get married Jack we can be together all the time."

Jack had no such intention but he held her tight as he answered. "There's plenty of time for that, my love - we'll have to save up."

Rose persisted. "I've got a bottom drawer saved up, Jack."

Jack decided he had had enough.

"We'd better be on our way, Rose. You've to be in by ten."

"When will I see you next, Jack?"

"Fortnight today - I'm on evening shift next week."

Rose was guided down the bank to the lane and she brushed herself off. She didn't want the staff at the house making any comments.

"Will you walk me back to the house, Jack?"

"Sorry, Rose. I must be off home, I've to be up for 4.30 in the morning."

Rose tried to hide her disappointment but it showed in her face; so Jack tried to soften the blow.

"I've got to be on time, Rose. It's for our future."

After giving her one last kiss, Jack made off down the road towards Bloxwich. Rose watched him till he was out of sight, then light of heart she made her way back to the big house, quite forgetting that every other night Jack had always walked her home.

## 1905

William was elated but was desperately trying not to show it. He had been in deep conversation with Dick Webb, the leading union man in the local lodge. "So there's the situation, Bill. It's all agreed by the committee. The job as full-time agent is yours if you agree, covering both the Pensal and Bloxwich mines. It's not a big area but we've got solid union support. You deal with all the day to day business and I'll keep the men in order. What d'you say?"

William had already accepted in his mind but was reluctant to be so obvious, so he put his left-hand fingers to his chin to show he was reflecting on the matter, Dick continued. "We badly need a full-time agent, Bill. All the committee are working full-time and we just can't cope with the detail. Besides which we need a man of letters. The paperwork has overwhelmed me."

"I'll need to give a fortnight's notice, Dick, will there be a contract?"

"Yes, we've got a standard contract from the Miners Federation. Too difficult for me to understand but you'll cope with it, I'm sure."

"I'll need an office."

"If you use your parlour, Bill, we'll pay you a rent. How about two shillings a week?"

"That's fine. What about wages?"

"The Federation have advised us on three pounds five shillings a week."

William's heart leapt, his wages doubled overnight. He spat on his hand and held it out. Dick did likewise and they shook hands on it.

"I'm your man, Dick."

Late that evening William and Jack sat in the parlour, two mugs and a bottle of stout between them.

"I've seen the paperwork, Jack, there's a lot of it. Also according to Dingle and Bradley, there are twenty-five cases in litigation - that's just the active ones! There'll be Lodge Meetings every month, minutes to prepare. I'll need your help Jack, at least for a start."

William placed a file on the table, boldly labelled 'DINGLE & BRADLEY'; Jack picked it up and leafed through.

"Its all been typed, Pa!"

"I know, it's the way of the world. Even offices are getting mechanised." The concept hit Jack immediately.

"That's it, Pa! We must get a typewriter. I'll get one. Carbon paper copies will reduce the amount of work by over fifty per cent."

William was impressed, thinking how good it would look to the committee. One in the eye for Hardcastle too.

"I'm a bit worried." Doubts had crowded in on William. "I think I'm too old to learn new tricks!"

Jack brushed it aside. "Don't worry, Pa. Leave it to me. I'll be your clerk till you can afford help."

William picked up a paper and showed it to Jack. "What do you think of that?" The paper showed the area accident statistics and the number of widows and families being supported by the union. Jack had to read it several times before answering.

"Good god, Pa! I never knew it was as bad as that!"

William looked sad. "I've just worked it out - it means one man in every seven is badly hurt each year. We've got our work cut out here. No wonder Dick Webb couldn't cope! Right Jack, let's get organised. We've a lot to do."

The next day Jack purchased a second-hand typewriter. Every spare hour for the next six months was spent at the machine, except of course for nights out with the girls. Throughout the next few years he watched, learnt and listened; changed his political allegiance to the emerging Labour party, feeling that the Liberals had little to offer the working man, especially when he discovered the extent of profits in the industry and the parsimonious distribution of wealth to the miners. On the typewriter, one finger became two fingers, became two hands as his skill grew. He also saw how fourpence a week from 3000 men became £50 a week and then £2,500 per year. Unimaginable wealth: and money was power!

## Chapter 3

## THE CANAL TAVERN

## 1908

The 'Canal Tavern' at Bloxwich was a hundred years old. Erected by ancient craftsmen, skilled in the ways of wood and inlaid with brick to follow the natural curves of beams produced by nature. It sat gracefully alongside the peace of the canal, untroubled by the noise of trains and rolling stock. Built by an enterprising brewery it catered for the needs of the bargees as they guided the laden barges from and to the Black Country and beyond. Coal, iron ore, bricks, pottery, china clay, potash and so on, passed by daily. Beside the tavern two barns had been built, one gave lodgings for the bargees and the other stabled their horses, the big dray and shire horses that pulled the barges. There was no room on the barges for living quarters or galleys for cooking so the tavern did a good steady trade. Large the barges might be but they glided silent as owls in the night, except for the muted clip clop of horses' hooves on the grassy banks. Even on a Saturday night the tavern was quiet. Busy yes, but alive rather than lively. A haunt of working men working a twelve hour day, including Sundays. Tonight was like every other night, quiet. But there was thunder in the air!

Thomas Peach had called "Time, gentlemen, please!" with greater insistence than normal, trying to hide his anger but keen to clear the tavern and put the large door bolt in place. No, he considered, he was more than angry, he was close to outrage.

After throwing the last door bolt in position he made for the parlour where Mary, his wife and eldest daughter Lizzie waited. In the parlour Mary sat, her mind in a turmoil, her arm protectively around Lizzie who was weeping. Entering, Tom first went to the window to check that the outside yard was clear. He did not want anybody to overhear what might be said within these walls tonight. Tom was not a violent man but tonight he was sorely provoked; turning from the window he drew a deep breath, trying desperately to calm himself. Despite himself, the words, when they came, spat out. A finger pointed accusingly at Lizzie.

"Is it true? Is it true what your mother has told me?"

Getting no immediate response, he continued with a roar. "I NEVER THOUGHT THIS DAY WOULD COME!"

Mary tightened her arm around Lizzie's shoulder; Lizzie looked at the floor. Early that morning Mary had come to the reluctant conclusion that something was seriously wrong. Lizzie's morning sickness and a thickening waistline could no longer be ignored. Suspicion had been growing for a number of weeks but her mind fought against a conclusion she did not want to reach. In the end however, she had to ask. "Are you pregnant, Lizzie?" I didn't even know that she had a young man. she had thought. Lizzie, no longer able to keep up the pretence of normality, answered, "Mum, I'm sorry, I'm sorry." Then she had broken down and cried and cried.

In response to Tom's question Lizzie nodded mutely and in misery.

"How could you do this, Lizzie?  SHAME ON YOU - SHAME ON US! I expected better from you!"

Mary pleaded, her mother love stronger than anger or shame. "She needs our help, Tom. Please, our help."

"HAS THIS CHILD GOT A FATHER?  GOD HELP ME I'LL HORSEWHIP HIM!" He raised his hands in despair but after a few moments realised that shouting would do no good so with great effort he forced himself under control. Even then anger got the better of him.

"I take it you do know who the father is? He has got a name, hasn't he? Who is he?"

Mary spoke very softly, hurt deep in her heart. "How can you say that, Tom? To our daughter! To your own daughter!" She paused, drawing on her courage. "It's Jack Elks. You know him. Son of the Miner's Agent. Works at Pensal Colliery."

Tom put a hand to his brow and closed his eyes. "Good god! Not a bloody miner - not one of those! Bloody Jack Elks of all people!" He banged his head with his hand in exasperation. "Everyone knows what a bugger he is! God, he must have chased after every woman for ten miles. This'll not be the first bastard he's fathered if what I've heard is true!"

Lizzie started sobbing even more "I - love - him, Dad. I really - love - him."

"How long have you been seeing him?"

"Since last September. I met him - in the town - when I was shopping for you."

"You never saw fit to tell us - or bring him here. Isn't that the right way?" As he spoke a terrible suspicion formed in his mind. "He has asked you to marry him, hasn't he?"

Lizzie made a great effort to compose herself before answering. "We spoke about it, Dad." As she remembered it now, she had spoken about it, about Jack she wasn't so sure. After she had told Jack about it four weeks ago he had been conspicuous by his absence.

"Does he know about the baby?"

"Yes Dad, I told him but I haven't seen him for a few weeks because he's been working."

Mary interjected. "She's about four months as far as I can tell, Tom."

"Right, get yourself to bed, Lizzie." Tom had made his mind up. "I'm sorting this out tomorrow!"

The next day Tom Peach thundered into William's parlour, which he still used as an office for the union, ready for a fight but was disarmed by William's readiness to listen and obvious candour. No, of course William hadn't known of Jack's association with Lizzie but then his Jack was a good lad. "I will speak to him. Please call me Bill; everything will be alright." he assured Tom. "We will both be by to see you tomorrow evening. Shall we say half past seven?" Beneath his composure William was more concerned than he conveyed, he had heard rumours about Jack but had dismissed them as idle gossip. After all, he considered, men will be men. But then he felt it was time that Jack settled down. Jack would be twenty-three shortly and William felt that, aged fifty-two, it was time he had a grandchild. In fact he quite relished the idea but decided to say nothing to Elizabeth yet.

On Friday evening, William and Jack entered the tavern and made for the back door of the bar room. The barman nodded them through. Wishing to impress and maintain appearances, they were both wearing their 'Sunday Best' with William wearing his bowler hat as befitted a Miners Agent, Jack with his cap. Tom, Mary and Lizzie waited in the parlour. Tom ushered them in, deliberately not shaking hands.

"We've met, Mr. Elks." He stared at Jack. "You'll be Jack then?"

Jack gave measure for measure. "That's me." Then when he saw William frown at him added, "Mr. Peach."

Tom introduced his wife and Lizzie to William.

When William first broached the matter with him, Jack had been annoyed but William had stood his ground, concerned for family honour. In any case and the more he thought about it the more he liked the idea of a grandchild. Though he had never said it, nor tried to show it overmuch, Jack was the apple of his eye. Jack had conceded to himself that Lizzie was attractive but he had no great feelings in the matter. Why be tied down, he asked himself, life as a single man was fine. Besides which a slump had set in recently and life was tough enough on reduced wages without the added burden of a wife. Why, only that morning he had been forced to redeem his suit from the pawnshop because unbeknown to him his mother had 'popped it' to get money for the weekend. Though much discussed, William could not take him on in the Agency because union fees were down and there was no chance the committee would countenance an extra clerk.

Slowly these thoughts had drifted through Jack's head. That had been when he really thought about the Tavern, obviously it was a thriving business, Lizzie was the oldest daughter, there was no son around. Plenty of opportunity for the good life. He could picture himself with a fine bottle of whisky to hand, convivial company at the bar. Smooth fine whisky; he savoured the thought. Things were bad at the pit, wages going down, working harder to keep up with the piece rates. If he weren't careful the good life would slip away. Hey presto! Welcome to the good life. Marriage wouldn't cramp his style but life might be easier and there could be money to make. The canal was never idle and every passing barge meant money. Yes, why not, he thought, take a chance, nothing to lose. He remembered, you've got to be ca-canny, lad!

"Don't worry, Pa. I'll do my duty - not let you down."

There was an awkward silence in the parlour for a moment, especially when Jack pointedly sat next to Lizzie and took her hand in his. Tom sniffed, unwilling to draw comfort from any sign; what he wanted were words and deeds, so he decided to start.

"I think we all know what we are here for - and what the circumstances are!" He glared at Jack while William fiddled with his wooden leg. "We may as well come straight to the point. What are your intentions towards our daughter?" Mary shuffled her feet in anxiety.

Jack didn't blush, he no longer knew how to.

"I love Lizzie, Mr. Peach. If she'll have me I'm going to

marry her - with your permission of course." He gave Mary a winning smile and squeezed Lizzie's hand.

Tom was somewhat taken aback so it was a few moments before he gathered his thoughts. "And what are your prospects, young man - where will you live?"

Jack was very serious in replying. "It's like this Mr. and Mrs. Peach. Things are a bit hard at the moment, there's no denying that, my wages have been put down to fifteen shillings a week, but it'll get better, don't you worry. We'll do fine, we'll manage."

William was about to say something then thought better of it. He knew full well that Jack earned more than that. Jack continued.

"There's a cottage on Wharf Street, rather small but we can manage there. It'll make a fine cosy home for us."

Tom and Mary were appalled. Fifteen shillings a week wages, rent to find and worst of all, Wharf Street! They knew Wharf Street; it was the worst kind of slum with cottages hardly fit for habitation! Before he knew it, Tom had burst out.

"No, no. I insist. You can both stay here. We've plenty of rooms. There'll be no need to pay rent so it will give you a chance to save."

He looked at Mary and could tell from her face that she approved, unreservedly. Lizzie was smiling in gratitude. Jack kept a straight face.

"That's kind of you Mr. Peach. I'll help you. Pa can tell you, I'm first rate at bookkeeping and accounts. Isn't that right, Pa?"

William nodded in confirmation as Lizzie gave Jack a kiss on the cheek. "Oh, Jack, lets get married soon."

Pleased that Lizzie was happy, Tom mellowed and Mary was smiling at last after days of worry.

"Right," said Tom, "there's a lot of organising to do. Tomorrow I want you both to see the vicar, arrange the church and get the banns posted. Mind you, Mary and I want a white wedding - and a proper reception. We'll have it here, in the tavern. Plenty of room."

Mary added her two pennyworth. "I will order the cake, get the invitations done. Oh, and there are bridesmaids to arrange."

She spoke from a deep happiness, her daughter was safe, and her grandchild would have a name. Jack was pleased but took care not to show it. Inside he was thinking that his invention of the cottage on Wharf Street had been a masterstroke. Ah, lad, it pays to be ca-canny.

Tom shouted through to the bar for drinks. William had a large brandy he felt so pleased, perhaps when he told her this would make Elizabeth smile at last. Later that evening as William stomped his way home and Tom and Mary made their plans, Jack took Lizzie for a short walk. Very short really as he stepped her into the stable where, unprotesting, Lizzie allowed him to make love to her. She was so happy she thought her heart would burst. "Oh Jack, I do love you. We'll be so happy together."

On the 14th March they were married at the Parish Church in Bloxwich and on the 27th August, two weeks overdue, 'Little Jack' was born in the tavern. His real name was John Thomas William but from the very beginning it was always 'Little Jack'.

## Christmas 1908

Elizabeth had not been at the tavern when 'Little Jack' had been born. She had not been invited nor did she want to be there, she had seen enough of babies. Just one more mouth to feed, more hard work. All the greater then her surprise when she fell in love and the object of her affection was 'Little Jack'. She had never loved William or her own children; then after being on this earth for nearly fifty years she was smitten. Earlier there had only been hard work and pain, even heartache, but 'Little Jack' had stormed the iron bounds of her heart with his trust and a simple gurgling smile.

At the tavern he was a fretful child and Jack had only to look at him and he burst into tears in a trice. Not that Jack bothered himself much. Lizzie had been grateful when Elizabeth visited, grateful that someone else would hold 'Little Jack' and coax him for awhile. Lizzie was two months pregnant and still sick by the day. Elizabeth was disgusted with Jack. Why, this little one was not even weaned yet! Elizabeth found, to her amazement, that she could calm 'Little Jack' by the merest soft touch or word so she would sit for hours cuddling and talking to him. Happy and contented in her presence he would immediately fret if she tried to leave.

As her heart softened Elizabeth learnt to smile and 'Little Jack' would dimple and smile in return. It's only wind, William would say but she would have nothing of it. 'Little Jack' was in her arms now and she was crooning in a low voice. With her free hand she opened the present she had bought him only days before. Daughters Ivy and Alice, the youngest of her children, could only stare at their mother in amazement; changed before their unbelieving eyes. Even Elizabeth had surprised herself when she purchased the small silver rattle. After a lifetime of scrimping and scraping till it had become a deeply ingrained habit, she had spent the half a crown without hesitation. 'Little Jack' took the rattle in his tiny hand, feet kicking in pleasure beneath the dress he wore.

"Don't you worry Little Jack, you're with granny now - granny will look after you." Her voice lowered as she whispered. "You're mine my little lovely - I will take care of you. I will never let you go."

'Little Jack' lay back, dribbled, kicked his legs and waved the rattle, deeply content.

## Late 1909

Tom Peach noticed that Jack had helped himself to a large whisky and drunk it with obvious pleasure. He wished that Jack wouldn't drink because he knew the obvious danger of a publican drinking and his plans, if they came to fruition, would put Jack into the tenancy of the tavern. Drinking the profits is the worst thing a publican can do, he murmured on a number of occasions. Mind you, he considered, Jack was a hard worker and when he helped with the stables and barn the work was soon done. Also if Jack was on duty no bargee escaped payment for his horse and lodgings. There was an undeniable friction between Tom and Jack but it was largely kept under control.

A week after Jack and Lizzie married, Jack had spoke about leaving the mine and taking over tavern duties. Tom sensed that Jack wanted more than to be an employee but Tom was unwilling to give up the habits of a lifetime. He was the master; there could not be two. So Jack would have to learn and bide his time till Tom was ready. Then slowly Tom had come to dislike Jack. Tom and Mary's marriage had been a love match from the day they met and still was. Apart from his daughters Lizzie, Ellen and Alice there was only one woman in the world for him, his wife Mary. Jack's dictatorial attitude to Lizzie and his indifference to their sons rankled with Tom.

There was 'Little Jack' still living with his grandmother and Jack showed no inclination to get him back or indicated in any way that he even thought or cared about the situation. Now Lizzie could hardly move out of the tavern but Jack would fly into a rage. True Jack still helped his father but Tom suspected this was just a cover for him to get out and about. Jack was still 'Jack-the-lad', as far as he could tell. William still viewed it as 'men will be men' but that was not Tom's way, so he laid his plans with care. Tonight was an ideal time to launch his campaign. The new baby, Leonard, had been playing up so Lizzie, tired from a day's work, had retired early. Jack was working and Ellen and Alice had been in bed several hours. Tom would have a quiet time with Mary when the tavern closed. An hour of peace and quiet.

When he and Mary settled in the kitchen for a cup of tea he casually launched his initiative. "I've been giving some thought to the future, Mary." Mary didn't react so he continued, "I think we deserve a change."

The conversation took Mary by surprise. "I haven't really

thought about it - I mean..... what about the girls?" Her voice faded away.

"That's it Mary, the future. Look, what have we got here? This Black Country is a disgrace, an industrial waste. What sort of men will they meet?" He looked sad. "I don't want another miner in the family - one's enough!"

"What do you think we should do, Tom?"

"Well, we've enough money saved up - we can go where we like."

"That sounds nice, Tom, perhaps we could go to the seaside."

"We've never had a proper holiday. How about making it a holiday, and an adventure?"

"I don't follow you, Tom."

"Australia, love, Australia. Sunshine and open spaces. A place where the girls can grow up in clean air. A growing country, not like here. I feel time is running out and we are not getting any younger. Why don't we go while we are still able?"

"We're too old, Tom. Fancy that at our age!"

"As long as I have you nothing else matters. I want you to think about it - give it serious thought."

"What about our Lizzie? What about our grandchildren?"

"Simple, we get the tenancy passed to Jack and Lizzie. He's dying to get his hands on this place. We sail with the girls and as soon as we're settled and get the lie of the land we get them and the boys to come out and join us."

Mary stared at Tom intently, as if trying to make sure he wasn't pulling her leg, as if at any moment he would start laughing and say it was all a joke. The look on Tom's face told her he was deadly serious.

"It'd get Jack away from the pit." He almost added, 'and his old haunts and habits', but thought better of it.

"Can I think about it for a few days." Mary closed her eyes in concentration. "Really think."

Tom crossed his fingers, "Wouldn't have it any other way. If you say no, we try something else."

The first stage of his plan accomplished he poured them another cup of tea. "Oh! And by the way I resent the inference that I'm too old - as I shall show you later!"

When Tom had gone upstairs, Mary sat in her favourite old cane chair by the fire for a while, thinking. Everything she loved was here but everything that she loved could go with her to the New World. She smiled to herself when she realised she was not afraid. This old chair of mine must go with me she resolved, then content in her mind she went up the stairs to bed.

When Mary got up in the morning she found Tom in the bathroom, shaving. She gave him a quick peck on the cheek. "I agree - Australia it is!" Tom almost cut himself in surprise, then gave a whoop!

There was a great hubbub in the tavern when they announced their plans. Lizzie was crying at the thought of losing them, even if only for a short while. Ellen and Alice were so excited they couldn't sit still. Even baby Len in his cot seemed to be happy. Jack was happy. It was to be his pub. Tom would leave the stock, fixtures and fittings. Jack thought with relish of the day when he could tell Hardcastle to stuff his job, maybe even invite the bastard in for a drink he thought. He'd had enough of mining. Mine host sounded so much better. Even the prospect of Australia was inviting, but first there was money to be made.

**Christmas 1910**

Lizzie was still weak and unable to do too much. Albert had been born only two months ago and Elizabeth had come to help though she made it plain that it was under duress from William. Jack held himself aloof from the domestic scene and several times had upset everyone by demanding that the children keep quiet. Lizzie was concerned that Jack's temper was much worse than usual and she couldn't understand it. Nor discern any reason as to why he was so testy. Jack had good reason to be worried. Over the last six weeks trade had suddenly, but steadily, dropped. The number of barges had tailed off and on some nights the barns were empty of travellers. Jack had cut back on the number of hay bales delivered and reduced the barrelage from the brewery.

Following Tom and Mary's departure to Australia the tavern had met his every expectation and there was a nice little sum in the bank for the future. Not a shilling had been added to that sum in recent weeks. It was William who supplied the first clue. "Hardcastle's cut the contract for the barges, reckons it's cheaper to use the railways by buying his own wagons. That way he gets the free-on-board price for the coal at the end of the line. Every time ten new wagons arrive another barge goes. Now I hear the foundry is to do the same with iron ore. Hardcastle's offered them a deal, coal out and ore back in the empty wagons."

Jack had reckoned that over eighty per cent of the barges would be lost eventually; and even though some would find alternative loads he was still bound to lose more than half his passing trade, at least. What if another works tries the same trick, they'd be bankrupt inside a year. He was good and mad and fearful all at the same time. Just when he thought he had found the good life it was being snatched away. Later when the children were abed and settled, he sat down with Lizzie, William and Elizabeth and explained what was happening and the effect on them.

Lizzie was aghast, she had been unable to help much with the business because of the babies. Besides which Jack had not wanted or needed her involvement. "You look after the home," he would say, "I'll look after the business." Business in Jack's view, had no place for women. William tried to be helpful and promised to circulate all the miners to persuade them to use the tavern. Elizabeth was quiet but triumphant. 'Little Jack' was still with her, now she thought nobody would want to take him away. So while the situation got slowly more difficult Jack started the painful search for an alternative. In good times the tenancy would have provided a cash sum on the open market but not now, Jack concluded. They would be hard put to get out with their skin intact.

## Christmas 1911

Throughout the year trade had steadily dropped with no sign of recovery. "This will be the last Christmas in the tavern, Lizzie."

Jack had reached a low peak. Despite all his efforts trade had fallen away and was now less than half that of the first year, when they had started. Lizzie tried to console him. "We'll be fine, Jack. We can manage."

Jack wanted to explain that it was no good, they were making no profit, almost working for nothing.

"Its not possible, Lizzie. We must get out before it sinks us."

The full implication of what he was saying was hard for Lizzie to accept. "But we can't leave. It's our home."

"If I could save it I would, but we can't halt progress. The canal has had its day."

"Could we go to Australia - be with Mum and Dad?"

"We haven't enough money." Lizzie went to speak but he stopped her before she could get it out. "And I'll not take charity from your mother and father - they'll not find it easy out there."

"What do we do then, Jack?"

"It's already arranged. We'll hand over to the brewery next week. Sell as much as we can. Pa has said we can go there for the moment."

Lizzie could only whisper. "So soon, Jack."

"Yes." He could not bring himself to tell her that most of the carefully hoarded savings had gone in a vain attempt to survive. Then he brightened up, putting a brave face on the situation.

"I've heard they're opening up some coal mines in Kent. Near Dover. Driving new shafts and roadways. Paying double and more wages. There are no miners in Kent so they're advertising for colliers. Pa has heard you can earn three to four pounds a week. If it's true then I'll be off in the New Year."

"But how will you manage, Jack?" Lizzie was stunned by the apparent quick turn of events.

"I'll manage, find lodgings. As soon as I'm settled I'll send for you." Jack had had enough of gloom for the moment. "Let's have a toast. A toast to the old tavern."

They raised their glasses. Lizzie shed a tear, while Jack thought that he was back to when he was eleven and the arse out of his trousers. Bloody hell, he considered, I'm twenty-six, a wife and three boys and starting at the bottom again. The good life would come again he vowed.

Chapter 4

THE GARDEN OF ENGLAND

1912

Jack had left Bloxwich early in the morning, on the 1st of January, leaving Lizzie and the boys behind. There had been tears as he departed and Lizzie had clung to him at the doorway demanding that he write soon. He had given her what was left of their money for safekeeping, keeping only ten pounds for himself. "Don't worry," he had told her, "if I can't find work I'll be back before the money runs out." With a bit of luck he reckoned he could manage for ten weeks.

After leaving London the train ran through beautiful countryside. Orchards and hopfields were lying fallow and oast houses nestled amidst the vales of scattered fields and hedgerows. Small quaint villages looked as if they had been there since the Doomsday Book, rustic, peaceful and untouched. The countryside had a look of richness and quiet prosperity but Jack knew that the huge numbers of farm labourers needed to maintain it, would be poorly paid. Jack sat in the third class compartment. The bench was hard; his bag was on the rack above his head. There was no corridor and he was wishing the train would reach Dover soon. In his bag Jack had a new pair of boots and his work clothes or rags as they were known. The call of 'rag-up' in the pit was the call to strike. Also there was a change of shirt with two collars and spare long johns. He thought about it. Nine pounds two shillings and fourpence in his pocket and a few clothes in a case. Not much for fifteen years of hard work. He had watched the other passengers and was grateful to see there were no men in similar circumstances on the train. A good omen, in his view, because he could spot a collier at two hundred paces and the less competition the better. He had no desire to wait in line.

It was two in the afternoon when the train pulled into Dover Priory Station. Only ten minutes ago it had started to drizzle and Dover was overcast with a leaden sky. Welcome to the Garden of England! Alighting from the train Jack made his way toward the ticket barrier. A porter danced alongside him.

"Take your case, sir? Shall I get you a trap, sir?"

Jack had no money to waste on the likes of that. The porter was obviously disappointed when Jack shook his head. Jack knew the porters desperately needed tips to supplement their meagre wages. Pointedly getting two pence from his pocket he stopped and smiled, then spoke softly.

"I need lodgings, comrade. Nothing expensive or fancy mind you, I'm a working man."

The porter smiled back. "I can tell, sir, from your accent. You're for the Shakespeare I'll be bound."

"That's right, comrade. Just a working man like you."

"I can recommend Mrs. Dilkes, in Military Road, Number 27. She keeps a good clean house and knows a man needs a proper meal."

The two pence disappeared into his pocket like a conjurer's trick. "Out of the station, sir, turn left and take the first on the right. Brings you out on Military Road. Tell Mrs. Dilkes that Bob Roberts sent you."

Jack went on his way leaving Bob Roberts pleased with himself. Mrs. Dilkes owed him another shilling.

Mrs. Dilkes was overweight, overbearing and totally uncompromising. She eyed Jack up and down warily.

"Bob Roberts directed me to you, Mrs. Dilkes."

"A bed is five bob a week. Sheets is extra for sixpence a week and are changed every fortnight. Baths are fourpence each and meals are a shilling a day!" Jack nodded, then was cut off as he went to speak. "No workmen's boots in the house, no drinking in the house – an' no wimmin niver!"

Jack gave her a smile. "I didn't realise this was a Salvation Army house, Mrs. Dilkes. That will do fine."

Mrs. Dilkes didn't smile and her hand thrust out. "An' a week in advance." Then just as Jack thought she had finished she unleashed her parting shot. "An' keep out of my parlour."

It was not until Jack entered the room that he realised there were no beds, only three mattresses on the floor, an untidy scatter of clothes and cases around them. A small wiry man raised himself from the floor and put his hand out.

"I'm Dai Powell, pleased to meet you, boyo. Welcome to our humble abode. I'm from Wales, from where do you hail?"

Jack was pleased to see a friendly face and he shook hands.

"Jack Elks from Staffordshire."

Dai inspected his palm.

"I can tell you're here for the Shakespeare?"

"Aye, you're right. I hear they're taking on men."

"Too true, boyo - what they need are miners, real miners! A big strong lad like you will have no problem."

Jack liked his melodic lilting accent and warmed to him. Men he understood. "What do I do, Dai?"

"Follow me, Jack. I'm a Shakespeare man, have been for two months. On the night shift. I'll take you to see the Butty Man this evening. Got your rags?" Jack nodded. "His name is Hewitt, real bastard but he needs men. Mind you he takes his dip, at least a shilling a day. Even if you lose a shift, mark you!"

Jack knew what a Butty Man was - he was the contractor who organised the labour. He had never met a Butty Man he had liked or met one that didn't exploit the men to the full. Butty Men sat on top, licking off the cream while the poor sods they recruited slaved below.

"What about tools, Dai? I shall need tools."

"Get those tomorrow, Jack. Morecroft, in the High Street,

only ten minutes walk away. Don't get a hammer, though. One between us will be enough but get some extra wedges. They don't know much, mind you - I asked for a 'spit' and they said they didn't stock them - and there they were, dozens of them!"

Darkness had already fallen when they reached the mine. It was unlike any other pithead Jack had seen. The engineroom had half a roof and no walls, there were no other buildings and only the pithead gear, with its two winding wheels, was in place. Nearby an old pump engine wheezed and groaned and pipes led from it into the darkness. Jack guessed it was pumping water from the mine. Way out in front was the sea, the first time he had ever seen it in his life. The area around the pithead was a sea of mud and muck, lit by oil lamps; through the centre there was a tramway. On the track were several low wagons, loaded with spoil, being pushed by several straining labourers. Dai led Jack into the yard passing a line of despondent men.

"Shouldn't we wait in the queue, Dai?"

"No, no, Jack. They're locals looking for labouring work. Bloody useless down the shaft, I can tell you. Good for nothing except as donkeys." He pointed. "There's Hewitt over there."

Hewitt looked the part, thought Jack. Fine suit, bowler hat, unbuttoned twill overcoat and pipe in his hand; obviously in the money. Dai removed his cap.

"This is Jack Elks, Mr. Hewitt. Fifteen years experience. Hails from Pensal in Staffordshire."

Hewitt stared hard at Jack, eyes like rivets.

"Come here, Jack Elks!" Jack moved closer. "Let's see your hands."

Jack held them out, then Hewitt felt his arm muscles. "You cleared roadways?"

"Yes, Mr. Hewitt."

"Night shift, six to six. Two gangs of ten, alternate half-hours, six days a week. Thirty pounds a yard. If you don't earn fifteen shilling a day don't come back!" A roadway would be nine feet by nine feet and a yard forward was a lot of rock. He hoped to god that the rock wasn't granite.

"I deduct one shilling for the first fifteen and ten per cent after that. There's no limit on wages."

"I understand, Mr. Hewitt, that's fair."

Hewitt looked at him suspiciously. "Fair! I'll say it's fair! You're not one of those union men are you? I'll have no troublemakers!"

Jack lied through his teeth.

"Oh no, Mr. Hewitt. I'll have no truck with that. I want work - not time out."

"Good." Hewitt was pleased. "Come with Powell at six tomorrow. Make your mark here." Jack made a bad JE. There were times to be careful and this was one of them. Hewitt turned away then called back. "By the way, you can smoke below." Hewitt walked away laughing.

"What's he talking about, Dai?" Jack was puzzled. "Surely they don't allow smoking, do they?"

"It's his sense of humour. You will see. There's so much bloody water it's like working in a bath. Coming in all the time like a spray. Mind you, I should have said something else. There's no sign of coal yet so we may be on borrowed time."

Four weeks later Jack and Dai caught the train to Womenswold to visit the Snowdown Pit. In those four weeks two men had died due to flooding and falls and with no sign of coal it was obvious the Shakespeare was heading for closure. A week ago Jack had put it to Dai. "We'll die if we stay here. These bastards are breaking every rule in the book."

Snowdown was one of the deepest pits in the country and often, because of the heat, they were reduced to working in their underpants. They put up with it as the wages rolled in. On the first of March Jack found a house to rent in Belgrade Street and immediately wrote for Lizzie to join him. Jack gave Mrs. Dilkes's cat a good kick as he left. He would have liked to have done the same to Hewitt but decided not to, word spread rapidly in the mines and he didn't want trouble.

## 1 March 1912

On the 15th March 800,000 miners and 200,000 surface workers across the country walked out on strike in support of a minimum wage. The wages of most men were based on piece rates but in difficult conditions, wages often shrank to very low levels. Management often refused payments when the men were unable to produce coal or get coal in reasonable quantities, even though they may have worked extremely hard preparing tunnels, clearing spoil or be faced with impossible situations like poor seams or excessive water. After some years of negotiation, latterly with the Government as well as the owners, the Miners Federation of Great Britain called the men out.

Dai Powell spat the dust from his mouth before speaking. "What are we to do, Jack?" Dai was apprehensive. "All the men in the valleys are out. Should we not stop in sympathy? I feel I am letting my mates down!"

"No, Dai, it would be a waste of time - like a snowflake falling on a wet street."

Dai was not convinced. "We must get ourselves a union as soon as possible otherwise the day will come when they will crush us."

"We will, Dai, we will. When there are enough men, when the coal starts going out. That will be the time. For the moment we must be careful, go slow. Mark my word, when this strike is over men will flood down here - men in other places will be refused work, you've seen it happen!"

"That's why I am here - the owners in Wales are real bastards!"

"That's our advantage, Dai. Every man that comes here will have known rough times and even rougher justice. Been cheated of pay, victimised and beaten when they protested. We won't have to make union men of them - they're already moulded."

Lizzie was in a panic. "Jack can't be there to meet me, Dad!" She sniffed and blew her nose as the tears came. "He's sent me the address but I've no idea where it is!"

William tried to calm her. "It will be easy, Lizzie. Don't worry. Get a porter to help you. Take a cab - you've enough money."

Lizzie was not mollified. "But there are five cases - and three boys. Albert can't walk properly yet." She started to cry again. "I don't know how I'll manage three boys?"

Elizabeth had been listening intently, letting the tension build up before she had her say.

"Two boys, Lizzie. Little Jack can stay with me. He's been with me for two years." She paused expectantly and turned towards the fire to hide the smile on her face. "Only till Jack sends for him of course." She carefully put some coals on the fire.

"Oh, I would be so grateful, Mum." Lizzie sounded relieved. "It would be such a help till we are settled." Elizabeth was triumphant as she turned from the fire, careful to hide her feelings. Little Jack was hers, she would never let him go.

*On the 1st November 1912 the first ton of coal was raised at Snowdown, within eight weeks 800 tons a week were being raised.*

## 1913

The Snowdown Colliery expanded rapidly once the main roadways and drifts were ready. By 1913 over 600 men were working and more were to follow as the field expanded; Tilmanstone Colliery opened shortly after. Initially only Snowdown was producing coal and to it were attracted a motley crew of men from every other coalfield in the U.K. Welsh, Geordies, Lancastrians, Scots, *et al.* There was not an area that was not represented. The overwhelming attraction was the prospect of steady work and the money that went with it. Men of Kent were of little use, being unsuited by lack of experience and inclination. Mining was alien to them.

There was no housing nearby for the new arrivals coming in such large numbers, so the men were spread over the surrounding villages and the towns of Dover and Deal. At that time Deal was a cosy little seaside resort much frequented by middle-class holidaymakers. The town was horrified at the influx of miners, and their families that followed; with their alien tongue and dialects and their even stranger culture. Boarding houses were full of signs saying 'NO MINERS'. Not only that but in the early years of the century twenty-nine boreholes were sunk in the search for coal. The area was like a 'Klondyke', attracting drillers, rigs and so on. The miners flowed in to exploit the underground riches discovered. Slagheaps rose in the peaceful Kent countryside. There were protests but the developments were unstoppable. Wealth in search of more wealth is rapacious in its demands. Miners displaced from their home areas moved south as mine closures and other causes of unemployment bit hard on the heels of the slump of 1909. Many of the arrivals were militants, hardened by years of oppression, ready to work but unwilling to turn the other cheek. Jack found fertile ground in which to work.

Along the coalface sixteen men sat down and relaxed, mixing in small groups. There was no point in hacking out more coal for the moment because the flow of empty tubs had stopped and there was no sound or sign of new arrivals. The men would dearly have loved to stand and stretch but the seam was only four feet high so there was no roof space for them to do that. Also the air was hot and clammy; water dripped constantly from the roof and the men were wringing wet from the high humidity. The floor was puddled with water. Much of the men's clothing hung from timber props supporting the roof. Heaps of stripped out coal were piled up on the floor, adding to it would only make the job of filling the tubs more difficult. Stripping out the coalface and filling the tubs needed to be a co-ordinated action. The men were disgruntled. They were paid on tonnage and there was no pay for waiting time. They could ignore the cold water coming from the roof when working but with no coal to cut, muscles would stiffen and boredom would set in.

The Deputy appeared. The Deputy managed the area and was often called the Fireman because it was he who set off the dynamite when needed, to loosen rock. "There's a bloody tub off the rails at the top end. I'm off to get it cleared. Take snap-time."

Jack had been working in the centre of the face, next to him was Dai Powell. "Keep an eye open, Dai. I've got business to do."

Dai took his snap-tin and went down the face. He knew that Jack was recruiting for the union and anything to do with unions was unacceptable to the owners, especially on company property. If Jack were found he would get the sack. The greatest problem in organising the men was the fact that they were so scattered outside the pit, over such a wide area. There was no tightly knit colliery village. Men found lodgings where they could, some even living in tents. Five new men had joined the face that morning at the start of the shift and now clung together in a small group. Jack took his snap-tin and joined them.

"Morning lads. We've not met before. I'm Jack, Jack Elks."

The men were a bit guarded and one of them muttered defensively. "We're not market-men!"

Market-men were the casual labour force recruited on a daily basis and often used as strikebreakers. Jack smiled at them.

"Plain to see, lads. You're pitmen through and through. Same as us."

They were still hesitant. One of them spoke. "We can pull our weight on the face, we won't drag the wages down, but we've been used to the stall, working in small groups."

The coal hewers at Snowdown worked in a line along a face, cutting and timbering as they progressed forward. It was essential to cut a straight face and timber up in line otherwise there was danger of a fall, also it meant the tubs could be aligned for filling.

Jack smiled again. "Don't worry lads. There's plenty of work for all of us. Where are you from?"

The group relaxed a little. "Glasgie." "Yorkshire." "Monmouth." "Lanark." "Fife." "We're from the ends of the world."

Jack replied and waved his hand over the other men, "You're among friends here. Have you got lodgings?"

They had all managed to find something but most were sleeping on floors, some with as many as six men sharing a room. Jack got down to business.

"I wanted to speak to you about our Association. There's a great need to stick together."

One man spoke up. "We were all union men back home but the Manager made it clear he'd have none of that here!" Another spoke up. "What's the tab?"

Jack was pleased. "We've formed a lodge, you know, a special friendly society arrangement. We pay two shillings a week. When the time is right and we're strong enough there'll be recognition."

One of the men wiped his brow. "God, its hot sticky and wet here. I've never known the likes afore!"

"It can be worse," said Jack, "the wages are reasonable at the moment because they can't recruit experienced men locally but conditions are poor, there are no houses built and the management have the whip hand. There's no chargeman on this face, or elsewhere, so we have to stick together and make sure we get our dues."

The deputies recorded events that made up pay, such as adverse conditions, amount of water, lost time, extra timbering up and so on. In unionised pits the chargeman was a union appointee who ensured fair pay and dues as a counterbalance to the deputy. That way it was more difficult for the men to be shortchanged.

One man was unconvinced. "Two shillings a week is a lot. I'm a family man. I've got to save to get them here, find decent lodgings."

Jack played his trump card. "We can help, organise a loan, tell you about fair lodgings. If you're hurt we provide compensation."

One after another the men knelt over, spat on their hands and shook on it. "We're with you, Jack."

Jack felt pleased. So far they had recruited ninety five per cent of the men. They were growing stronger by the day. When the committee met that evening he would have five more men in the bag.

"See me outside the pit gates later. I'll give you directions, some notes and some cards. If you haven't got the cash, don't worry, it'll wait till after pay day." Several men looked embarrassed and one spoke out.

"I'm not good with the letters, Jack - never did get much schooling."

Jack made a point of being serious. "You leave that with me. If there's owt you need, anything, you come to me. Union matters, a letter home, best shop for boots and tools - you see Jack, I'll see you right."

At the end of the face Dai started singing, he had a beautiful Bardic Welsh voice, so Jack knew the Deputy was returning. Dai had seen his distinctive bullseye lamp up the tunnel, slicing through the gloom. The Deputy was in a temper.

"Tubs coming down! Up you lazy bastards! What the fuck are you doing Powell?" He had noticed the men grouped together and didn't like that - that's how trouble started. Dai gave him an angelic smile, somewhat wasted by the grime on his face.

"Just recruiting for the choir - trying to bring a little culture into our poor lives."

"Get back to work you Welsh cunt!"

The men picked up their tools, the tubs rolled into place and the fillers started shovelling coal.

An Association committee had been formed some months before and Jack had been a natural nominee. He had got articles of association from William back in Staffordshire and argued with passion for the immediate collection of dues, now nearly sixty pounds a week was mounting up in the bank. With funds they were no longer just a talking shop. They must bind together and help each other for mutual support. Many of the men had not worked for months prior to coming to Kent. Some had walked for hundreds of miles in all weathers just to get here. More importantly they had known oppression and hardship. Their desire for solidarity was self-evident. What was needed was an organisation to bind them together. Jack worked every possible hour outside his shift to get that organisation going, but he kept every piece of paperwork in his hands and guarded it carefully. There was no argument from the others on this. Jack had proved time and again that he was the best-educated man among them. For the moment he was content to let things grow. Their chance would come, his chance would come.

It was already late when Jack got home. Lizzie was waiting for him, hot meal ready and water warm for the bath.

"You look so tired, Jack."

"There's nowt wrong with me, girl. It won't always be like this."

"But I see so little of you. All these meetings, keeping records. There's no end to it, even on Sundays."

He started to undress. "Don't worry, hard work never hurt anyone."

Lizzie put some hot water in the tin- bath, looking anxious.

"But I don't know anyone here. The shopkeepers are so off-hand. The local people don't talk."

"It's early days, Lizzie. They don't realise the miners are

here to stay - they'll change when they realise where the money is."

Lizzie paused awhile before speaking, winding up her courage a little. "I had hoped we could join Mum and Dad in Australia. It's weeks since we had a letter. I hope they're in good health."

Jack had not forgotten either. "I know we said we'd go but we need money. We need a year to save, at least."

Lizzie looked sad. "The boys are growing fast. Mum and Dad have never seen Alice. I'm not even sure they know she is born."

Jack placated her. "I've still a mind for us all to go."

He knew one day he would have to make a decision but that may be years from now, in the meantime it was best to work at what he knew best. Lizzie relaxed when Jack indicated an open mind on the matter. Jack got out of the bath and dried himself.

"Come and see the babies, Jack. You've not seen them for more than ten minutes over the last few weeks."

"Sorry, must have my dinner, then I've got a meeting. Must go."

Lizzie dutifully put his plate on the table and returned to the sink feeling a mite dejected. The people around here are not like us, she thought. There was no sense of community like in Bloxwich. Then she remembered. Len, Ernie and Billy, together with their families should be arriving over the next month or two. Then she would have folk of her own.

## October 1913

### THE MORNING POST

*Yesterday Magistrates fined the Colliery Manager of Senghennyed Pit, Glamorgan, a total of £22 for offences under the Coal Mines Act of 1911. Senghennyed has a history and reputation as a dangerous pit and in 1901 many men lost their lives in an explosion. As recently as 1910 it had to be evacuated for several weeks because of a dangerous build up of gas, or fire damp as it is called. In the latest accident 439 lives were lost in a single explosion. Giving evidence, the Mines Inspector said that, despite repeated notifications, there had been a failure to provide apparatus to reverse the direction of currents of air throughout the mine and also a continued use of unprotected electrical signalling apparatus. The Colliery Manager was found guilty on four charges, one of which concerned the failure to make daily reports and conditions as to coal dust in the working*

*The Colliery Owners were acquitted on all charges. So far this year over 1300 miners have lost their lives in underground accidents in the coal mines of Great Britain. There have been a total of 164 prosecutions for offences under the Coal Mines Act and only 94 convictions, giving rise to fines totalling £295 in all. It is vital that safety conditions be raised if many more lives are not to be lost in our mines.*

## 1914

Lizzie hesitated before knocking on the parlour door, she knew Jack hated interruptions when he was working on the union business. Quietly opening the door she peered in. As usual Jack was there, surrounded by a mass of papers, the old typewriter clicking away. Jack didn't look around.

"I'm busy!"

"I thought you might like a drink."

"How do you spell 'conciliation'?"

Lizzie shrugged. "I'm not sure Jack. Shall I look it up for you?"

She entered the room to go to the dictionary. Jack squinted at the paper. "I think I might need glasses."

Lizzie was looking for an opportunity. "You need a break from this, Jack. We haven't been out for over a year. Why don't we go to the picture house tomorrow? Len's wife will look after the children."

Lizzie was pregnant again and wanted to go out before her tummy ballooned and became uncomfortable. Jack pushed his chair back and stretched, looking up at her.

"Can't! There's a very important meeting on tomorrow."

He leaned forward and looked at her more closely. "What's that you've got on your face?"

"Just a little powder and rouge, Jack. Doris showed me how."

Doris was Billy's wife.

"Get it off, woman! Can't abide the stuff!"

"Doris thought it might brighten me up, you know how my skin goes when I'm expecting."

"I don't care. I will not have my wife looking like a music hall trollop!"

Lizzie went to wash her face.

Saturday evening in the seaside town of Deal was quiet, but then every night in Deal was quiet. It was one of those places. So a large assembly of men in the Town Hall was bound to cause notice. Especially working men, some still in dirty pit clothes and with grimed faces. Buses and lorries had transported miners in from all the towns and villages around Snowdown. Promenading passers-by looked askance, many passed over to the other side, men looking aloof and women tut-tutting. What is the place coming to! Inside the hall Jack and other members organised tables and seating, arranged papers and got prepared for the first public meeting of the Snowdown Mineworkers Association.

Jack had been acting as secretary in an unofficial capacity and like all the senior members had not been formally elected. Over five hundred men crowded the hall. Previously it had been agreed that Jack would initiate proceedings whilst all others remained on the floor. A call was made for nominations and very quickly the President and Chairman were elected. Then Jack stepped down and the President and the Chairman took over. Bill Haseley and

Albert Wright stepped up,

Albert was the Chairman so he took control of the meeting.

"I want nominations for two committee men and a secretary. Do I hear names please? Nominations must have a proposer and seconder."

To Jack's intense gratification and relief he was given almost unanimous support as secretary and he stepped up to the top table. There was great clapping and cheering as the committee assembled. Albert banged for silence.

"Order please, gentlemen." He was held up for a few moments as various members inquired where they might be. "I call on the Secretary to make his report."

Jack had spent days preparing for this moment and he gave himself the satisfaction of waiting for the noise to abate and he checked his papers before getting to his feet.

"Fellow members, I will put before you in a moment an agenda that will take us from our present position of weakness to one of strength. One that I am confident is in your best interests. Before I do let me tell you of what we have achieved to date since our small beginning twenty months ago. Today we have thirteen hundred members, nearly every pitman at Snowdown. There is seven hundred pounds one shilling and fourpence in the bank. Since we formed we have paid compensation to members amounting to seven hundred pounds, fifteen shillings and sixpence. We have helped, by way of loans, one hundred and thirty men to move their families to Kent. That is what we have done and will continue to do. Also we are helping to organise the union at Tilmanstone.

As from today onwards I propose we no longer be the passive organisation of the past, afraid of shadows, skulking in the dark. We have elected officials, we have substance, and we have overwhelming support. I propose the following eight motions. That we apply to the Miners Federation of Great Britain for membership, that we authorise the executive to send delegates to Federation conferences. That we incorporate our Federation membership into our Articles of Association and accept the Federation rules and negotiating rights. We authorise the executive to negotiate with the management of Snowdown in all matters concerning wages and conditions of work in accordance with Federation Rules. We authorise the executive to conduct ballots concerning any Association action and to bind all members' actions to a two-thirds majority. That the executive represents all members in matters of dispute and representation with the management. We authorise the executive to distribute association funds in support of any action for which a ballot has taken place. That we appoint auditors. And lastly we retain the articles of a friendly society for the protection of our funds, with the title 'Kent Mine Workers Association'."

Albert rose to his feet. "I move a vote of thanks for Jack. Carried. Put that in the minutes, Mr. Secretary." There was a burst of applause. Albert continued with pride.

"Jack has put in endless hours of work on our behalf so that we might arrive today in strength and good shape. From my own knowledge I can tell you that he has taken many personal risks so we may stand here today, the strong organisation that we are. It is beyond my wit to repeat all he has said so I will cut short my embarrassment by asking for a vote on all propositions. Those for? Those against? None. Carried unanimously. I will now ask the President to give his inaugural speech."

Bill Haseley rose, showing obvious emotion. He was a proud, quiet Welshman of fifty and had spent all his working life as a pitman.

"You have given me the great honour to be your President. Forty years ago when I started in the pits as a doorboy such an honour could not have passed my mind or be thought likely. There is so much to be done there is a fear in my mind that I may never see it all come to a conclusion and I may pass on before the work we must do is complete. These are the rambling words of an old man who never had much schooling but I clearly see what must be done to bind together our men who come from so many parts of this island bringing with them an ark of cultures. There is a need for schools for our children, recreational fields, teams to be built to reinforce our spirit of comradeship and foster our pride, more homes and better homes. I ask you, can the Kentish man play football and rugby as we? No, they have not the spirit to play with passion as we do and that is our strength because we will build a community they will envy. This is not the Promised Land but we will try to make it so. We want a chapel and a hall. Yes I hear men say we need pit baths, better ventilation for the hot place in which we work and we must face and pull up a management that cares nought for the lives of men. All these we can achieve if we build with our hearts as well as our muscle. There are children and grandchildren to come and I do not want them to say we burked the situation. Before I go I wish in my old age to sit by a field and watch our young play as pit ponies romp at summer leave. When that is done I will go happy. With your support we can achieve all. Thank you."

From the hall Dai Powell gave Jack the thumbs up sign. Jack was content. They were on their way. He was on his way.

War was declared in August and the British Standing Army of regulars departed for France, many pouring through the port of Dover to Calais and beyond. Many would not return but at the time that was not known and the widespread jingoism and flare of patriotism lured many men into the arms of the Sergeant Major. Many miners joined, especially the young men and boys. Just as coal supplies were most needed, production began to fall. The situation was made worse by the logistical operation of conveying coal from the mine and bringing timber in. Also the movement of coal and supplies in the mine was the work of young men and boys, an operation that was a hard, grinding, monotonous, slog. Without families to support the young men were first away to war and recruits from other mining districts dwindled to a halt.

Jack was concerned that Association membership was falling but realised that this could be turned to advantage. Some weeks previously he had written to Clarence Pike, the General Manager, on behalf of the Association requesting a meeting.

On the appointed day Bill Haseley, Albert Wright and Jack arrived in hopeful expectation. Pike received them brusquely and had quite deliberately not invited them to sit down. They stood cap in hand before him. Bill Haseley showed their credentials and explained the extent of membership, and then he handed over a copy of the minutes of the Association election meeting.

"We ask you to recognise the Association in accordance with the wishes of our members."

When he had finished Pike lent forward, and, with evident contempt, flicked the papers onto the floor, causing Jack to kneel to retrieve them.

"That is what I think of your paper. That is what I think of your bloody union! I will have no part in recognising it! I resent your attempt to meddle in the management of this colliery. Bugger off!"

Jack saw Bill stiffen at the response and it was a few seconds before he replied. "Mr. Pike, the men have by democratic means elected me their President and spokesman, together with our committee. It would be in all our interests to come to an agreement. We do not wish to progress by devious and hidden means but meet man to man, in the open."

Pike screwed up his face. "Bollocks! Let me state plainly. I will not deal with your Association as you call it. What do men like you know about running a colliery? What can I learn from an old fool such as you? Piss off and get back to your shovel. Fuck off!"

Bill Haseley stood his ground with quiet pride and firmness

"I have been on this earth for full fifty years and I know my upbringing was with lowly folk but never have I been so spoken to by any man. My way is to give full courtesy and respect to all and I cannot reverse that which I have been taught and followed all my life. We came in good faith because we thought there was common ground in the growth of harmony and trust. There is no seeking or thought to take your place. Can you not see in this endeavour the mutual benefit to us all and we are not here to advantage ourselves over all else."

"I said, fuck off!"


Twelve months later Jack was ready. More men had enlisted and he knew from the Checkweigher exactly what the production levels were. Profit margins must be being squeezed. With that thought in mind he sought a meeting with Pike. A private meeting, let me buy you lunch, in Canterbury. Jack mentioned his concern about the loss of men. He had proposals to staunch the flow. In preparation Jack bought a decent suit from the pawnbrokers.

"I take it you're paying for this?" Pike growled it out. Jack nodded. "In that case I'll have a bottle of wine and the Beef Wellington!"

Initially Jack confined the conversation to war events in general, he wanted Pike to relax. Eventually Pike came to the point. "You mentioned the loss of men in your letter, what have you to say?"

"Call me Jack. I think that's appropriate for a private lunch on neutral ground, don't you?"

"I don't think so, Elks. You may be the Secretary of your so called Association but I won't have that familiarity."

Jack shrugged. It was no more than he expected. "As I see it men have left and are still leaving. Profits are going down."

Pike raised an eyebrow. "That's my concern, not yours."

"If I thought it was only your concern I shouldn't be here. But if the pit closed we would lose. If the transport boys go other men lose wages. If the coalface is denuded the men lose money. Everyone loses."

With a small gesture with his wine glass Pike conceded grudgingly. "Maybe."

"Don't misunderstand me," said Jack, "but when wages are lost men's minds turn to other matters. Small issues become big issues. Bad situations get worse. Even my role as Secretary gets more difficult. I certainly don't want to lose wages!"

Jack poured some more wine. "Don't take this as a threat because that is not my direction but if the men decide to take action we have the funds to back them. Our executive has great respect from the men but if events blow up we are bound to action by democratic vote."

"Lot of bloody socialists! That will bring this country to its knees."

"Our men don't know what a socialist is! Ask them, they'll stare at you in wonder. Ask them a different question though it might be different. Ask them if they can feed their family properly or if they have a decent home for their children? Then you'll get an answer."

"Yes, yes!" Pike waved his hand, "Get to the point! What's your proposal?"

"There are a number. We will appeal to the men to stay at work. Don't forget we speak to the wives as well, mining communities stick together. Coal is as important as soldiers, otherwise steel, railways and munitions will grind to a halt. I have made contacts in the Federation to bring in extra men. We can get the rail wagons returned faster, the NUR will listen to me. So will the dockers. The quicker the coal gets away the sooner you get paid. The timber needs to be delivered on time. I know how to do it."

"I can do all that!"

"No, I speak to the men on the ground. You can only go through management, they'll not help, not at this time."

"What's your price?"

"There's no price, no money to be paid - only co-operation."

"Spit it out!"

"Recognition of the Association. Full negotiating rights as in other districts. Details are here." Jack passed over the papers that had been flicked on the floor. Pike picked them up and rapidly read through. As he went to speak, Jack raised his hand.

"Also we want more houses, a safety committee, union chargeman on the face. Clear rules, binding rules regarding disciplinary action and help with community projects."

Pike re-examined the papers. "That's not here!"

"Yes, that's the beauty of it. When you meet Haseley and Wright you not only accept their request but also pledge yourself to these other matters. A concord. It will have to be in writing of course. Here's a suggestion." Jack passed over a note.

"How do I know you can deliver?"

"You have my word, I say nowt that I don't mean."

"There'll be no mention of this meeting?"

"This meeting never took place. I'm as keen on that as you."

"What's the alternative?"

"Chaos! We can either strive for harmony or disagree." Jack deliberately kept his voice low and flat so his words did not sound like a threat.

"That's a threat, I cannot take that. It will do no good to strike!"

"There will be no strike, Mr. Pike. Why should I risk beggaring our own members or throw away hard saved funds? No, it is not them we are talking about. Just keep in mind what I can do for you, what I can do against you; but I do not want to do that. That is destructive and would help no one."

"I could sack you!"

"That would give me twenty four hours a day to work against you because the men would back me."

"Do Haseley and Wright know of this?"

"They have no knowledge whatsoever."

"How do we proceed?"

"Simple. You invite the lodge committee to meet you. They will take it as a magnanimous gesture. Bill Haseley will take it like the conversion of Paul on the road to Damascus. You will get all the credit and good will."

"Agreed," said Pike, "I'll need a week."

"Agreed," said Jack.

After a while and the last of the wine, Pike said he must go to the lavatory. Jack went with him. They stood facing the wall. Jack made sure they were alone then he spoke quietly.

"One or two small things, Clarence. When Bill Haseley comes to your office you will offer him a chair and treat him with respect. He is the finest man you will ever meet, naturally honest and honourable. If you ever treat him as you did before I will put your teeth in your throat!" Surprised, Pike pissed on his shoe.

"Oh, and one last thing. Don't make me kneel again. I kneel to no one."

Two weeks later the Association was accepted. How right you were Pa. Ca-Canny, Ca-Canny!

## 1915

Mr. Gilliland, senior partner of Gilliland and Plunkett sat at the top of the table, staring around myopically, whilst cleaning his glasses. That job done he replaced them and stared quietly around the group. His hands, untouched by hard labour, were smooth with nicely rounded nails. Everyone waited on him to speak. Jack noticed the hands and self-consciously placed his below the table, trying to hide his blackened fingernails and workworn fingers. Mr. Gilliland started.

"Good afternoon, gentlemen. This is my first day as the independent chairman of this Joint District Board. Our task is to decide the agreed minimum wage in accordance with the Act. At the present time this is four shillings per day. That seems to me to be a considerable amount of money to pay a man for doing nothing, however I do understand that, once decided, our decision becomes law and thereby enforceable. Now, it is Messrs Downley, Pike and Conrad acting for the owners and Wright, Elks and Pritchard for the men?" There were nods of agreement all round. "Perhaps Mr. Downley will put the owners case?"

"Yes, Mr. Chairman. The position is very simple. The

present four shilling minimum is satisfactory to the owners. During the last year this minimum has had to be paid on only a limited number of occasions, ten per cent in fact."

Gilliland wrote down a few notes. "What do you have to say?"

He glanced over at Wright, Jack and Pritchard.

Albert Wright spoke up. "Mr. Chairman, this minimum has held for three years but circumstance and times have changed. It must be updated."

"Why is that?"

Jack took over. "Mr. Chairman, piece rates have risen whereas the minimum rate has been static, its value has therefore fallen. Wages in all industries have gone up. In any case the current minimum was set without regard to the prevailing piece rates at the time."

Mr. Gilliland shook his head. "Perhaps Mr. Downley will explain this 'piece rate'."

"Yes, Mr. Chairman, the men who get the coal are set a target of how much they should produce. If they reach that target they get a full wage. Should they not reach the target the wage falls but cannot go below four shillings a day."

"So the men are paid by results, is that it?"

"Exactly, Mr. Gilliland."

"I do not see what the problem is." He looked at Albert Wright. "A man can produce nothing and get paid twenty four shillings a week!"

Albert sighed and returned to the fray. "There are dozens of reasons why a man may not produce coal. There may be none there, there may be too much water, the seam may be poor quality. It is against all these reasons that the minimum wage was to act as a buffer otherwise a man may work all week and get nothing."

Mr. Gilliland looked triumphant. "That's it, the very point. In those circumstances the man gets the twenty-four shillings!"

Jack stepped in again. "Twenty four shillings is not a fair week's wage. The act states that the minimum must be set in relation to the prevailing piece rates. That is not the case. Also the minimum is only paid if the man has had a one hundred per cent attendance record over the past six months, again that is not stated in the act. Not only has this board failed to observe the letter of the law but the management often delays payment for as much as three weeks."

Gilliland looked hard at Jack. "As a lawyer of thirty years standing I do not consider I need instruction as to the law. In my view the raising of the minimum rate can only encourage idleness and that I cannot support especially at a time when the flower of our nation's menfolk are dying on the field of battle to protect this Island and those who work safely at home, buttressed by a minimum wage."

Henry Pritchard tried hard to keep the anger from his voice. "Neither do I feel we need advice on patriotism when our men have willingly foregone both their Easter and summer holidays. Men die daily in the pits, not only in wartime but all the time. Injuries are commonplace but we do not let up. As has been said, ten per cent of our men are reduced to the minimum. There is not a man here who could keep himself and a family on twenty four shillings a week."

Gilliland was unmoved. "Mr. Downley, why are there delays in payment?"

"Very simple Mr. Chairman. The events that cause minimum wages to be applied occur in a haphazard manner and it takes time for payments to be checked after the paperwork has made its way to the office. Our job is to get the coal out for the country, not to delay it by chasing paper."

Gilliland looked at Jack again. "There you have it, there is no unreasonable delay. I quite agree with you that the Act does not say that attendance should be ignored, neither does it say that it cannot be taken into account. I judge it to be perfectly fair that a man's attendance record be taken into account!"

Jack was terse, too terse. "Even if he has been injured or ill or bereaved?"

Gilliland drew himself back. "The contract between master and servant is clear. We are paid to work, not otherwise, insurance is paid if a man is injured or ill and in other circumstance there is the Board of Guardians. The Minimum Wage Act is not a charter for the helpless or the idle. There is no point in setting a high wage rate for doing nothing because that will only encourage idleness or be an incentive to loaf and sit about. I will have a vote on the rate of four shillings per day. Those for? Three. Those against? Three. As Chairman I vote for a continuation of the current rate. The meeting is closed."

Jack was in a bad mood when he got home, Lizzie could tell from the set of his jaw and pursed lips.

"Have you had a bad day, Jack?"

"Yes. I've been spoken to as if I were a bloody boy - a stupid boy! They give us a lawyer for a chairman who has never done a day's hard work in his life!"

He sat down, seething.

"I'll get you a drink, Jack. Help you to relax."

"Yes, then I must write to the Federation and get reading."

"Read what?"

"The law, woman, the bloody law! I'm told I don't know the law. Well, I damn well soon will!"

Lizzie wanted to tell Jack that she was pregnant again but decided that today was not the day.

## 1918

The inaugural meeting of the Snowdown 'Joint Pit Committee' met in this year. This arose through the mechanism of the 'State Control of Mining Act' which had been enacted late in 1916. Overall production was failing to meet the nation's need in wartime so the government announced that each colliery must appoint a committee of equal numbers of owners and men to meet to promote productivity. Jack, Albert Wright and Tom Enfield represented the Association. Headquarters man Richard Edward Rowland aided by Clarence Pike and Ted Burrows, an Overman, represented the owners.

Rowland took the chair at the head of the table and opened the meeting. "As chairman of this committee I will...."

Tom Enfield interjected. "Who appointed thee?"

"Aye, who appointed you?" Albert rapped his pipe on his boot to remove the dottle.

Rowland sounded surprised. "I was appointed to this committee by the Chairman of the East Kent Colliery Association. The owners have the greatest interest in this therefore it must be me!"

"You may see it that way, I certainly don't." Tom weighed his words carefully. "According to the note passed to our Secretary from the Federation we are equal numbers. This meeting is to decrease absenteeism and raise output. Is that not true?"

Rowland looked flustered. "Yes, but..."

"We should vote for chairman." Tom cut in. "I think that's fair!"

Jack and Albert nodded support. They had agreed their tactics before today, although as Jack had pointed out it may be better to let them provide the chair at this first meeting. "Let them propose, put the onus on them, go careful at first." Pike proposed a vote for chairman.

"I propose, Mr. Rowland." Three for. Three against. Deadlock. Jack led off.

"I propose a rotation of chairman. That way everyone gets a turn. Fair to all sides. If that is agreed then I propose Mr. Rowland takes the chair today."

A minute later it was all agreed, so Rowland asked for proposals. Jack, Albert and Tom remained silent.

"Come, come, gentlemen. Let's have some positive proposals. That's our patriotic duty."

Albert puffed at his pipe. "What's patriotic got to do with

this?"

Pike said his piece. "Surely, it's clear. If we cut absenteeism that will increase output. That's our first priority. Then we explore other means of getting more coal out. The nation needs it."

"Well put, Mr. Pike," Mr. Rowland enthused, "For King and Country. Cut absenteeism and produce more coal."

Tom deliberately kept his voice emotionless. "I think you've the nub of it. So how do you consider we will cut absenteeism?"

Jack cut in. "Firstly, do we have absenteeism? If so, how much? We must deal with facts."

"Do you have any figures, Mr. Pike?" Rowland asked.

"Yes, we lost over 5,000 man days in the last year."

"What were the causes of absence?" Jack asked.

Pike did not like the way this was going. "I'm not sure. I did not know this would arise!"

Got you, thought Jack. "Mr. Chairman, as the secretary of our Association I keep figures of the compensation we pay our colleagues who are absent sick. During the last year 3,600 days off work related to accidents at work. As that represents the main cause of absence then surely it is the causes of those accidents we must address."

Rowland smiled. "Thank you, Mr. Elks. I regard that as an excellent suggestion. What do you think, Mr. Pike?"

What Mr. Pike thought could not be repeated at this meeting. Moments ago he had consoled himself that only half the meetings would be controlled by the Association. Now they were trying to control the agenda and this damn fool was playing into their hands. He gritted his teeth.

"Yes, of course this must be carefully considered. May I ask for this to be put to the next meeting so I can present detailed statistics?"

Ted Burrows spoke up. "There were 5,800 days lost according to the box hall office records so that leaves 2,200 days unaccounted for Mr. Chairman."

The box hall office was the timekeepers and manager's office at the bottom of the pit.

"Yes, we understand that," said Jack, "but my figures relate to compensation payments, illness in the ordinary way does not count. Also in wartime there is an irreducible minimum due to family bereavement and so on that we can never eradicate. The analysis and elimination of accidents in the workplace must remain our priority. Do you not agree, Mr. Chairman?"

Rowland thought he was getting the hang of this job. "Yes, I feel that is a fair point. We cannot speak individually to each man!"

Pike nodded, concealing his annoyance. Jack returned to the fray.

"There is another point, Mr. Chairman. I feel sure your wife will have mentioned to you that the price of everything has increased. If she has been as indignant as my wife she will have mentioned it."

Caught off guard Rowland conceded. "Yes, you're right, Mr. Elks. She has mentioned it on quite a few occasions."

Jack tried to hide a smile. "With regard to the lost time, does it seem likely that a man would absent himself without reason and lose wages if his wife was asking for more money."

Rowland looked around the table. "Yes, that seems a reasonable and natural conclusion. Mr. Pike, if you will provide the analysis of accidents as agreed then that seems the best area to concentrate on."

Jack continued. "It is rather urgent, Mr. Chairman, if we are to meet the government objectives, for Mr. Pike to give all of us details of matters referred from this meeting prior to future meetings. I can promise that from our side we will study them and arrive back with solutions."

"Yes," said Albert, "complete co-operation. That's a promise."

Rowland looked at Pike. "Mr. Pike, I am sure you will help in every possible way. I look forward to getting early details."

Pike was thinking there might be murder before then. As Rowland sublimely returned to the meeting, Pike got in first.

"Output is a management matter so I propose you hear me first on this."

Tom had been briefed on this. "First, Mr. Chairman, we must decide what 'increased output' means. That is a fair question, is it not?"

Rowland stared in amazement. "Surely gentlemen, surely we all know what more output means. It means getting more tons of coal onto, what do you call it - yes, the bank."

"Ah!" said Albert, "I understand now. You will excuse me for being a foolish old man. You do not mean getting the men already at work to produce more. That is fair."

Pike kicked Burrows under the table, then led off. "Clearly the Chairman means we must produce more - by any means available!" He was getting testy.

Jack stepped in. "There are two issues here, Mr. Chairman. How to increase the overall output of the mine and secondly, how to get each man to produce more."

"Yes, yes, that's it!" Rowland was pleased, "Perhaps Mr. Pike or Mr. Burrows could take the first of those two points."

Mr. Pike ground his teeth in annoyance. "Mr. Chairman, I do not consider the first point to be a matter of consideration for this meeting. I cannot table proposals at this committee."

Jack jumped in. "Mr. Chairman, we came to this meeting believing we were serving our country. We want to co-operate as Mr. Wright has said. We want to contribute and will make the greatest endeavour to support you in whatever must be done - but we cannot do that enveloped in darkness!"

"Yes," said Rowland, "the government instructions gives no limitation, it specifies that we raise output. Mr. Pike, only the other day at headquarters you spoke on such matters. It would be most valuable if you put your intentions to this meeting."

Pike was on the point of rebellion but thought better of it. "If you consider that correct, Mr. Chairman, then I will do that, except for matters outside the mine bounds, of course."

"Mr. Chairman," Jack kept on, "in view of our pledge should we not consider matters outside the mine bounds if they have any effect and consequence on the work here. While we are not businessmen and would not want to meddle in those matters beyond our ability, we assure you that our links with other labour organisations are strong. All our resources are at your disposal."

Rowland felt he was on a winner. "Yes. I agree. Mr. Pike, let us be as frank and open as possible," he gave Pike a winning smile, "in all matters pertaining to the organisation and development of the mine." Taking Pike's silence as agreement, he went on. "Thank you, Mr. Pike, that will be most instructive. Now, let's move to the next issue. Getting more out of the men."

Albert clamped his pipe in his teeth. "Mr. Chairman, if we produce more who will get the benefit?"

Poor old man thought Rowland. "Why, Mr. Wright, the country will benefit - the nation will benefit."

Removing his pipe, Albert scratched his head. "Ah! I see. The nation will benefit!" He smiled. "That's good. Free coal for the nation. I am satisfied."

Rowland looked puzzled, "No, I think you misunderstand me, Mr. Wright. The coal will be sold in the normal way."

"Oh!" said Albert, "that's a horse of a different colour. The men won't benefit from this! I'm to go to them and say 'do this' and 'do that', get more coal and they must do it for nothing. Whereas the owners will be paid for it. Is that what you mean?"

Rowland went down the slippery slope. "No, Mr. Wright. I didn't mean that, of course the men must receive a fair reward for their effort."

Jack had his lead. "That is very fair, Mr. Chairman. If the men can produce more and get more on to the bank then they must get a proper return for their effort so we must consider the means of doing it and examine wage rates to ensure the fairness of it all."

Pike was beside himself with rage. "That is not part of this committee, wage rates are another matter. Mr. Chairman, I protest."

Rowland felt he had to uphold his position. "No, Mr. Pike. I have said, extra output, not the same, but extra output can be rewarded. Otherwise why will the men help us?"

"Yes", said Jack, "that is fair. Men at the coalface get more coal, other men work harder to get that coal to the surface. Other men get it to the transports. As Mr. Rowland has said, that extra output should be rewarded. Mr. Chairman, my colleagues and I will give you the utmost support in all matters we have discussed. No stone will be left unturned."

Pike rolled his eyes at the ceiling as Jack continued.

"I feel we have done an excellent days work. We will come to the next meeting with many proposals, so we look forward to getting the information from Mr. Pike. May I suggest we close the meeting so we can get to our task and meet again in two weeks? We propose Mr. Wright as chairman on the next occasion but are happy to let Mr. Rowland continue, he has our utmost confidence."

"Good", said Mr. Rowland, "if there are no dissenters I shall be pleased to continue. Thank you gentlemen, I look forward to the next meeting."

As Jack, Albert and Tom walked down the road to the nearby village pub they could barely contain their laughter. Tom kept blowing his nose to stop his eyes watering.

"Oh, my God! What a meeting!"

"Was that a cabbage or was that green!"

They had won everything they could have hoped for, and more. An examination of all work practices, safety issues, details of management plans, spending on productivity which would include mechanisation, transport arrangements, rates of pay for all men, above and below ground and the cost of living as an issue. And all in a day, no, an hour!

"That fool from the headquarters," said Jack, "he really is

well named isn't he!"

"What do you mean, Jack?"

"Why, Richard Edward Rowland, that's who. Richard Edward. Dick! Ed! Don't you get it - 'Dickhead' Rowland."

They laughed the more.

"Did you see the look on Clarrie's face - it was a picture." said Albert, "I thought he'd burst. He's probably kicking Burrows all around his office at the moment!"

"By gum!" said Tom, rubbing his hands, "I can't wait for the next meeting!"

Albert was still chortling. "Hey Jack. I heard you had another son. We haven't wet the baby's head yet. This is the occasion for it."

"Just wait till we tell Bill Haseley!"


## May 1918

Several times Lizzie had experienced disappointments that the war had stopped them going to Australia.

"Will this war never end, Jack? We will never see Mum and Dad, I fear."

"We can't go until this war is over, whatever happens."

Lizzie sighed. "At least you had the good sense not to enlist."

Jack nodded in agreement. "I've started at the bottom three times – that's enough for me."

Albert, the third son, appeared in the doorway. "The postman gave me this letter, father."

Absently, Jack took the envelope. "Get off to school now."

Jack did not like the look of this envelope, made of white paper with a black edge. He could tell it was from Staffordshire with his father's clear copper plate address. Wondering what it could mean, he opened it and read.

*Dear Jack and Lizzie,*
*My heart is sad as I write this letter. Yesterday we were told that Bertie has been killed in Belgium. In all the confusion letters have been delayed and it is only now that we have been notified. He was buried on the battlefield, we know not where and there can be no proper funeral so I grieve but have only a letter to hold. I asked him not to go but he was so proud to serve his country and see the world, there was no holding him back.*

Jack passed the letter to Lizzie. "I didn't even know he had joined - we've dozens of lads joining, they think the army will be better than the pits! Damn, damn, damn!"

Lizzie was weeping. "He was so young, Jack."

"He was only twenty-two."

Jack threw the letter on the fire and it flared up and withered away.

## Walsall Observer

*Private Bertram Lawrence Elks is officially reported to have died in France on April 13 from gunshot wounds in the abdomen, received the previous day, after a year's active service with the South Staffs. A single 22 year old miner, his home was at 32 Wallington Heath, and he was employed before joining the colours in 1917, at Great Wyrley Colliery. (27 April 1918)*

Bertram Lawrence Elks is buried at Poppennye in Belgium

# 1918

## THE END OF WORLD WAR 1

*'I believe that men are beginning to see, not perhaps the golden age, but an age which is brightening from decade to*

*decade, and will lead us to an elevation where we can see the things for which the heart of mankind is longing.'*

*WOODROW WILSON*

PRESIDENT OF THE UNITED STATES OF AMERICA

# Chapter 5

## HONEST JACK FROM KENT

## 1920

The combined executive committees of the separate lodges of the Kent Miners Association met early in 1920. There were now three collieries in the area, Snowdown, Tilmanstone and Chislet. As the new collieries opened, Jack and other members of the Snowdown lodge visited and helped form new lodges under the auspices of the association. That association was unco-ordinated and the loosely knit ties made it difficult to meet and formulate common policy and action. Also each group tended to be jealous of their independence. In all this Jack had only a few advantages. Firstly, he was the longest serving and most experienced secretary, secondly, he had met many men and recruited them and thirdly, he controlled the central fund which paid Federation dues and so on. Last but not least Snowdown had the most men so in a total vote it would dominate. That situation would, Jack knew, rapidly change as Tilmanstone and Chislet took on more men. Jack decided to act before it was too late. With that in mind he sought a meeting with Bill Haseley and Albert Wright.

"Lets go in the Snug, what will you have to drink?"

Bill shook his head, Albert wanted a pint. Jack got two beers from the bar and sat down. Bill filled his pipe, he sensed this was not meant to be a short meeting so he loaded his ammunition. Jack wanted to reassure them. "I've not asked for this meeting here to be underhanded."

Bill, as usual was very solemn. "That is good. I do not feel easy with secrecy."

"No," said Jack, "I have real concerns. At the moment there are three lodges but each goes its own way. There will come a time when, if we don't stick together, we'll be cut up piecemeal. There are three owners, three managements and three lodges. That is a weakness for us that they will exploit and take advantage of. We must bind together, have a central body that can talk for all. Then there is the Federation. We pay our dues but have no representation. We need to be seen as a district not three separate mines."

Bill puffed his pipe. "You mean have only one lodge?"

Albert lifted his pipe. "We'll not get agreement to that!"

"No, we need the lodges to organise local matters. Act as a focal point for the men. An overall executive would consider and control issues that apply to everyone and then represent all in those matters. Like district minimum wage rates, Federation policy, political funds, legal matters and so on."

Albert conceded. "You have a point, Jack. That is the arrangement we had in Yorkshire."

Jack kept quiet as Bill pondered for a moment.

"How do we go about it?"

Inwardly, Jack breathed a sigh of relief. "I think it is best if you and Albert approach the other committees. Suggest we consider new rules and organisation but stress that 'local' remains just that. There is strength in numbers but only if we are all on common ground. I can prepare new articles defining the rules of the area and local committees, we must also separate central and lodge funds."

"We must have a joint meeting but that means more work. An agenda. And minutes as well!" Albert looked worried as he said it; paperwork was not his strong point.

Jack pressed the point. "If you can set it up, Bill, I can give you an outline agenda for discussion and organise a conference to follow on from there."

Bill looked pleased. "I like the idea of binding all the men together, in all our mines, with one group for we shall be the stronger for it. I remember how it gave us unity in the Rhondda all those years ago."

Albert got another two pints. Jack pressed on. "There is talk that the National Mines agreement will end soon, a new wage proposal is being prepared. There is talk of ending the control on hours worked."

Jack stopped, he could see that Bill was lost in thought. Bill had heard all and understood, but he understood more. Three rugby teams, a special cup, more fields, children playing, a bigger community, filled his mind.

"Yes, you're right, Jack. We must build Jerusalem not Jericho. Give me the words and your papers and some wise words on this 'Sankey' matter."

Albert didn't understand that. "Yes, Jack. Explain this Sankey report I hear about - and this triple alliance!"

A month later all the lodge committees met in the County Hotel in Canterbury. Bill Haseley opened the conference.

"I only sit in this chair at the request of you all and until ballots have been presented to the men. During this process of democratic change we can either split asunder or become one. Each man must have his say as that is fair and while my feeling is for unity I would force no man to a situation that his heart rebels against. An agenda and revised articles of association are before you. I have asked Jack Elks to keep notes. The meeting is open to comments."

"What do we gain from being members of the Miners Federation?"

"We have a say in negotiations, contribute to the political levy that puts Labour members in Parliament and share in the strike fund."

"What if we don't want to strike?"

"As now, we are bound for the common good, there is

strength in numbers and the owners negotiate with a single body on national pay issues."

"Why do we need Labour men in Parliament?"

"To promote legislation for our betterment - better working conditions and safety measures. Oh, and the Coal Mines Act."

"What will be the work of the local committees?"

"That is defined in the revised articles. All matters relating to one mine only will be handled locally. All matters that have a district definition will be handled centrally - by a central committee."

"How do you tell which is which?"

"That is well defined but remember most issues start locally, it is for the local committee to sift and either hold or pass on."

"The central committee will need to handle many matters. How will they cope?"

"That well may be true. I put it to you here, has anyone a suggestion or idea?"

Albert spoke up. "In Yorkshire we employed a Miners Agent to deal with daily matters and to advise and inform the committees of events. He also looked after compensation claims. We called it 'add-minnie-trashun'."

Bill reflected on that. "The agenda and articles do not allow for that. I do not like that word Agent. At the Federation that is called General Secretary. Mindful of the fact that we have nearly one hundred men hurt each year there is great value in the suggestion. May we have a vote to include such a person be put on the agenda for inclusion in the ballot."

"Do we have the funds?"

"Our funds are sufficient to allow this support and it will free committee men from considerable irksome duties. Those for? Those against? Carried."

The conference went on for several hours then broke for dinner and drinks. Bill collared the men from Tilmanstone and Chislet. "There may be an impression in your minds that I have done all this work to prepare for this day. That impression would be false, I could not do it. The man we must thank is Jack Elks who has spent several weeks preparing everything. May I ask that one of you propose and the other second a vote of thanks to him at the end of the meeting."

Four weeks later Bill Haseley was elected President of the Association by all collieries and Jack was elected as the full-time General Secretary. Lizzie was pleased but made the wrong assumption that she might see more of Jack. Well she did in a way, because her front parlour became the new Secretary's office but Jack's hours did not diminish. Lizzie got on with the children and housework. A son had been born in the previous August and what with a new baby and another two little ones not yet at school her days were full to overflowing. Every now and again Jack would appear demanding quiet and it was worse when the four eldest came home from school.

## 1920 October

Throughout the war and afterwards the cost of living soared and because miners wages were held back, their standard of living inevitably declined. War-time appeals to their patriotism had kept wages down. When the war was over the miners starting agitating for better wages. Since 1917 the coalfields and production had been under state control and it was felt by the majority that nationalisation was entirely feasible. Total state control had certainly proved more effective than the previous operation of 370 separate owners. The Miners Federation put forward a claim and the government offered two shillings a week and a board of inquiry. That board was called the Sankey Commission and it reported that miners should get rises of up to 30%, reduced working hours and proposed public ownership of all coal mines. The report also concluded, 'There are numerous houses in the coal districts which are a reproach to our civilisation.'

Whilst the miners were jubilant, the government was concerned and changed some members of the commission but even that did not seriously modify the proposals. The mine owners were incensed at this outcome, so the government rejected any proposals for nationalisation. After going to the TUC for help, which was rejected, the Miners Federation went to the National Coal Board, set up in the war, to negotiate for an increase in wages. This was refused so the miners formed an alliance with the National Union of Railwaymen and the Transport workers. When the government responded by offering yet another tribunal the Miners Federation acted, called a conference, and the miners voted for a withdrawal of labour. Jack was the Kent delegate at his first conference, following the ballot.

Jack had expected calm, efficiency and organisation. What he got was confusion. He was confused and he was surrounded by confusion. Delegates split into groups. Leaders on the podium flitted back and forth; sometimes disappearing for hours, nobody seemed to know where. Rumours spread around the floor. Jack could fathom little sense to it. Vainly the Chairman tried to keep order but the debate had broken down. Jack eventually found a group of men from Staffordshire and introduced himself. "Yes, we remember your father." " Where have you been?" " Who are you representing?" "Right Jack, bugger this lot, lets have a drink!" "Your first time here is it? Stay with us, Jack, we'll put you right." Jack relaxed. He was among his own so he didn't mind as the conference dithered on for several days.

Rumour, rumour, rumour. The NUR were in, then they were out! The government had given in. Then it hadn't. The owners had agreed a rise! Pigs might fly! The man in the moon ate green cheese!

Jack had thought there would be concord and solidarity, but he noticed there wasn't even agreement amongst the men on the podium. Resolutions flowed back and forth for discussion, getting nowhere. Jack got worried wondering what he could say to the committees when he returned home, back to Kent. "Nowt but waffle lads!" "The whisky was good."

Helped by the Staffordshire men Jack slowly got his bearings, starting to understand the nuances and political groupings. It was the group of executives on the podium that fascinated Jack. That was where the power resided. Jack made up his mind. That was where he wanted to be, he wanted to be a "Homburg" man. All the men on the podium wore a " Homburg", a nice grey Homburg hat with a black band. It was they who were really dictating events he could tell, doing deals, meeting powerful people, manipulating. Down here on the floor, he concluded, they were just so much cannon fodder. If he was to achieve anything he had to get up there. But how? In a vote he would lose, he held only 3000 votes in over three quarters of a million! He needed friends, if possible powerful friends.

So he watched and listened, talked to as many delegates as possible. Gradually he started to understand and see the way things were done. Jack was nothing if not a fast learner. He picked up the gossip that Robert Smillie, the President, was an ailing man and there were deep divisions between him and a group of younger men on the executive. It would be those younger men who would grab power if Smillie faltered. Smillie was for peace whilst the others wanted to fight. Jack's basic instinct was for a fight, use the power of the Federation, which had nearly a million members. By the third day Jack knew who the fighting faction were, but he needed them to come to him. There was no advancement in being a humble supplicant with only a few thousand votes in his pocket. If he were to gain those powerful friends, there was only one chance, he must speak.

On the third day he saw his chance when Smillie made an error and appeared to be supporting the government and the NUR and Transport Workers representatives withdrew, shattering the Triple Alliance. Even from a distance Jack could see the annoyance on the faces of a number of the executive members. When those men left the stand and went amongst the delegates during an adjournment he watched. When the Chairman reconvened the meeting there was a barrage of demands for a motion to strike and so it was ordered for debate the following day. Jack fought his way to the secretary's desk. He knew tomorrow was the final debate so he put his name down to speak. It was obvious, the alliance had broken in pieces and the miners were on their own. Smillie was too old, thought Jack, he has lost his stomach for a fight. Somehow they must show that they would not be given the runaround. If they lost the National Wage Agreement, Jack knew, coming from a small field, that his members would be in a nutcracker. It was stand and fight time and Jack was for fighting. The secretary had treated Jack's request with indifference. "You'll have to go first, the graveyard spell!" Jack accepted - it was that or nothing.

Next morning the hall filled, delegates entered and sat in listless postures, conversing in subdued tones. Gone was the bluster of the last few days, days of getting nowhere. Smoke from a hundred pipes drifted around the ceiling as the Chairman called for order.

"The chair recognises the conference. The proposal is that we continue the fight in accordance with the ballot of the 2nd September, which gave the necessary approval for the withdrawal of notices. I call John Elks, the Kent Secretary and delegate, to the stand."

Jack took a deep breath and went forward. Nobody clapped. He had never spoken to such an audience before and his hands were clammy, It's now or never he told himself, no going back - shit or burst. He reached the stand and ordered his papers, resisting the temptation to cough. There was a quiet in the hall but he knew that was not respect; they were just jaded, tired and fed-up. He looked around the hall before speaking, willing them to listen. When he spoke it was slowly and with emphasis.

"My name is Jack Elks and I speak on behalf of the Kent mineworkers. Our numbers are small but we are in good heart and will always fight with determination and fortitude for what are only our basic rights - as all men should and as we have done for years. Our men have worked a ten-hour day for years, not in a selfish way, for themselves, but in the hope and certainty that it would bring succour to their country in its hour of need in that terrible war. They, like the men who returned from the Great War seeking a better future for themselves and their families, find themselves thrown to the mercy of owners who do not know humanity. Do not forget that the war was not only fought on the battlefields of France but dogged our footsteps in our daily work. Keep in the forefront of your minds that in recent years one in six of our men has been involved in an accident that resulted in death or a lengthy time off, to be relieved only by the poor law or our brotherly donations.

Consider all that against these proven facts. Over the last five years that coal industry profits have risen fourfold, coal prices threefold and the wages of our men only twofold. It is not our men who have benefited from these events and it is clear that unless we stand united together we will fail - and the forces of capitalism and greed will grind our people into the ground. The men of Kent stand for action in the common good and WE are for the withdrawal of notices. We stand firm on this ballot. WE ARE READY! WE WILL FIGHT! WE WILL NOT YIELD!"

As he finished there was spontaneous applause and shouts of "Hear, hear!" He paused at the stand for a moment and as he did so two men from the executive lent over and clapped him on the back. "Well done, young man, well done! We'll see you in the bar later, Jack"

As he made his way back to his seat, delegates stood up and shook his hand. "Good speech!" "Well done, Jack!" "We're with you, Jack!" When he found his seat a nearby delegate beckoned to him.

"You've made a friend there, Jack. That was Arthur Cook who slapped your back."

Jack was pleased, he was a name, there must be no going

back. A chink in the door of power had opened. He had spoke from the heart. He wanted power, he needed power if he was to help the men he represented. There was one thing of which he was sure, deals were not made in conference. They were made behind closed doors, in corridors and in bars. He must open the door. Arthur Cook was widely known and respected as a strong man. That was too good a chance to miss.

At the end of the conference the owners' terms were rejected and on the 16th of October the lock-out began. It lasted fourteen days. The miners gained two shillings a week and an hour off the working day, a poor return for their efforts. At the start of the strike the Emergency Powers Act became law, an act which gave Ministers and Police powers of suppression and arrest never known before in peacetime.

When Jack returned to Kent he purchased a grey 'Homburg' hat and it sat in its box on the top of his wardrobe. Waiting. Should the day come Jack would be ready.

## November 1920

Only two days previous Jack had won a small victory at Chislet in persuading the company to provide a travel allowance for the men who journeyed daily from Ramsgate. The few houses in the surrounding villages had filled very quickly and only Ramsgate had houses available but it lay at the far end of a convenient railway line. When he got back to his office the telephone call came through - the lodge secretary at Tilmanstone had been sacked and the men had all walked out. He knocked on the door of the Colliery Manager and entered.

"Good afternoon ,Mr. Spriggs, Jack Elks from the Association."

Spriggs indicated a chair. "Please sit, these are not the best circumstances to meet with all the men out, especially after being out for two weeks in October." Easing himself into the chair, Jack commenced.

"I've heard two sides to this story, perhaps you will give me your version."

"Yes, it's very simple.   Four days ago I went to the Enginehouse. Evans was the duty engineman - he was not there. Two days later I called in again. Evans was missing, so I looked in the yard.  There were ten men waiting in the cage so I went back to the Enginehouse and still Evans wasn't there.  When I found him I sacked him!"

Jack frowned. "What did you state as being the specific reason?"

"Failing to be in control of the engine while there were men in the cage. A clear breach of the mining regulations."

"And after you sacked him all the men walked out?"

"Yes, in clear defiance of the agreement!"

"I'm sorry about that, Mr. Spriggs - we should have given notice. Returning to Evans, he states that on the 13th he went to the men's. There was no call on the engine.  On the 15th he needed a fitter so he went to find him.  When he left, the cage wasn't loaded.  He had no idea the trafficman would load the cage."

"So he said but I will not overlook a breach of the regulations. The men should go back. What I did was clearly for their safety."

Jack chose his words carefully.  "That might have been acceptable but for one thing.  You have made it abundantly clear before this that you disapprove of Evans and his union involvement.  The men take it you are making an example of Evans rather than addressing the fault - that is why they are out."

"The regulations are clear - the engineman must be in control of the engine if men are in the cage. The men should go back! I think you should take them back."

"Unfortunately I'm the Association Secretary not a dictator. The men have voted. They'll stay out till they see fairness."

"What do you suggest?"

"Firstly, you must reinstate Evans, but fine him, read the riot act to him about future conduct. The men will go back."

"No, this is a matter of law."

"If you had evidence that Evans left the engine when the cage was full or loading there would be no problem. The men would be demanding he be sacked for their own good. No such evidence is available!"

"Evans is not the sort of man we need. He has broken the law and he is sacked and he stays sacked."

"Then we must disagree, Mr. Spriggs. The men and the committee are adamant - nothing I can say or do will alter it."

"As I see it I am threatened with a strike over a safety matter. A safety failure one of their own men committed. I will not be threatened!"

Jack got up. "Good day Mr. Spriggs. I am available to you at any time - day or night, if you wish to talk."

## 20 February 1921

Jack was back in the Tilmanstone Manager's office again. "As we are no further forward the men have voted to call out the safety men. The Committee feel you acted out of spite."

Spriggs voice rose. "That will destroy the mine - two weeks without pumping and the mine will close. Do you agree with this?"

Jack put his hand under his chin, his forefinger touching his cheek. It was something he did unconsciously when thinking.

"Speaking man to man?"

Spriggs nodded and then added, "Yes - of course," to emphasise the point.

"There's no sense either side. You've lost fourteen weeks output, the men have lost fourteen weeks wages. Why?"

Spriggs went to speak but Jack put his hand up. "I don't agree you're right but let's just say you are - Evans was at fault.

We still come back to this point, does the punishment fit the crime? If Evans stays sacked he'll not get another job – that's a lifetime punishment. That is what the men see as unfair especially as they think you act from malice. There is no evidence that Evans acted improperly."

"Failure to pump will destroy the mine – that's also malice!"

Jack shook his head in sorrow. "Do we or don't we get this pit working. Was Evans there when the cage was loaded or was he not? Evans states no. Nobody had come forward to say otherwise. Even if you bring someone forward at this stage the men will not believe you."

"What do you suggest?"

"Reinstate Evans. Tell him off, dress him down - give him letters about what he can and can't do - whatever, but reinstate him to start on the next shift."

"What about the men?"

"Do nowt. With Evans back they'll just walk back. A suggestion. I'll be witness when you speak to him - make sure he has a letter about his past and future conduct. That way there can be no misrepresentation."

"Let's hope you're right!"

All the men returned the next day. Jack had the advantage. A management who owed him and a committee that would be more inclined to follow the agreed rules in future.


# 1921

The economic crisis of early 1921 had a devastating impact on employment right across the country. Unemployment reached 1,300,000 among insured staff, those covered by the early National Insurance scheme, but a million more had to resort to the poor law or the workhouse. As coal prices fell the government wished to drop all aspects of state control, which they had maintained since 1917 to the nations advantage and return the mines to the owners. In addition they wanted to decontrol coal prices. The miners' leaders were in a turmoil, running between owners and the government in an endeavour to maintain wages and conditions for their members. Jack attended a belated Federation conference on the 22 February. Over the past few weeks he had spoken to many of the Kent men and their wives. The vast majority were for strong action to protect their families. At least, he thought, my motley army is behind me. To Jack's dismay the first day at Conference was a dismal affair. Prevarication, uncertainty, confusion and bickering filled the day. Arthur Cook lamented the loss of fighting spirit. President Bob Smillie would give no lead and in a dismal speech at the end of the first day he said, "Both the other unions and our men are against a strike." Not that it had been put to the test.

At the end of the day Jack retired to the bar for the consolation of a drink. That is where Arthur Cook and two other executive members found him.

"Hello, Jack, this is Noah Ablett and John Potts." They shook hands. "Get some drinks in, John." Under his breath he murmured. "Committee men, Jack."

Jack was pleased but remained quiet, he wanted to see which way the wind blew. The drinks arrived, Arthur continued. "It's been a dismal day, Jack. You must have been as disappointed as we were."

Jack had his clue so he felt able to speak openly.

"I am. If rumours are right the owners will be back in harness any day now. An immediate strike might give us a chance before the government hands everything over. If we fight later it will be like advancing on the Somme. This damn talk, talk is getting us nowhere!"

Three faces stared intently at Jack. Arthur spoke.

"Tomorrow's crucial. If we can get a strike ballot agreed tomorrow we might have a chance." There was a short pause before Arthur continued. "We've got to get around Smillie. Can you help, Jack?"

Jack felt helpless. "I will if I can but I don't see how."

Arthur's voice lowered. "What if I said there's a group of us anxious to move forward - but we need an opening. Not a revolt, mind you. No, not that, just a gentle prising open of the gate. Smillie has had it but if we try to smash him there will be an outrage - but if we can open up a debate from the floor then we can follow opinion. How do you put it.....?"

"Reflect the views of the delegates." John Potts ended it for him.

"Yes," said Arthur, "that's it - follow the mood. A call to arms from you Jack, would, shall we say, steer things in our direction."

"But subtle, Jack," Noah spoke for the first time, "subtle. No Bolshevik nonsense, just a nice clear plea for action."

"Yes", said Arthur, "persuasive. Enough for the Chairman to steer the debate."

'Christ!' thought Jack, 'How many are in this? These three, the Chairman?' "I'll do what you ask," he tried to sound confident, "but surely one man isn't enough?"

Arthur smiled and the others relaxed. "Spot on, Jack. There'll be another two men to follow you. Smillie has to leave at ten tomorrow for a meeting." He tapped his nose as he looked at Jack.

"I haven't got my name down, I'll need to register."

"Don't worry, Jack. It's all arranged, you'll be the first call to speak after ten. Here's your order papers."

Arthur put his hand on Jack's shoulder. "We'll not forget this, Jack! Now come and join the others in a drink."

'Yes,' thought Jack, 'little by little, doors were opening.'


Next morning the conference opened to the usual divisive talk, with several speakers arguing for support for the unemployed. Jack tried not to fidget whilst the minutes ticked by. He saw Bob Smillie leave the podium and thought, if all is going to plan, I'm on next. Within minutes the Chairman was standing.

"Gentlemen, I have to attend with the President. I call Mr. Ablett to the Chair."

Noah banged for order. Jack was called and he strode forward with confidence. He noticed Arthur look at him but he avoided any eye contact or acknowledgement. Drawing a deep breath he started.

"My heart is sad for the unemployed and their families. I feel sure every man in this room feels the same. I would make any personal sacrifice in order to help the unemployed in any industry or our own. Notwithstanding that, not to concentrate on our own members will only multiply the misery. Without careful thought on our part we shall only add our men to the millions already cast aside and out of work. We will not achieve much unless we lead. I hear the lament that we lack fighting spirit. NOT HERE, FELLOW DELEGATES," he tapped his chest, "NOT HERE. We are told we should vote against drastic action yet I hear no alternative."

There was a great stir around the hall at this perceived attack on the executive and there were shouts of "Hear, hear!" Jack paused for effect.

"There is good reason to believe that the mines will soon be passed back to the owners. The government may have been difficult but do you doubt when I say that the owners will not come bearing olive branches. That they are planning action to our detriment while we debate and bicker. Do the owners love us and wish us well! We must clarify our actions. We must fight against district wages, for it will set one man against another. We must pursue nationalisation and a fair wage policy. I will not willingly go back to my members simply to wring my hands when they ask what they must do, or what we do. What are the virtues of our men? I will tell you, they are courage, comradeship, endurance and self-discipline. ARE THOSE VIRTUES NOT PRESENT HERE IN THIS HALL? There are those who say that nationalisation is beyond our reach, that we cannot ask for a minimum wage to keep a man off parish relief, that we cannot ask for a central wage authority or a rise in pay. Tell me when we have asked for more than a fair share? Fellow delegates, I ask you to show the same virtues as the men we lead. Let us pursue a sensible strategy with vigour and clarity of aim. STRIKE NOW WHILE THERE IS STILL TIME! I AM FOR OBJECTIVE AND EFFECTIVE ACTION - NOT WORDS."

Two speakers later, John Potts moved a motion for strike action. During that debate Bob Smillie arrived back to say that the government had told him that control would be handed back to the owners on the 31st March. The motion was lost as the conference decided that the executive committee should be sent to negotiate with the owners. With deep regret an old and ailing Bob Smillie announced that he was retiring, knowing that he had won the day but at the cost of deep divisions; also in his heart he knew that despite the events of the day, the Government action to return control to the owners meant a strike was inevitable.

On the first day of March the government announced that coal prices were to be decontrolled and the owners announced new terms of employment. All existing contracts were null and void with effect from 31st March. The miners were unwilling to accept and the great lock-out started on 1st April. A million miners were idle and the government enacted the Emergency Powers Act.

Long before that Jack was back in Kent. Praise ringing in his ears, thanks in his pocket. When he got home Lizzie told him she was pregnant again.

## 21-22 April 1921

Jack travelled to another Federation delegates' conference on the 21st April when the lock-out was in its third week. The owners were adamant, return on their terms or stay out and no ground was given on either side. So the miners had to decide whether or not to continue or give in, having gained nothing as well as losing three weeks pay in the process. Giving in now meant accepting massive wage cuts. When Jack arrived, Arthur Cook sent a message asking for a meeting.

"If we give in Jack, we've lost everything and gained nowt. Mind you there are those for giving in. We'll have to push and shove to keep going. There's a lot of pressure from three areas, especially Nottinghamshire, to back off. Go cap in hand!"

"My men are still solid, you have my support."

"Christ, Jack, if you ran Durham and Nottingham there'd be no problem. We must get you on the Executive but I can't get enough votes lined up. But don't you worry, we're growing all the time. We need your help."

"What do I do?"

"It's all organised, Jack. I've got your name on the order paper to speak tomorrow just after lunch. It's important we get off to a good start then, the vote will be at four thirty. I've got five speakers lined up behind you so fire 'em up Jack. Give us a good start then it doesn't matter what's said in the morning."

"We've got to keep the pressure on the government, Arthur."

"I know, Jack, I know. The buggers will only intervene if we get a good solid vote to go on."

"It'll mean the soup kitchens - our funds will be wiped out! Will the Federation help?"

"It's the only way, Jack. My friends and I are working on the NUR delegates, our fraternal friends. When this is over, get back to Kent and keep things going. I've got to stay here and keep the pressure on otherwise there'll be back sliding!"

Jack looked pensive. "There's one thing, Arthur. When I speak I mean what I say. There's no other way."

"That's what makes it so perfect, don't you see. Folk can see through a phoney a mile off. Honest Jack, that's you."

On the morrow Jack was called to the stand and for the first time there was applause, not total but he was winning friends.

"The men of Kent are behind you in this hour of greatest peril to our cause, and we are solid in our belief of the fairness of our claims. In a few hours you must vote. When the destinies of our men and all their comrades in all the mines, together with their families, are in OUR HANDS, we must hold together as one. There are reasons why the railwaymen will not support us - if so I cannot see them. I pray they will see the sense of solidarity and the mutual comfort and benefit of giving us aid. Notwithstanding that we entered this alone and we must pursue that course to a conclusion.

This I do believe, that without a National Wage Board we are thrown piecemeal to the wolves. Even now as we are at this meeting our comrades are being arrested and families evicted. For what reason I ask you? BECAUSE MEN ARE LOCKED OUT UNTIL THEY ACCEPT A WAGE WHICH CANNOT SUPPORT THEIR FAMILIES. My men have sent me here with the clear understanding that they will not give in to these monstrous demands made on us. Continue with the battle because our survival is at stake. We hold to our pledge not to return to work until our just, reasonable and fair demands are met. FIGHT ON, I SAY - FIGHT ON!"

At the end of the day the delegates voted overwhelmingly to continue the struggle. Jack had made more friends, men sought his company. Arthur Cook expressed his gratitude. "Good, well done. They'll be shouting for you to speak soon. Come and meet a few more of my friends."

## 12-14 June 1921

When the tenth of June arrived the strike was already in its eleventh week and the owners at Snowdown had posted the latest lower pay rates, inviting men to return to work. On 12<sup>th</sup> June, at six in the morning, 300 pickets assembled outside the local railway station as a few men tried to return to work.

"Scabs! Scabs! Scabs!" The shouts echoed in the stillness of the early morning. Already the sun was shining. The ten policemen on duty were overwhelmed by sheer numbers and the strike-breaking men stayed on the platform rather than face the men outside. An hour later the returning train took the men off and peace resumed.

The next day the police were ready and seventy men stood in the station yard, truncheons ready to deal with the pickets. Against a sullen background a dozen men were escorted to the Pit gates. The day after, the 14th, the police waited in vain, alone in the morning cool. No one appeared on the early morning train and the pickets were missing. Police patrols were heavy for the next two weeks.


## 21 June 1921

The strike had begun officially on the first of April and was now in its twelfth week when Jack was notified by the Federation that a new ballot was to be held to vote on the latest government proposals. Now he was on his way to Snowdown, to meet the first of the local lodge committees and to pass on the bad news. The officials were waiting when he arrived at the Welfare Centre. Dai Powell made Jack welcome.

"Will this take long, Jack? We're organising a soup kitchen for the families in a short while. Let's sit under a tree, it's a fine day."

The lodge had built the Welfare Hut on a small piece of land purchased from their weekly subscriptions. There was a grassy area in front, with a few trees. Several of the wives were tending a large cauldron hung over an open fire. Jack noted the presence of the local vicar and took that as a good omen of community spirit. Jack commenced.

"Have you issued the compensation payments, Mr.

Chairman?"

Dai Powell reported promptly. "It's all done, but we are down to ten shillings a week for a family of four, that is why we are doing the soup kitchen."

"Good!" said Jack, "Now these are the latest proposals. I will get you the ballot papers tomorrow so if I explain what is being put forward it will give you a chance to talk to the men. If we return to work now the government will pay a grant of ten million pounds to the owners. Wages will reduce by two shillings a week for a man for four weeks and after that the Federation will agree a further reduction until the ten million is exhausted."

Several of the committee could not understand it. "Why do we have to take a reduction in wages if the government is giving a subsidy?"

Jack noticed a straggle of women and children coming down the road each carrying a bowl, plate or jug. That didn't concern him, it was the body of police behind them that worried him. He kept a wary eye on them. He continued, "The owners' wage offer is lower than the Federation will accept so the ten million pounds will top up that offer but ......... Why are those police here, Dai?"

"What police, Jack?" Dai looked down the road. "Can't imagine, they've not been in the village before!"

"I think you had better get your people off the road, Dai. Get them behind the fence."

As Jack watched the committee got all their folk in, while the police formed a line across the road and drew their truncheons.

"Are we ready?" called Dai, "Let's get the soup served. Only one slice of bread per person. Will you serve Vicar? Don't push now, there is plenty for all!"

He turned to the gate as the Police Sergeant strode forward.

"Are you in charge here?" His truncheon waved at Dai. "You will all disperse, this is an unlawful assembly!"

"This is a soup kitchen, Sergeant, on private grounds."

The sergeant stared around the throng. "All I see is a load of bloody lawbreakers, up to no good!"

"Vicar!" Dai waved the vicar over. "The vicar will tell you, this is a soup kitchen for hungry people."

The vicar hurried forward. "Can I help you Sergeant? These are my parishioners, hungry people to be fed."

The police sergeant wrinkled his nose. "This is an unlawful assembly within the meaning of the Emergency Powers Act."

The vicar raised his voice, "This is private property, Sergeant. These people are interfering with no one!"

"You had better leave, Vicar, otherwise I cannot be responsible for your safety." The truncheon jabbed out. "There were men having a meeting and now they have been joined by a crowd."

"I shall report this to your superior!"

The sergeant opened the gate. "You do that, Vicar. NOW YOU LOT - DISPERSE. THIS IS AN UNLAWFUL ASSEMBLY. YOU HAVE TEN SECONDS TO DISPERSE!"

"Forward men!" The police lined up along the fence as the vicar ran for help. The sergeant counted while most of the crowd stared, many had not heard the order so they were still intent on getting food. Dai just had time to scream, " GETAWAY – BACK TO YOUR HOMES", when the police charged. The fence went down with a crash and women and children screamed as the police ran at them. In the confusion people tripped and fell, bringing others down. Some stood rooted to the spot. Truncheons fell and all the food went over onto the ground. Men tried to save their families and were beaten down.

Jack charged forward. "Get them away, Dai! For God's sake run!" Several men and women ran into the hall for cover but the police followed them in and smashed the interior into ruin. People ran for their lives.

It was all over in a minute and the sergeant was calling to his men. "STAND FAST! FORM COLUMN!" Only a few small children were left standing, crying aloud. Two men were down unconscious and Jack knelt, shaking his head, a bash across the ear had nearly stunned him. He was surrounded by debris, broken plates and jugs, tables and the remains of the food scattered on the ground. Only the fire remained intact.

"COLUMN SHUN - REPLACE TRUNCHEONS - QUICK MARCH!"

As the Sergeant passed Jack he bent over. "That'll teach you bloody agitators and communists to obey the law!"

Jack said nothing, his head hurt too much for arguing, though he silently cursed the vicar for leaving, if only he had stayed he would have made a powerful witness to events.

On Friday, July 1st, Jack got a telegram ordering a return to work. The government terms had been accepted. They had lost.

## October 1921

The Relieving Officer of the Board of Guardians shuffled his papers and peered anxiously around. He was used to dealing with individuals not groups of men so before speaking he cleared his throat several times.

"Please excuse me, gentlemen - am I to assume you will speak individually or is there a spokesman?"

Jack spoke up. "Mr. Modley - if you will allow, I am the spokesman but these men are here to answer individual questions as you may direct."

"Why is it necessary to have a spokesman?"

"The men present are only ten in number but in fact there are one hundred and seventy men all told so we felt it best to establish a general case with you before all applied direct. The need may vary from man to man, family to family, but the circumstance under which so many cases arise is common to all."

"This is a most unusual approach! Why cannot each man make representation on his own?"

"Time, Mr. Modley, time - unless we can cut down the processing time some of these men may not see you until after Christmas."

"I cannot promise on the outcome but you may proceed."

"Thank you Mr. Modley - I will proceed as quickly as possible. Please stop me if you have any questions."

Jack stood up; he had learnt from experience that it was the more authoritative stance.

"All the men I represent are currently employed at Tilmanstone Colliery, however they are working only five days a fortnight instead of twelve. This is not by choice but a condition imposed by the management due to lack of demand for coal in the current economic situation."

"How long has this gone on?"

"Since July of this year."

"That was at the end of the strike, was it not?"

"That is correct, Mr. Modley, but the current circumstance do not arise from that lock-out."

"I see - the men were not responsible for the strike?"

"No, they were not. Wages were set between the National Negotiating Board and the Miners Federation. When that could not be agreed the owners voided the men's contracts."

"Did not the men vote for this action?"

"Some certainly but the numbers of men at Tilmanstone could not sway the matter in a national ballot of one million members. Nor have the owners said that the changes in the working week or the lock-out have been the cause of short-time working. It is caused solely by the lack of demand in the country and overseas. The request for relief stems from the lack of income today, not from previous loss of income."

"When considering relief I must take into account any money that a person may have - from whatever source, including savings."

"Yes, we understand that Mr. Modley, that is why it is urgent to see all men quickly. I am only trying to establish the common background to this."

"If the need for relief arises now why cannot each man make application?"

"I regret, Sir, that this has been a problem for over three months. Here is a report from the local doctor, you will see that he has attended eighteen men who have collapsed while working. His diagnosis is lack of food. It is beyond my understanding why men will not ask for help but it is necessary to see that pride has prevented the seeking of assistance. It is that pride that will also cause men to withdraw from assistance the moment proper working recommences."

"Are these men available for work on those days when the colliery is closed?"

"Yes, except in those cases when the doctor may provide evidence of illness or incapacity."

"If the Board provides work will the men take it?" Mr Modley suddenly looked most severe.

"I see no reason why not. This list," Jack passed it over, "gives the name of every man with a family currently on short time working who has a contract with the colliery. I would be grateful if you will agree to see the one hundred and seventy men as quickly as possible. If you are agreeable the men here will help organise attendance and can direct you to the most urgent cases first - those with the largest families."

"I fear it will take at least three days even to do as you ask!"

"Three of the men here represent the local lodge committee - they will give you every assistance."

"I will commence at two p.m. If you will have the first thirty men here there will be priority treatment."

"Thank you, Mr. Modley. You will find that all the men have their pay dockets to hand, children's birth certificates and so on."

## January 1922

Lack of capital and the effects of the lockout came to a head in January as the owners dismissed all but the safety men and closed the Snowdown Colliery. Since the end of the last strike the colliery had been limping along on short weeks. The effect on the miners was catastrophic as short-time working led to low wages and that led to hunger. When the pit closed the men had no option but to resort to the Board of Guardians and seek relief. Jack and the lodge committees got to work helping with the transfer to other pits but not all could be accommodated and 200 men were out of work. Other miners in the area, who were still working, paid a levy to help the men out of work but it was touch and go for those men and their families until Snowdown re-opened in 1923, under the ownership of Pearson Dorman & Long Ltd. With the effect of the levy and reduced numbers of men working, union income dropped well below the 1918 level and Jack had to take a pay cut to eke out the union funds.

## June 1922

Lizzie was in the kitchen baking when Len and Albert got home from school. "Anything to eat, Mum?" they chorused.

"No, it will be your tea-time soon."

"We're off to play football." They dashed for the door. Halfway there, Albert skidded to a halt and returned.

"The Headmaster said I was to give this to you, Mum!" He fished a crumpled letter from his pocket and thrust it in her hand. "We'll be back in an hour!" Then off he dashed shouting to Len to wait. When they had gone Lizzie wiped her hands on her apron and opened the letter.

*Dear Mr and Mrs Elks,*

*Four weeks ago I entered your son Albert Edward Elks for the public examination held for entry to the Dover Grammar School. Your son has an excellent academic record as well as being an enthusiastic team sports player. On the basis of his proven record I considered that he had an excellent chance. Notification has been received today from the examining body that he has been awarded a scholarship, which will commence on the 28th August of this year. The scholarship period is five years.*

*We are very proud of Albert's achievement. Please notify me of your acceptance of this offer within two weeks of receipt of this letter.*

Lizzie tucked the letter in her apron, she was so pleased. Her son with a scholarship! Who would have thought it! Her father would be so pleased when she wrote to tell him. Two days later Jack was home and she gave him the letter when he had finished his dinner.

"What's this?" He scowled at the letter. "This letter is addressed to me. Why is it opened?"

"It was addressed to both of us. Its from the school, I didn't think you would mind."

He picked up the letter. "Don't open mail again - unless it's personal!"

Silently he read and then put the letter down.

"What do you think, Jack? Isn't it wonderful news."

"Waste of time - absolute waste of time!"

Lizzie's heart sank. "I thought you would be so pleased that Albert has done so well."

"We've no money to waste on schools." Jack scowled and his voice hardened. "It may say scholarship but there are fees to pay. Books and uniform. Money doesn't grow on trees!"

"I could make economies, surely we could manage."

Jack gave her the letter. "You can burn that. Grammar school won't help him. In a few years him and Len can get to the pit - learn to pay their way like I did. If he wants education he'll find it without my help."

Lizzie hesitated, Jack returned to his paper.

"I'll hear no more about it!"

## June 1923

In the month since Lilian May had been born Lizzie had been ill, not desperately ill, but generally felt unwell, constantly tired and depressed. Reluctantly she made an appointment to see the doctor. The examination over, the doctor sat her down.

"You have had ten children, Mrs. Elks?"

"I have but I've never felt like this before."

"I'm not surprised, there is so much the body can take then it starts to complain. Babies drain the body, your body is telling you its time to stop."

"I don't think my husband would accept that."

"My concern is your kidneys. They are starting to fail. That shows up in the urine test. More babies will put intense pressure on your kidneys and there is a risk of failure."

"What will that mean?

"You will die - the body cannot function without kidneys." Lizzie was quiet so he continued. "Can you not speak to your husband? The contraceptive devices available are very safe today."

"He won't use such things." She stopped, searching for words, clearly embarrassed. "He says they ruin his pleasure."

"If you have more children it will kill you, the kidneys will slowly fail and poison will build up in your bloodstream."

"I don't know what to say."

"Should I speak to your husband?"

Lizzie was horrified. "No, no, don't do that Doctor - he would never forgive me. He would go off the deep end if he even knew I had spoken to you about this."

"You must speak to him, Mrs. Elks. I am sure he will understand. Try and get him to see me."

"I will try."


As a troubled Lizzie walked home she knew it was useless and would only provoke a row, even possibly a violent one. She could not face that.


**December 1923**

There was a Miners Federation delegates meeting called for late in the month. Jack received a call asking him to come to a meeting, a hotel away from the area, on the eve of the conference. Noah Ablett, John Potts and Tom Richards were waiting to speak to him.

"Welcome, Jack." Noah shook his hand. "Arthur can't be with us, you will understand why in a moment. You've met John and Tom? Good, lets find a quiet corner."

Tom studied Jack for a few moments. "How do you find Frank Hodges?" Hodges was the Secretary of the Federation and he had been elected to Parliament several months before.

"Truthfully?" They nodded, so Jack continued. "He did a bad job for us in that last agreement with the owners. Not that it matters, he must resign now he's an M. P."

John Potts glanced around before speaking, making sure they weren't overheard.

"He wants to stay on. Tom Henderson, the Labour Party Secretary has made representations. The Executive has agreed to a motion tomorrow to waive the rules, so Hodges can stay on."

"Why would they want him to stay on?"

Noah sniffed. "We don't. Truth is he's too clever by half. It will split the Federation Executive. If he stays he's a problem, if we refuse a vote we offend the Labour Party. We've the best chance ever of getting the party in power at the next election so we want to remain friends."

Tom broke in. "We've only one chance to clear the air, we must discredit him. Make it appear we have no choice!"

"How do we do that?" Jack was puzzled.

John Potts placed three papers on the table, then he turned to Tom Richards. "Get some drinks, Tom, while Jack digests these."

Jack read quickly. "Where on earth did you get these, are they genuine?"

"Absolutely. Guaranteed!"

"There are three highly paid part time jobs here." Jack was

astonished. "Any one of those would be more than enough for one man! How did Hodges get them?"

Noah picked the papers up." Beauties aren't they. All non-executive directorships of private companies so no one will know. These two, the Water and Electricity companies are owned by the Enstones. The third one, the shipping company, is owned by the Northfleets. Now do you see?"

Jack nodded and sighed. "They're major coal owners in the Midlands and Lancashire!"

"Exactly!" said Noah, "He's been bought! Even the Labour Party doesn't know."

"What do we do?"

"We've tried the quiet way – so now we blow him out of the water."

"Arthur is the best man," said Jack.

"No, can't do that. That's why he's not here tonight. Arthur is going to be the next Secretary. We'll make sure of that. First, though, we must get rid of Frank!"

"We were hoping you'd take on the task, Jack," John Potts hesitated, "but we would understand if you say no."

"What do I do."

"Tomorrow, the first item on the agenda, there's a proposal to waive the rules, let Frank do two jobs at the same time. Tom Henderson has been invited to speak. If you oppose I'll put your name down to speak after Henderson."

"What if I fail?"

"You won't. As soon as you mention those jobs, there'll be eight delegates up and passing around copies of these notes. I doubt he'll get a single vote. We'll have Arthur in by the end of the conference."

"Honest Jack from Kent!" Noah raised his glass. "Let's drink to the Federation."

As befits a Political Party Secretary, Tom Henderson was an eloquent and persuasive spokesman. A gifted man, tall and with tawny hair, he rose to the rostrum with complete confidence.

"Delegates of the Federation. Today you have a chance to make history. With great distinction, your Secretary, Frank Hodges, has served you honourably and faithfully for five years. During that time the number of mining members of Parliament has risen from five to forty, a clear indication of your strength and sense of purpose. In that endeavour Frank Hodges has been a tower of strength. Today he stands in front of you both as a Labour M. P. and your Secretary. I do not doubt that he has the ability, single-mindedness and skill to do both of those public services, because mark my word, being your Secretary is a public service. His influence with the owners is immeasurable and he has worked in harmony with all for the betterment of your members. He is held in great esteem by the Party, our Party - and your Federation. I ask you to modify your rule for the good of everyone so that we gain and you do not lose a man of outstanding personal attributes, oratory and accomplishments. My confidence in you is only matched by my confidence in Frank Hodges. Please again, for the good of all approve this motion."

There was loud clapping as he sat down next to Hodges and they shook hands.

The Chairman called Jack to the stand to little applause. Jack was making a wrong move many concluded. He took his time in starting.

"Fellow delegates. Our rules have existed for thirty years and served us well. Should we modify our rule, where does it end? Do we have a part-time President, I ask you? A part-time Treasurer? No, I say! Single-mindedness IS a virtue. That is why our officials serve us and us alone. When Frank Hodges stood for Parliament he knew the outcome of success. A man cannot serve two masters. Or is it three, OR FOUR!"

Some delegates were on their feet and shouting. "Shame!" "Shame!"

The chairman intervened. "The Kent delegate will refrain from making wild allegations! This is most improper. You will withdraw those comments!"

Jack passed him copies of the three papers.

"Mr. Chairman. I will not withdraw. No man can serve five masters without his loyalties being torn asunder. The very secrecy of these appointments," he waved the copies in the air; in the hall he could see the papers being passed around, "points to untrustworthiness. We need a Secretary who will cleave to us, whose honesty and integrity are beyond question, who will fight for us! We have men of character here - and they will be ours alone."

As Jack finished speaking Frank Hodges was getting up to leave. Arthur Cook was elected as Secretary to the Federation three days later.

## 25 October 1924

Ramsey MacDonald's Labour government lasted only nine months before it went to the polls in October in search of a proper majority. Labour were in power but could only function with massive Liberal Party support. Polling day was to be on the 29th October.

Although it was a Saturday, Jack got up at his usual time to go to the office at nine. The Association was not a political party but they naturally supported Labour and had invested a good deal of time supporting and promoting the local Labour candidate. Not that he stood much chance in a mainly rural area but they felt that it made a contribution to the whole countrywide effort. The Association Lodges had pressed the case; without a Labour Government with a majority they would get none of the social and work changes for which they had been pressing. Lizzie served his breakfast and put the daily papers on the table, in front of him.

"Will you stop those children making so much noise!"

Lizzie felt quiet unwell, she knew she was pregnant again.

"Sorry Jack, it's the boys but I'll tell them. I know it's difficult but May is teething. I'll do the best I can."

"She can go upstairs."

Lizzie hurried off while Jack unfolded the top paper and was hit by the headline.

DAILY MAIL, 25 OCT 1924

# MOSCOW ORDERS TO OUR REDS

GREAT PLOT DISCLOSED YESTERDAY

**'PARALYSE THE ARMY AND NAVY'**

AND MR. MACDONALD WOULD LEND RUSSIA OUR MONEY!

*A "very secret" letter of instruction from Moscow, which we publish below, discloses a great Bolshevik plot to paralyse the British Army and Navy and to plunge the country into civil war. The letter is addressed by the Bolsheviks of Moscow to the Soviet Government's servants in Great Britain, the Communist Party, who in turn are the masters of Mr. Ramsey MacDonald's Government, which has signed a treaty with Moscow whereby the Soviet is to be guaranteed a "loan" of millions of British money.*

*The letter is signed by Zinoviev, the Dictator of Petrograd, President of the Third (Moscow) International, and is addressed to A. McManus, the British representative on the executive of this International, who returned from Moscow to London on October 18 to take part in the general election campaign.*

"LIZZIE! GET MY COAT! I must be off."

Jack left hurriedly, leaving Lizzie to cope with the baby who would not be consoled. Luckily she had Alice and Ivy to help her. Alice was the first to speak when things were quiet.

"I'll take baby May for a walk, Mum. Donald can come with us."

"I will feel better in a moment."

"You don't look well - you were sick this morning. Are you expecting again?"

Lizzie shook her head. "No, no. Its nothing like that, I just need a rest." She was wondering what the doctor would say when she plucked up the courage to go and see him. "Don't worry now, I'll go to the doctor next week if things don't improve. I just need a pick-me-up, then everything will be fine."

As Jack proceeded to the election office it was only force of habit that made him hurry. It was already too late, the damage was done. The small Communist Party was no part of the Labour movement, it was in fact specifically banned; but publicly put like that in a national newspaper then tens of thousands would believe it.

The letter referred to was, thereafter, never claimed to be anything other than a forgery but that didn't matter. Voters were driven in shoals to vote against the 'Bolshevik menace' and the Conservatives won the election with an overwhelming majority. With the Government, Owners and Press against them the Miners would face hard times in the days ahead. The miners last lingering hopes of nationalisation were destroyed as Labour was swept from power.

### December 1924

Tilden Smith knocked on the door and entered. The five directors of the Tilmanstone Mining Company waited on him.

"I will be brief, gentlemen. As the principal debenture holder I have to say to you that as you have failed to pay the debenture interest for the last twelve months, you leave me no choice but to call in the Receiver."

The managing director responded. "We have arranged a plan

to raise further capital to exploit the field, we ask that you hold off for four weeks to give us an opportunity to resolve this."

"Four weeks it is but I hold by my word."

"We can assure you, sir, that we will succeed and the guarantor of the overdraft backs us". Four weeks later the capital issue failed, the guarantor withdrew and the Receiver was called in. When the Colliery was sold and a new company formed, Tilden Smith was the Chairman.

Now it was the turn of the Tilmanstone men to go through the grinder as uncertainty, short-time working and refurbishment took their toll over the next year.

## 1925-26

When Arthur Cook took over as the Secretary of the Miners Federation in 1924 he used all his influence to get Jack elected to the Executive Committee. The last lock-out had been resolved by a government subsidy of ten million pounds to the industry to ameliorate the effects of wage cuts but this was a temporary measure due to run out on 30th April 1926. During that interim period the Miners Federation negotiated but made no progress. The government refused to provide further support whilst the owners insisted that wages must fall and hours increase. Arthur Cook found himself increasingly involved in a welter of meetings and correspondence with Government, Branches and the TUC. What he needed was friendly support from the executive, support from trustworthy friends and supporters to advise him in matters of fine detail, political manoeuvre and strategy. Using all his influence he added Jack's name to the election list and on the 1st April 26, Jack was elected. He was a 'Homburg' man at last. On the 14 April the mine owners posted notice of a "lock-out", all existing contracts of employment were withdrawn and unless the men accepted new contracts, on the owners terms, they could not return to work. Initially details of the new terms were not given but on the 30th these were stated as a twenty per cent wage reduction, an extra hours work per day and a return to district bargaining. Prior to April the government started preparing plans for dealing with a strike, the Emergency Powers Act was to be supported by detailed arrangements for the country to be under the direction of Regional Controllers. The miners gained the support of other unions and entered into an agreement with the TUC council that gave the TUC the authority to conduct negotiations and control actions, in effect control the conduct of the dispute. The unions were mindful of the fact that when Welsh miners had struck in late 1925 there had been wholesale arrests and severe sentences. So the owners stuck rigidly to their guns, the government havered and as the attitudes of all sides hardened it was like the start of a war. Like the mobilisation arrangements before the Great War, once started, the drift to war seemed inevitable, like a self -fulfilling wish. There seemed only one likely outcome. In this case a 'class' war.

## THE TIMES
5 October 1925

*Liverpool will be the starting point in a new move on the part of the Fascisti. Arrangements have been made for members in the Liverpool area to become special constables and to drill at the hall of the City Police. Captain W. J. Lewis, Commander of the Fascisti in the Lancashire and Wirral area stated that officers of the organisation were to take the oath at Police Headquarters today, the swearing in of other members in due course. He said, if we should be called out we should act as special constables under the command of the Chief Constable of Liverpool. So far Liverpool is the only place where arrangements have been made with the police. Inquiries indicate that the arrangements will allow the Fascisti special constables to be under their own officers.*

*(At this time the Fascists were called the Fascisti)*

## March 1926

Jack sifted through the reports arriving on his desk. Tilmanstone was suffering from a lack of orders and the management had responded by stopping and starting production in a haphazard manner. There had been two roof falls and two men badly injured, while another had a thumb amputated after his hand had been crushed by the haulage tubs. Jack made a note to get the hospital reports preparatory to submitting legal claims. In the meantime the men would need compensation to keep going but that could do no better than keep their heads above water. There was a proposal from the Tilmanstone management for the erection of pit-head baths but the majority of the money would need to come from the men via the Welfare Society funds. A ballot must be organised. At Snowdown the situation progressed slowly. Coal production had stopped at the end of October in the previous year and men were engaged in creating new roadways. On top new winding gear and flywheels had been installed and these were being tested. Coal was targeted to be produced starting on the first of May. That troubled Jack, he knew the current contracts would need to be renewed about that time. Already the owners were pressing for lower wages and longer hours. The good news was that after several years of patient negotiation with Dorman Long they had agreed to build a new village of 1200 homes between Adisham and Shepherdswell. Also new homes were being prepared at Deal in anticipation of the new Betteshanger Colliery opening within a year. There would be new hope and new jobs if only this present crisis could be averted. He had high hopes of the next Federation delegates meeting. Arthur had virtually guaranteed his seat on the executive. The thought gave him great pleasure.

## 5 April 1926

Jack had called the Executive Committee of the Kent Association together in his office, what had to be said was not for prying ears. Around the table were Albert Wright, Bill Haseley, Dai Powell, Harry Pritchard and Tom Enfield.

"My congratulations, Jack." There was pride in Bill Haseley's voice. "It is a great honour to our Association that you are an Executive Man."

"Must be nice to be feted in Downing Street!," piped up Albert. There were handshakes from all before they took their seats.

"Thank you all," said Jack, "but our problems are only beginning. That's why I want you all together. The mine owners are solid, they are going to force new contracts on us. Our information is that they want a reduction in wages of at least twenty per cent. There seems to be no chance of getting a peaceful agreement, it's everyone's opinion, and mine, that a strike is inevitable. Though that is for your ears only for the moment. With Tilmanstone on short time and Snowdown not producing coal we are not best placed. I suggest we make some plans as how best to deal with it. Also I don't want our men in prison or arrested."

"Yes, I agree, Jack." Bill Haseley looked serious. "I am concerned for the younger members. They can be so hot-headed and unafraid of danger."

"Very true," Dai agreed, "I suggest we take advantage of our surrounds. Plenty of farms will take on boys – pay is terrible of course but it will keep them out of harms way. Also there are casual jobs in all the resorts getting spruced up for the holiday makers."

"Yes, said Harry, "there will be harvest work later if this dispute goes on, we must take every opportunity to get some money in."

"I am concerned about many of our Snowdown men. There are still two hundred without work and there is a chance they will not be taken back quickly even when the pit is ready." As Albert spoke he puffed out great belches of smoke from his pipe.

"We could organise a meeting with the Guardians. We have a right to demand work or relief for men without jobs - strike or no strike!" Jack made notes as he said it. "But what about Chislet - the men are so scattered there?"

"We'll think on that Jack", said Bill, "during the last strike we had food centres. It is better elsewhere - we can plan the soup kitchens and such like"

## 14th April 1926

Arthur Cook had sent a telegram to Jack asking that he join him in London and to be prepared to stay for a few weeks. When he arrived Arthur was waiting, looking harassed.

"God, am I pleased to see you. We've just had the latest notice from the owners and it needs close scrutiny and interpretation. Are you prepared in Kent? Can they manage without you?"

Jack put his valise on the floor, put his jacket on the stand and rolled his sleeves up.

"Yes, I saw the notice this morning, had a good read on the train. We've got first class men in Kent, they can manage without me for a while. It's been agreed we'll get as many of the boys and young men out to the farms and seaside towns as possible to keep them out of harm's way. Young ones can be brave but sometimes foolhardy."

"Good! That's good." Arthur looked relieved. "There's a meeting this coming Sunday in Staffordshire. Ernest Bevin will join us. Come yourself, we need a good speaker. If you can arrange that, it will help. I've a meeting with the TUC and there's a mountain of correspondence. Unless there's a miracle our men will be out on the 30th. Now I must be off."

Jack sat down.

"Leave this with me, Arthur. You weld them together and

keep the TUC solid. I'll spin and you can delve but don't expect to find any gentlemen out there!"

## 20th April 1926

When next Sunday arrived, six hundred men crowded the football pitch on the edge of Bloxwich. A colliery band played in the background as a dozen or so policemen patrolled the perimeter but wisely kept a respectable distance from the crowd. There was a sharpness in the air but it did nothing to subdue the assembled men because this was Arthur's day. Their respected leader, Arthur Cook, the General Secretary of the Miners Federation had come to raise their spirits, so they gathered around the stand. Ernest Bevin, from the TUC council and one day destined to be a Minister of State, got up on the stand to loud cheers and called and waved for order.

"Men of Pensal and Bloxwich Collieries, thank you for your presence and support. As you know, your leader Arthur Cook will speak to you." He paused as loud cheers echoed around the field. "But let me first introduce you to a man who will be known to some of you but if not of whom you will have heard. He comes from you and was born in your midst. Please welcome Jack Elks."

There was clapping and calls of "Remember me, Jack?" as he mounted the stand. Every weekend Arthur visited different areas to meet, encourage and harangue the miners. "We must put fire in their bellies, Jack. Soon we will need all their resolve."

Jack didn't mind a bit. As members of the Executive they stayed at first class hotels and travelled first class. He loved the hustings also. Speak from the heart, Jack, as always. He began.

"Men of Pensal and Bloxwich, it is good to be home among the men I worked and played with those years ago. I have never forgotten you. Is Percy Ibson here?" He paused to look around and a man called out "Yun here, Jack." Jack continued. "Are you still up to your arse in horseshit?"

There was a loud roar of laughter and Percy waved his arm, pleased with the attention. Jack knew instinctively they were on his side.

"I am pleased you are in good spirits as soon we will need all that you can offer and we shall have to dig deep in our resolve if we are to win the current battle. Last year we had a battle and you may ask with reason why we fight it again. But on the last occasion we did not win - it was only an armistice. Do not doubt that those who lie in wait for us are preparing to meet us head-on with the full powers of the law and the military. The government and the owners say we lack patriotism but I remember the numbers of our men who fought in France, my own brother died there. Did not those remaining forego holidays and work extra hours without pay; did we do it for selfish or unpatriotic reasons? NO BUT ALL IS FORGOTTEN WHEN WE ASK FOR A LIVING WAGE OR IF WE OBJECT TO A REDUCTION IN WAGES. The notices have already been posted for a lock-out, not just here but all over the country. We will fight in unity or perish. On your behalf we have pleaded for a meeting of minds and hearts but our foes are implacable. They would drive us to a killing ground and destroy everyone of us. That will not, cannot, happen if we stand together. TAKE COURAGE - STEEL YOUR HEARTS - STAND TOGETHER!"

There was load cheering as Jack waved and stepped down. Ernest Bevin stood up. "Thank you Jack. Put your hands together lads." Ernest paused a moment for effect and let the noise die. "I CALL ON ARTHUR COOK." As Arthur rose to mount the stand the noise was tumultuous and caps were thrown in the air. Arthur stood very still for a moment then his arm pointed out over the crowd.

"Comrades! - You should not hear me speak for I am a common lawbreaker fit only for His Majesty's Prisons." There were loud jeers directed at the police, everyone knew that Arthur had been in jail three times for agitating and leading strike actions. "But they can send me there again because I will never give in unless we right the wrongs that fall on us, that fell on our forefathers and fall on us today! When did we get ought but we had to fight for it and starve for it. Not only as men but our families even more so. I can remember the children crying to sleep for lack of food watched over by a mother who had nought to give except a mother's hand. When we ask for bread they spit on us as if we were nothing, not part of humanity. Therefore I tell you - we will never give in, bow the knee or be beaten into submission. What do they expect from us? TO DIG THE COAL FOR NOTHING? We go to negotiate in good faith, bolstered by our certain knowledge of boundless profits and royalties for men who never put a sweat on their brow and what do they say to us - take a reduction in wages and blow away the minimum wage. Yes, they offer a share in profit but who can read the book? Nor will they let us set their wages to see that the accounts are just! No, that is a commercial secret so we must take the fag-end that they throw on the ground. There will be no change until we strike back - THERE MUST BE A REVOLUTION! I see no other way.

Our great strength is our unity of purpose, our solidarity. All working men must stick together and the spirit that binds us must be strong as mortar. Today the miner is the worst paid man in the country so what do they propose? They propose to destroy our wages agreement, that which we fought so hard to gain. We will be cast down should we agree. We protest about bad safety and conditions that will kill a man and what are we told? It is the hazard of the job! There is no pity, no care - they will not even barrow us to the poorhouse. We must prepare to fight - WE MUST SWEEP ALL ASIDE! There is only one way to end this fracture - WE MUST MEND IT - OR END IT! Get ready, stand fast! NOT A PENNY OFF THE WAGES - NOT A MINUTE ON THE DAY!"

There was a tremendous roar all round the field. "NOT A PENNY OFF THE WAGES, NOT A MINUTE ON THE DAY!"

As Jack left the field a young woman rushed up and threw her arms around him. It would not be like Jack to protest at such a sign of affection but he was puzzled. "Who are you?"

"Ivy, Jack - your sister Ivy!"

When Jack had left Bloxwich she had been an eight-year-old girl now here she was grown up. She took his arm.

"How are the boys? How are the girls? I have so much to ask. That was a fine speech, Jack. A very fine speech, I was so proud of you."

Off they went, arm in arm. "Let's go have a drink."

## 30th April 1926

The Federation Executive sat whilst Arthur Cook gave his latest report. Pipe smoke filled the air and the hotel manager had been given strict instructions no one was to disturb the meeting. Arthur started.

"You will all have read the Royal Commission report published on the 26th March. That called for immediate pay cuts and we rejected it. The owners offer we know about and I am grateful to Jack Elks for the careful analysis and report he has made to us. Every district notice has been scrutinised and the varying effects of proposed changes noted. As you can see the notices vary from district to district. We have exhausted every avenue of negotiation. Neither the owners nor the government will agree to any single one of our proposals however small. An hour ago I had a letter from the Prime Minister, suggesting an agreement. That letter is in front of you, you will see it is cleverly worded. I have asked Jack if he would analyse the proposals. Jack!"

Jack checked his notes, then commenced. "In each district there will be an agreed national minimum wage but is conditional on working, on average, an extra hour per day. The effect of the new minimum wage is that all men will receive a lower actual wage of between ten and sixteen per cent. The average is thirteen and a half per cent. If you take into account the longer hours and lower wage it represents a downward adjustment of twenty seven per cent to the hourly rate."

Herbert Smith, the President took over. "Gentlemen. I have in my hands telegrams to the effect that already two-thirds of our men are locked out. Already! At this hour the Prime Minister intervenes. Then I am informed that the owners will not accept his proposals! What do I say?" He paused. "I propose to go now to the TUC council and say we have totally failed to reach an agreement and ask their support of us. For? Against? All for."

The battle had commenced. The TUC issued the call to the unions for a general strike to commence. On Monday the 3rd of May there were no passenger trains, no coal or heavy goods trains, no evening papers, no trams or buses.

## 3 May 1926

The speaker of the House of Commons called on Mr. J. Thomas, Labour Member of Parliament, in reply to the Prime Minister.

"Mr. Speaker. The General Council of the TUC had never asked for a subsidy as a permanent solution of the present difficulty. The only thing the General Council had asked the Prime Minister since Monday last was that negotiations should be given a fair chance, because they could not conduct negotiations under threat of a lock-out. The breakdown took place on that and that alone. The lock-out came into operation at midnight on Friday night. There were forty thousand men who finished their shift on Friday afternoon, and it was not until 1.15 on Friday afternoon that the first national offer was made by the employers. What they then offered was eight hours a day and 20 per cent minimum wage. The meanest part of the business was in demanding that the miners' representatives should agree in advance to a reduction of wages.

What the miners asked for was a chance to discuss the whole situation. The position taken up on behalf of the miners was that there should be no lock-out of men without giving a chance for negotiation. I do not believe two per cent of the people would vote for a revolution, but he was a blind fool who could see that these people were driven by circumstances into courses they did not desire. This was not a revolution; it was merely a plain economic industrial dispute where the workers said they wanted justice. Is it not too late to avert what I believe to be the greatest calamity to befall this country. I appeal for one last effort to be made."

## 4th May 1926

The Miners Federation office was a mass of papers, telephones constantly ringing. In the middle of it sat Jack, tirelessly working away. Arthur bowled in the door. "We're winning Jack, winning I tell you. Men are out from John O'Groats to Lands End. What's the news?"

"The good news is we've received donations to the value of £10,200 today. Money is coming in from overseas unions. Discipline is good but there have been about 20 arrests."

"Excellent Jack. As long as the TUC hold firm we can mend this fracture!"

Jack returned to the administration. Lizzie had contacted him to say that Len and Albert were fine. They were both working on a nearby farm and when they weren't milking cows they were honing up their football skills and showed signs of getting a suntan. "I will be home tonight," he'd told Lizzie, "there's a meeting tomorrow."

## 5th May 1926

Rain threatened as the Dover strikers assembled in the Pencester Road. There were mainly men, with a small number of women, and Jack wished they had a band to proceed the banners.

However even if they could get one the Police Inspector on duty had made it plain that martial music would not be allowed. Robbie Stokes, the NUR leader helped Jack create a semblance of order and at last the banners led off the procession. Turning around Jack called out "Get 'em singing lads. Sing-along, now!"

"WE'LL MAKE A BONFIRE OF OUR TROUBLES, ALL OUR CARES WILL BLAZE AWAY", struck up along the line as voices sung out.

"Heads up, lads. Show a bit of pride!"

Up the Folkestone Road they went singing, past the Priory Station, their numbers increasing all the time.

"Are we down hearted? No - No - NO!"

As they reached the football ground the rain started. Jack didn't have to call for quiet as the singing stopped as the rain came. Jack stepped up on to the rostrum.

"The entertainment comes later - for now you've got me! We stand here together, the railwaymen (Cheers!), the tramway men (Cheers!), the locomotive men (Cheers!), the miners (Cheers!). Our men owe you a debt of gratitude that cannot be repaid. The present terms for the miners in Kent will mean every man will lose one pound three shillings a week and have to work five and a half hours extra to get it. There has never been a finer example of union solidarity than we see here today - or across the country.

What do we do now? Nowt I say. DO NOWT! They want us to cause trouble so they can make an example of us. Why do you think those police wait over there? But I want no martyrs - no broken bones - no arrests!" He took off his Homburg and shook off the water.

"That is the most violent action I want to see today! Until the football match starts, that is!

Now, please give a warm welcome to Robbie Stokes from the NUR".


**8th May 1926**

The Prime Minister's broadcast to the nation.

".... employers must do all in their power to keep works running.  The government position is that the strike must be called off, absolutely and without reserve.  This mining dispute can then be settled.  A solution is within the grasp of the nation the instant the leaders are willing to abandon the general strike.  I am a man of peace, I pray for peace but I will not surrender the safety and security of the British Constitution.  You placed me in power eighteen months ago.  Have I done anything to forfeit that confidence?  Cannot you trust me to ensure a square deal, to secure justice between men and men."

## 11th May 1926

Herbert Smith, the President, spoke to the Executive Committee.

"I have had proposals passed on to me from the Chairman of the Royal Commission, Sir Herbert Samuel, regarding a settlement.  He proposes the government renews the subsidy for a reasonable time, a National Wages Board under an independent Chairman, and will seek a settlement with no revision of wages. Do you consider his proposals meet our demands?"

Arthur was quick off the mark.  "Does he say the government accept his proposals?  If so, why haven't we heard from the Prime Minister?"

Herbert shook his head.  "He doesn't claim that, they seem to be his own proposals.  However, you all heard Prime Minister Baldwin the other night.  If you believe him then we must go and negotiate.  If not we must continue as we are.  Those for acceptance?  None.  I will go to the TUC now and tell them of our decision."

## 12th May 1926

Jack and Arthur listened to the BBC noon news bulletin. "We must break for lunch -we've been going six hours already."

Jack got his 'Homburg'. "Let's just hear the news finish."

Arthur turned in astonishment. "Good god, Jack - did you hear that?"

The newsreader went on "The nation has just passed through a period of extreme anxiety.  It was announced today that the General Strike has been brought to an end."

Jack threw his hands up. "How did this happen, there's been nowt said to us!"

Arthur could not contain himself.  "We've agreed nothing. Nothing!  You get on the telephone to Herbert while I speak to Ernie Bevin to find out what they know at the TUC."

"What about the men, Arthur?   There'll be chaos, not knowing what to do!  Shall I send telegrams to the districts telling them to hold fast while we get organised?"

"Aye, be quick, Jack - what a bloody mess!"

Jack went as fast as he could.

An hour later he was back to find Arthur and Herbert waiting.

"I'm calling an executive meeting as quickly as possible." Herbert clenched his pipe firmly in his teeth, almost biting through the stem in his frustration, before continuing.  "From what I'm told, the TUC believed that Samuel was acting officially and they believed that Baldwin was sincere the other night.  That he was sending them a message that all was agreed - all they had to do was bend the knee!  They went to Baldwin and surrendered! They've already sent out notices to all the other unions calling it all off!"

"But they never spoke to us!"   Jack's temper was rising. "You went and told them we didn't believe the proposals, that Samuel was acting unofficially!  You went personally and told them for God's sake!"

Arthur needed reassurance. "Jack, have the telegrams gone out?"

When Jack nodded Arthur went on. "Even Ernie Bevin assumed that the lock-out notices would be withdrawn and the subsidy renewed! My cat could have read the situation better!"

"We're on our own," said Herbert, "Baldwin has already said that Samuel could not bind the government. We must fight on. You two had better get fund-raising, this is going to be a long battle."

"They will try to smash us," Jack was taking off his jacket, "it will be the soup kitchens again."

Herbert got up. "I want nowt said about the TUC. No recriminations. You can think them - but not say them. Not after what their men have done for us. The owners will squeeze us dry, we must try and keep what friends we have."

## 1st July 1926

Jack collated all the reports together, coming in from the Kent lodges. After weeks without work the men and their families were suffering but there was no sign of a return to work. At Eythorne the Lodge was organising daily tea for the children. Miners selected by ballot were digging coal at all three pits to raise fuel for the boilers to keep the mines in good order. The Thanet Guardians were supporting 150 families in Ramsgate; food centres had been set up in Canterbury, Westbere, Sturry and the new village (later called Hersden) for the scattered miners of Chislet. Snowdown management were threatening to close the re-furbished mine for seven months if the men did not return now but both the Lodge committee and the men refused to concede. Jack made a note to address that matter, there would be no harm in letting a token number of men return as some of them had been laid off since November in the previous year. It would do no good if there were a permanent closure and with Betteshanger due to open in the next year, the Snowdown owners, Dorman Long, might cut their losses and mothball the pit.

In desperation several hundred men at Tilmanstone had approached the Guardians and demanded relief or work so they were now breaking roadstones for Eastry Council. Jack was pleased at that. Angry desperate men might take extreme measures in frustration without enough money coming in for their families and the last thing he wanted was for the men to get into trouble with the law.

Good, he concluded, everything in order. Now he could get ready for Arthur Cook's visit tomorrow.

## 2nd July 1926

The procession of fifteen hundred people, headed by banners, slowly made its way down the Dover High Street towards the sea front. Behind the banners strode Jack and Arthur Cook. The miners had now been out for nine weeks with no end to the conflict in sight. Jack had appealed to Arthur to come and speak. When they reached the sea front it took over twenty minutes for all the procession to arrive. Men had come from as far away as Ramsgate. Jack got on the stand.

"Ladies and gentlemen, fellow-workers and miners of Kent. Only one man could have come here today and raised a crowd such as this. He needs no introduction but introduce him I will. Please welcome a man who has given his life in support of the miners of this country. ARTHUR COOK!"

To great cheering Arthur shook Jack's hand and mounted the stand, his arms flung out over the crowd.

"We are told we use our weight in a selfish way to get what we don't deserve or work for. If that is believed then I ask the British public to vote to say whether they believe the miners ought to get a living wage or not. Is it wrong that I want to see every man off the dole, earning his own living? No one on unemployment or supported by the Guardians can be happy or healthy.

Working in the pit is no joy ride. On my first day underground I saw a man die and over the years I have had to carry many an injured or dead man home. I was in the rescue team at Senghennyed when 439 men and boys died in a single explosion - we carried no live men out that day. When the manager was found guilty of flagrant abuse of the safety rules he was fined a week's wage. And the owners? Scot free - not a penny in fine or stricture.

Danger goes with the job but we object to unnecessary danger, but neither the Tories nor the Liberals will pass a safety act unless forced to by disaster. Before this stoppage a quarter of a million of our members were taking home less than two pounds a week! Now we are told to accept less! At the last stoppage the government gave a subsidy of twenty million pounds to the industry but I show you this White Paper. The owners got eight and a half million while a million miners got only two and a half million. That's two pounds fifty a man spread over nine months! I see someone disagrees with me! Yes, you sir! The figures I have quoted are not mine - they are the official government figures!

To produce a ton of coal costs fourteen shillings in direct costs, including wages. But it retails at nearly three pounds a ton. Where does all the difference go? It is not going to our members. The Prime Minister told you in a broadcast that he has tried to get the two sides together. I consider three sides make a triangle. When we get there what do we find? He argues for the owners so we are back to two sides again. The coal owners say they will starve us out. That is why I have appealed to miners in other countries to help us because there is no doubt of the owners' intentions. They have said it publicly! Now they say it is politics to accept help. I tell you it is simple defence. The Prime Minister tells me to take the men back - take you back - I say I follow your democratic ballot. The men pay me to defend their interests so I will not say in Downing Street one thing and say another to you.

Others have done it and Frank Hodges attacks us daily.

We are beset with blacklegs - they are all around. Well I say this. If the OMS* and the Fascisti want to work in the pits - well let them! They may go down once - I will bet my soul they'll not go twice!

We must stick together - without unity we will be broken and hunted down. But I say this, if I am to be broken then let it be in defence of what I believe in - justice and fairness. Not just for miners but for all working men!

STAND FAST - STAND FIRM - STAND TOGETHER!"

Later in the evening Jack took Arthur to the station for his return to London. "How long can we last, Arthur?"

"I think about five or six weeks. The appeals are going out and some money is coming in. Hodges opposes everything we do and say at the Miners International. I've never met a turncoat like him!"

"The men here are worried, the management are threatening to close Snowdown until the middle of next year. I feel sorry for the local men who supported us. Both the NUR and the Tramway men backed us to the hilt. Now they're being victimised - refused jobs and being offered lower wages. Damn all we can do about it, either!"

"Sorry Jack. They're going to starve us out - make no bones about it! If the men stay out we must stay with them. You saw them tonight. They'll not go back till they are ready - whatever we say."

*OMS—An organisation called the Organisation for the Maintenance of Supplies, formed by Lord Harding of Penshurst to arrange volunteers to act as strikebreakers.

A porter came striding down the platform. "Attention please!

The company apologises that the 10.30 train to London is cancelled, I repeat………"

Jack picked up Arthur's bag. "You'd best come home with me. They've run out of coal!"

## 11th November 1926

Jack was discouraged but not downhearted. After over six months the men of Snowdown and Chislet had given up the struggle and most had returned to work even though the Federation had not officially sanctioned an end to the strike. There was no point in recriminations, the men and their families had given their all and many were in a poor state. Jack wanted the men at Tilmanstone to return as well but they were proving more stubborn, especially as the company operating it had changed hands. Things generally were so quiet that even the soldiers at the local gas and electricity works had been withdrawn because no threat was perceived. There had been no arrests or incidents amongst the miners of Kent. On 9th November, Jack received a letter asking him to visit the Tilmanstone Colliery to discuss the work situation.

As Jack entered the Tilmanstone office he muttered a quiet prayer, though it sounded more like an oath. The new Manager, Beck, offered him a seat.

"Good morning, Mr. Elks, we've not met before"

Jack sat down. Through the window he could see the few men on picket duty and thought how miserable, cold and downhearted they seemed.

"Mr. Elks, this is our first meeting, let me explain my position. At great expense the new owners have refurbished the mine and we are ready to start producing. Either we start work soon or we face closure. How do we sort this out?"

"What do you offer?"

"Standard rates and hours, the same as the other mines in Kent."

"May I see them?" Beck passed over the price lists. Jack glanced through them, he could see almost instantly they were the same terms as at Snowdown. "What if these are not accepted?"

"I'm sorry, there can be no negotiation - if our costs are higher than others we'll go out of business. For a single mine company like ours, parity is essential."

"I want all our men back, Mr. Beck, there must be no victimisation. How many will you take?"

"Every man on the old payroll, provided they are back in ten days and accept the standard contract."

"What about recognition of the Association?"

"As I said, there will be no victimisation but I will not recognise the union until the district wage rates and conditions are signed."

"What if the men won't go back?"

"Unless I get a reassurance from you within six days then the owners have instructed me to put advertisements in all the coalfield newspapers offering jobs. I have no option. Once that is done every man will have to take his place in the queue and old employees will get no preference."

"What are your future plans - do you expect to take on more men?"

Beck hesitated. "Can I speak in confidence?" Jack nodded.

"I am expected to double output within two years."

Jack considered. That would mean a near doubling of the work force.

"What about union recognition?"

"If the men come in and sign the new contracts, then we'll see."

"These wage rates and conditions will have to be approved at the District Bargaining Committee." Jack passed the lists back

"I know that but I can't wait. We must get started."

"Should I get the men back now I want a promise of recognition of the Association and that all men working here will be required to be members."

"And if we don't?"

"As I see it, Mr. Beck, we have a good chance of peace and harmony. I do not want my men beggared more than now. It will take years to repair the damage. You are starting new. Let's try and work together. There will be no fighting except against injustice. The lodge committee here are honourable men and provided there's no victimisation then we get off to a good start. If all the men are Association members there will be no squabbles and arguments over market-men and blacklegging."

"I cannot sign such an agreement today, we must get started first so how do we proceed?"

"A gentlemen's agreement. The men will go back and you agree to full recognition as soon as the district wage agreements are signed. Union dues to be deducted from wages and no man taken on without a card. I can promise you a high level of co-operation. What do you say?" Jack held out his hand.

"I've heard you called 'Honest Jack from Kent'," Beck held out his hand, "let's make a new start."

"If this was a pub", said Jack, "I'd buy a round!"

"Strange you should say that, Jack, I was saving this bottle till the first full tub of coal came up." Beck went to his cupboard and got out a bottle. "Let's have a drink to the future!"

One week later Tilmanstone was in full production.

## December 1926

The Federation delegates had voted for a return to work, their funds were almost exhausted, the miners in the fields beaten down. They had lost the battle and had to eat the ashes of defeat. It was not even a defeat with honour; they had gained nothing and lost nearly everything.

On the first day of December, Jack caught the train back to Dover, passing through the same countryside he had seen those years before on his way to the Shakespeare. The bitterness of defeat rankled but he knew it was pointless to dwell on such matters; but they had lost all they had fought for and more besides. He knew that the funds the Federation had built up over a decade were exhausted, they were all but smashed. Naturally the Federation would recover slowly. The miners still had faith in it because it was the only means of making progress but with a declining economy, unemployment rampant and their loss of prestige it would be a decade before they could regain their old position. He thought of his own members, his men as he called them, those who had started with such hope, fearing the worst but willing to stand stoically when surrounded by hardship. They were faced with more years of hardship. Because not only would they now get lower wages but few had managed to survive the last seven months without borrowing from the Board of Guardians, the overseer of the Poor Law. All must be repaid. Then there was the back rent and the victimisation. There would be a mountain to climb, he would need all his skill and statesmanship if they were to endure, if he was to endure. He could not let those men down, he had made them his own, he would fight.

Looking out of the window he could see that the Kent countryside was unaltered, as if great events simply washed over it and passed it by untouched. His thoughts turned to his last meeting with Arthur Cook, a man beaten down, worried and concerned.

More than anyone else Arthur had nailed his banner to confrontation and he had taken the failure personally.

"I let you down, Jack. Let us all down! I never thought it could come to this. What do we do? We ask, we get nothing. We negotiate, we are turned away. We concede, we are told it is not enough. They spend more on imports of coal than we ask in wages and they tell us we know nothing of economics. They turn this country into a police state and all we can do is bend the knee!"

"There was nowt else we could do, Arthur. Even a rat will fight if backed into a corner!"

"I don't care for myself, Jack but what about the men? What will happen to them? They stuck by us for seven months! We had everything against us. The fight is over but the conditions the owners have imposed will bring no goodwill or any spirit of conciliation."

Jack sighed. "There's no peace by forcing longer hours and lower wages. The fight was unequal, I think I shall hate police and soldiers all my life. There are some lessons to be learnt though."

"What do you say, Jack?"

"We must get the press on our side, prove all these accusations of Bolshevik collusion are false. Get more political, concentrate on strengthening the Labour Party, get more mining M. P's."

"Will you stay to help me?"

"No, Arthur. I must get back to Kent. The lads are in a terrible state. The owners won't negotiate with me at the moment. They say take it or leave it."

"You're right, Jack. Get back to Kent and fight for justice. I have to remain here, the knives are out for me. Do you recall the words of that American Indian Chief when they had lost all their lands and the tribe scattered and defeated? He said the 'Hoop of the Nation' had been broken and could never be repaired. Well it must not be so here if I have to give my life for it."

As the train pulled into Dover, Jack could feel his energy returning. For the moment his work was here and here he must concentrate his efforts. The basis of district agreements must be enforced; his clerk had told him that there was a mountain of individual cases to pursue. He would need to be 'ca-canny' as never before, he would work even harder. With mounting confidence he swung down off the train and headed for his office.

During the prolonged strike George Spencer had frequently been on picket duty at Snowdown Colliery so his face was well known. Not that he had done much more than stand, cold and bored, for most of the time. Except towards the end of the seven-month stoppage when a few 'blacklegs', driven by deprivation had returned to work. George had almost wanted to join them but had relieved his feelings by joining in the chant of 'Traitors' with the rest of the picket. The large number of police, who outnumbered the pickets three to one, had kept a tight control so the 'blacklegs' went in to work unhindered. George just bided his time, kept his nose clean, and hoped this would all be over soon. He knew that to get arrested would condemn him as an agitator and lead to dismissal. It came as a great shock to him, when on the first day back the management team at the gate had refused him entry.

"You're trespassing, Spencer, bugger off!" George was so flummoxed he could only say that he needed the job. "Thou didn't need it last week! You're a troublemaker, so bugger off. You'll not be told again."

Ten days later George sat in an office temporarily used as an Employment Exchange to attend for an interview. He thought the interview had gone well. He had paid all his dues and he answered all the questions as fairly as possible. As he said, he was an unemployed miner so getting alternative work without experience was very difficult. He was greatly surprised to be refused benefit on the grounds he had not been genuinely seeking work. When asked if he wished to appeal he was told to come back the following week to meet the 'Court of Referees'. When he returned he was ushered in to meet Mr. Snow.

"Sit down please!"

George removed his cap. Mr. Snow appraised him for a while before speaking. George sat, very nervous, on the edge of his chair. It was so quiet that he was startled when Mr. Snow interrogated him in quick succession.

"You are George Spencer, aged twenty nine, unemployed collier?"

"Yes, Sir."

"You claim you were dismissed on the 1st of December?"

"Yes, Sir, I have...."

"You were employed at Snowdown Colliery?"

"Yes, sir."

"Why were you dismissed?"

"As I said before, sir, they just turned me away at the gates."

"Why did they do that?"

"They said I was a troublemaker, but I...."

"Just answer the questions put to you."

Snow thumbed the papers.

"What have you done to find employment?"

"I've tried all over, sir, but I've no experience out of mining."

"Hum. Perhaps if you find employment you'll be more careful of it in future. Now, exactly where have you been? Where did you go yesterday?"

"Nowhere, sir. It seemed so pointless and I was unwell."

"So you haven't been genuinely seeking work?"

"I tried everywhere, sir, been turned away each time."

"Where did you go last Monday?"

"Waxted Farm in the morning."

"What was the name of the owner?"

"I wasn't told, Sir."

"What about the afternoon?"

"I went to the foreman on the road gang."

"What happened?"

"He told me the clear off."

"Have you been back to Waxted Farm?"

"They had no job, sir."

"That was on Monday, what about today?"

"I don't know, Sir."

"No, but how can you tell if you don't try. Have you been to Canterbury?"

"No, Sir. It's a ten mile walk and my boots are fair worn out."

"So you haven't tried."

"No, Sir."

"What about the other coal mines?"

"They're not taking on men."

"Have you tried, been there?"

"They're even further off, Sir. I haven't had a decent meal in weeks, I couldn't make it there and back, day in, day out."

"Why haven't you had a decent meal?"

"The union compensation was small, Sir and there are the children to feed."

"I can see no evidence that you have sought work on a constructive or daily basis. Application dismissed. You may go."

That day George saw the chairman of the Snowdown Branch of the Association. "Sorry, George, try not to worry, we'll support you for the moment. I'll ask Jack Elks to help."

A week later Jack and George sat in front of the referee. Jack commenced, "I asked for this appeal, Mr. Snow, which you have said you will consider. It seems to me that a man such as Mr. Spencer, who has never asked for assistance before, may in some way, because he is not an educated man, have failed to make his case properly or plainly. That he may, because he did not explain properly, have put you in the invidious position of arriving at a conclusion, that in your normal high standards of judgement, you would not have arrived at."

Jack put his best smile forward as he said it. Mr. Snow looked severe.

"I do not see how, Mr. Elks but I am a Christian man and would not want to be party to an injustice."

"May I submit some points to you? Go over the issues and events so that you will feel certain you have not been misled and unwittingly been drawn to an unfortunate conclusion against your natural inclination for fairness."

Mr. Snow havered for a few minutes but eventually conceded that Jack could explain. "Appeal granted. You may proceed."

'You're a miserable bastard,' thought Jack, 'anyone would

think it's your own money you're giving away.' In the background he knew, of course, that instructions had been passed down that men such as George Spencer were to be given short shift. Honest men like George were so gullible, they actually thought the system was there to help them.

"I would like to start with the matter of Mr. Spencer's dismissal. During the mining strike Mr. Spencer did nothing illegal. He participated in a legal picket."

"Mr. Spencer's claim was not rejected because of the dismissal!"

"We are certain that is true, Mr. Snow, but in its manner of presentation the matter may have led you to the suspicion that Mr. Spencer acted in a way that led to his own dismissal."

"I admit I had my doubts but I do not think that swayed me."

"Of course not Mr. Snow, but just to clarify the matter I have a letter from the police sergeant on duty that Mr. Spencer's actions were at all times that of a law-abiding man and on the day of his dismissal, although the words 'you're a troublemaker' were used, no evidence was presented in support of that."

Jack handed over the letter.

"I never said Mr. Spencer was a troublemaker!"

"I appreciate that, Mr. Snow, but I just wanted to clear the matter up in case it might have seemed that Mr. Spencer had done something to cause his dismissal."

"But he did cause it, he went on strike!"

"That may appear so but it is not true. Here is a note from Dorman Long Limited, the mine owners, stating the colliery would close on the 1st May, revoking the men's contracts because the Miners Federation and the owners were in dispute over new contracts. At that time agreements were controlled by the National Wages Council, a matter over which Mr. Spencer had no control, so he was unable to work. Rightly, Mr. Spencer did not claim insurance benefit in that period and has only done so since his dismissal. I hope that clears up the matter leading up to his claim."

Snow polished his glasses and fidgeted with his papers. Jack was pleased because he hoped that a conscience was being pricked.

"Coming to the information given by Mr. Spencer. You asked Mr. Spencer if he had been to Waxted Farm. All the farms around Snowdown are fruit and hop farms and they only provide work on a seasonal basis in the later summer months, casual labour at harvest time. The few winter jobs are available only to experienced horticulturists. Mr. Spencer will be unable to find farm employment. Here is a letter from the owner of Waxted Farm, and a number of other farms, stating the case. They will of course consider Mr. Spencer in the summer."

Jack handed over more letters.

"You also asked Mr. Spencer if he had been to other collieries. The local vicars, who you know are gravely concerned at recent events, here state that every coal mine has continuously, since 1st December, displayed notice that no jobs are available and also that in the last two weeks they have laid more men off."

Mr. Snow began to wilt but failed to say the magic words so Jack ploughed on.

"You also mentioned the council road gang. Here is a letter saying that they have been unable to take on new men for over three months because of the high unemployment in the area and because of the economic climate are having to lay men off."

Still no magic words.

"You asked Mr. Spencer if he had been to Canterbury. I have here a letter from the Panel Doctor saying that Mr. Spencer's health is poor and in his view he is unable to walk the round distance needed. Were Mr. Spencer able to find employment in Canterbury at the level of his ability, which would be restricted to labouring, the cost of travel would take two thirds of his wages so he would be unable to feed his family. Here is a survey of prevailing labouring wages in the area, you can see that the average pay is fifteen shillings a week. Then there is the matter of his boots, they are in such poor condition they would fall off his feet on a long hike."

"He could perhaps go to the Guardians?"

"That is true, Mr. Snow, but they advance loans, not wages or benefits, and that would put Mr. Spencer into deeper debt than he is already. Mr. Spencer is an insured man and has paid all his dues so to provide him with insurance benefit is his reasonable legal right. As a Christian man and a regular churchgoer whose honesty and hard work are self-evident, surely he also has a moral right to help"

"Will you have me believe there is no work in this area, Mr Elks?"

"There are hundreds of men seeking work, chasing after one or two jobs. If you care to name any farm, works or estate and so on in the area I can give you or get you proof there were no jobs today, or yesterday nor will be tomorrow. I can assure you that Mr……..."

Mr. Snow brought him to a halt. "Application granted." The magic words said Jack picked up his case and guided George out.

The work of the committee men scouring the area, buying pints judiciously, bending the knee to the clergy and so forth had paid off. A few weeks ago Jack had been in the corridors of power now he was back pounding shoe leather, fighting the spitefulness and victimisation of petty officials. Lots more men waited on his help.

## January 1927

Jack had lost his seat on the executive. After the defeat in the great strike and as a supporter of Arthur Cook it was only to be expected. Besides which, there was much work to do in Kent and he could hardly afford the time. His last action was to sign the memorandum drawn up by the executive outlining the events from 4th May to the end of the strike. That memorandum concluded: *'The fight is not over. The conditions of the owners are imposed conditions and bring with them no goodwill or spirit of conciliation. Longer hours and lower wages cannot bring peace in the coalfields. Nor will we allow district agreements to shatter our strength and unity. Our Organisation is still intact and we are determined to recover the ground that has been lost. In this endeavour we look with confidence for the full support of the whole Trade Union Movement.'*

The memorandum was to be Arthur Cook's swan-song, except for one small triumph in June 1927 when he forced the resignation of Frank Hodges from the International Miners Federation. When Hodges died in 1947 he left an estate of £132,959, a fortune at that time.

## February 1927

Not until February 1927 did Jack manage to get a meeting with the Kent owners and that was only grudgingly agreed after he threatened to take legal action. There were no handshakes or greetings, just a curt nod and a hand waved towards a chair. They were the victors.

"You asked for a meeting, Mr. Elks, what have you to say?"

"There are a number of issues. Shall I outline them?"

"Go, on!"

"I am here as the officially appointed representative of the Miners Federation to be a member of the District Negotiating body. In that capacity I represent all members of the Kent Mine Workers Association."

"You do not represent all the men!"

"I represent over ninety five per cent of the men."

The Snowdown representative butted in. "Who represents the other men? Why are they not here?"

"Mr Elks represents all the men at Tilmanstone." Jack was grateful to Beck for that comment but did not address him direct. He also knew he was close to that recognition at Chislet but nothing could be said at this meeting. The very nature of the owners grouping demanded solidarity at this meeting, as none of them would willingly concede higher rates of wages. Unfortunately the Snowdown man was the Chairman.

Jack continued. "As I said, I am the official representative appointed under the agreement with the central board. In that capacity it is my job to negotiate all wage matters in the district, irrespective of union membership."

"We reserve our views on that matter, what else have you got to say?"

"I wish to discuss certain matters regarding conditions of work and contracts. There is the matter of the period of agreement, the ratio of wages to profit and the minimum percentage increase on base rates. There are also the matters of victimisation and unfair disciplinary procedures."

"We are not prepared to discuss any of these last matters, they are matters for us alone!"

"Then you leave me no choice. As the accredited representative, as I stated, I have sought legal advice at the highest level and will tomorrow serve writs on all of you. Both as owners and individuals."

"You cannot do that!"

"I do not wish to, I would rather we arrive at an amicable conclusion. That would be to the benefit of everyone."

"Your union is broken, you have no funds. It will cost you thousands of pounds to bring us to court."

"That works two ways, gentlemen. You cannot break the law of the land and get away with it. The agreement between the Federation and the National Negotiating Board is a legal contract. That contract, to which your body is a party, and forced on us, specifies that district wages agreements are to be approved by the Secretary of State for Mines and we must be a party to it. Whereas you gentlemen have businesses to run I will have little to do except pursue legal action. Do you want to spend your time in court for the next ten years?"

"How will you fund such action? Who will represent you?

We will get the best legal brains in the country!"

"All the better, gentlemen, the better the brain the higher the cost. As for myself, I shall conduct our case, so it will cost my Association very little. I can get legal assistance from my Federation. During the last six years I have spent more time in court than out. Furthermore I will issue writs against each individual owner. If you want a legal fight then you shall have one, the writs will be served tomorrow."

There was a hasty whispered conference.

"We will not agree to anything else other than the agreement regarding a district wages agreement. We can discuss nothing outside that agreement."

Jack was pleased, he had got all he had come for, all other matters would follow on. His toe was firmly in the door; he had won the first skirmish. He drew two documents out of his case.

"Here are the formal rules and memoranda applying to District Wages Councils. You will see that it allows for representation by the men. I propose to bring three committee men to future meetings. Their names will be notified in advance."

The Snowdown man was not mollified. "I feel strongly that non-union men be represented."

"I have no difficulty with that", said Jack, "but as they are only five per cent then one man would be fair."

Beck interjected. "Mr. Chairman, I cannot see the advantage of that. The wage rates and conditions are complex, highly complex. I move we should limit the meeting between us and the Association."

The Chislet representative added his weight. "I agree ,Mr. Chairman."

When Jack left the meeting two hours later he had got all he came for. He was not a beaten man with a beaten organisation. There was a way forward with the law and politics. His confidence grew. The days of tub-thumping were over. The years of struggle lay ahead.

\* \* \* \* \* \* \*

*Arthur Cook, the most revered mine leader of his day, hung on for a few years but died prematurely in 1929 at the age of 46. During those last few years the Federation took a more passive role but Arthur worked hard on the political front. When a Labour Government came to power in 1929 there were forty-three M.P.'s sponsored by the Miners' Federation. The pits had their final revenge on Arthur. His leg, that had been injured in a pit accident, became cancerous and nothing could be done to save him.*

*When he spoke about the 'Hoop of Nation' being broken he was speaking from the following quotation.*

*"I did not know then how much was ended. When I look back from this high hill of my old age, I can still see the butchered women and children as plain as when I saw them with my eyes still young. And I can see that something else died there in the bloody mud and was buried. A people's dream died there. It was a beautiful dream. But now the nation's hoop is broken and scattered, there is no centre any longer and the sacred tree is dead!"*

*These words were spoken by Black Elk of the Oglala Sioux, late in his life. As a boy of thirteen he had been at the battle of the Little Bighorn in 1876.*

## 1927 to 1939

In 1927 there were over 200,000 miners out of work across the country. There were two reasons. Firstly demand for coal fell; in fact it fell every year for 5 years up to 1933. The number of miners dropped from 1,000,000 to 780,000. Secondly there was an increasing introduction of mechanisation. Unemployment reached its peak in the early 30's. These unemployed often ran out of normal insurance benefit and were reduced to living on the 'dole'. The dole was the term used for the benefits then in operation. To get the dole an unemployed man had to prove need, the so-called "means test" that applied to the whole household. It took into account the entire earnings of the house, including sons and daughters, any savings, pensions or other assets. Families often broke up under the strain. However, whether on the dole or at work, wages and income were often extremely low. The men may have suffered but the wives suffered more; if anyone in the family went short of food and clothes it was the mother.

By 1936-37 a recovery had started and this was accelerated at the approach of World War II, as the country rearmed.

## Chapter 6

## THE YEARS OF STRUGGLE

## March 1927

Jack eased himself into the chair with some relief. It had been a long hard day so far, now there would be a long afternoon of negotiation. Across the table was Mottram, secretary for the owners, the East Kent Colliery Association. He stared hard at Jack and cracked his fingers.

"Right, lets get as many cases done as we can. I know you're prepared to stay till all hours but I have a home to go to!"

"Then I suggest until six p.m. The court hearing will be in five days and there's a lot of paperwork to do."

Agreement on compensation cases seemed to take forever, meanwhile the men involved suffered. Jack picked up the first file.

"This is the Dunn case. Severe Nystagmus. It is accepted that this eye complaint occurs only in miners, so that is established. The eye specialist has said he's totally unfit for work."

"Our eye specialist has diagnosed naturally occurring short-sightedness and cataract as well, so there cannot be full compensation." Mottram frowned to show he was digging his heels in. Jack was not impressed and sniffed. "Possibly, but it is on the basis of the Nystagmus alone that the specialist has said he is unfit for work, the man is practically blind!"

"I suggest £300 in full settlement."

"No," said Jack, "as a rule of thumb we take five years earnings if a man cannot work again. That would be £800."

"Apart from his eyesight this man is fit, he can find some other work!"

"He's been unemployed for four years.  No, I cannot accept less than £600."

"Agreed.  Next."

"Tester.  Crushed when he was fourteen."

Mottram looked at his file.  "I see his age is 18 now. His father will have to come to court.  He was paid weekly compensation for two and a half years, now he's got a job training in the lamphouse.  I see no need for compensation."

"The lad cannot walk far and his arms are twisted.  He could have been on top wages for many years - which will be denied him. He will lose two pounds a week for the rest of his life. He must get compensation for loss of earnings at the very least."

"I suggest £200."

"Agreed, subject to review when he is 21, then if he's on top rate in the lamphouse there will be no need for adjustment."

"Agreed.  Next."

"Walker.  Suffered a rupture at work."

"He was paid compensation while off and is now back at work.  Working normally as I see it."

"The hospital specialist has said that his stomach is weak and the rupture is liable to recur.  There must be agreed compensation against that eventuality."

"In that case we would offer him light work."

Jack persevered.  "There must be linkage between the previous rupture and any in the future otherwise the case is liable to go on and on.  I suggest we agree on £100 against future events and a guarantee of light work.  That really costs you nothing!"

"Agreed.  Next."

"Kemp.  Lost an eye from a metal splinter in 1921. He's been getting eight shillings a week since.  His present wage is two pounds ten shillings a week against potential earnings of three pounds ten.  I suggest a lump sum payment of £200."

"I will offer £150."

"Accepted," said Jack, "next is Luscombe. Unfortunately he has just died."

"The judge won't agree a settlement until his legal representative appears. Do we have one?"

"No, I'll put that in hand immediately. Mrs Luscombe needs support urgently. Next is Smith, suffering from miners' dermatitis. Medical opinion is that he must not work down the mine again."

"How old is he?" Mottram searched his papers. "Oh! Yes, 22. I think it fair to say that we don't want him back. Our specialist has said it could lead to complications. What do you suggest?"

"£700."

"I agree £600."

Jack agreed quickly, he would have settled for £400; he continued.

"Next is Ruddick. Injured left knee and cartilage removed. He has been getting one pound ten shillings a week compensation. He was a hewer but that is impossible now, the specialist has stated he cannot kneel and the ligatures have tightened. He has been offered work on the coalface but such work is impossible! I suggest light work on the haulage, he will be all right provided he doesn't have to kneel, and £200 compensation."

"Will he take the haulage?" Mottram looked puzzled.

"I see no reason why not," said Jack, "according to the reports."

"Will you accept my word if I say he's been offered work as a trammer and refused it!"

Under his breath Jack cursed. "Can we leave this while I talk to him?"

"I will give you a week, Jack," Mottram made a note, "but if he doesn't accept, then the compensation will drop to seven shillings a week."

"Next is Heath. A trammer, knocked down by a runaway tub."

Mottram peered over his glasses. "Has the specialist reported from the latest X-Rays?"

"Not yet but initially he received three broken ribs and severe lacerations and a broken ankle." Jack checked his notes. "The original X-ray and notes are available."

"Yes but that was three years ago and we must get an up to date assessment before we can agree compensation."

Jack was annoyed at this delaying tactic. "Will you continue to pay the eight shillings a week disability he's been receiving since he came back to work?"

"I see no reason for that!"

"The man was out for two and a half years. There were considerable loss of wages and it is your medical adviser delaying matters."

"Agreed, we will continue."

"Next is…………………………….."

Mottram got home late at nine to a cold dinner, cold shoulder and cold comfort.

**1st April 1927**

Letter to the Editor: Daily Herald

Dear Sir,

People everywhere, especially those whose views gain so much publicity, need to be properly informed about the so-called 'dole'. Last week a Coroner said this about an unemployed man who had committed suicide. "This man preferred death to the dole. In his circumstances I feel great respect and sympathy for him. This man represents the very best of Englishmen who feels his pride demeaned to take what he has not earned. If only there were more like him there would be less abuse of the system."

Let me say this, the dole is simply an extension of the National Insurance Act. Whilst it is true the scheme has been extended by state aid owing to the current economic collapse, that is not the fault of workless people. When they worked they paid contributions as required by law. What is an unemployed man to do if he cannot find work?

There must be no dishonour to any person in accepting the dole; it is a small compensation for the loss it replaces. To even hint or suggest that suicide is acceptable rather than accept the dole is the most dishonourable statement I ever heard. These are bad times for many and the nation should be proud that our Insurance Scheme is helping many get through circumstances over which they have no control. A true Englishman gives succour to the needy and the helpless when he has ought to give; a true Englishman will take the offering hand when he is down. That is how we are taught to play and how we should conduct our life. Therein lies true pride. It is a comfort to know it still exists in our country and there is daily witness to it.

Yours faithfully
Jack Elks.

## June 1927

Tilden Smith, Chairman of the Tilmanstone Colliery Company, gazed around the table. "Gentlemen, please allow me to say how pleased I am to meet you all, there are some proposals I wish to put to you."

Jack and the Tilmanstone Lodge Committee Jim Evans, Ernest Withers and Sam Cresswell sat on one side of the boardroom table. Facing them were Jim Davenport, the Colliery Manager, supported by his underground manager and Will Furness from the Deputies Union. They were all silent,

Tilden Smith pressed on. "I have been Chairman of the Tilmanstone Colliery Company these last eighteen months. During my life I have been a director of many companies, both in coalmining and out but I have never been part of a company with so much dislike between management and men. The atmosphere here is not one in which we can all prosper. I could ask for your views as to why it is so, no doubt there would be a multitude of answers. We could rake over old ground but that would get us no further forward. My proposal is rather like cutting the Gordian knot. With your agreement and understanding my intention is to create a Joint Management Committee. That committee will have power to oversee the management of the mine and to make recommendations directly to the board of directors. There is only one condition, the committee will have access to all, I repeat, all information relating to the operation of the Colliery, so members must sign a confidentiality agreement. There is a second condition which I trust will not give offence as I want this committee to represent employees, whether management or workers - all members must be colliery employees."

He looked at Jack. "Does that give you any problem, Mr. Elks?"

"Not at all Mr. Smith, I came because you invited me. Your proposal is an admirable one which I have no hesitation in endorsing. Is it your intention that the people present constitute the committee?"

"The committee will comprise five members, Mr. Davenport as chairman, one other management member, one appointment from the deputies and two from your association. The deputies and the association may vote, if they wish, but appointments must be for one year."

"Workmen members will lose pay by attending meetings. How will that be dealt with?"

Tilden Smith smiled. "Fairly, Mr. Elks, fairly I hope. That will be for the committee to decide." He tapped on the table and eased his chair back. "Mr. Davenport, there are notes in the folders on the table, may I suggest you discuss any matters arising from the delegates. Mr. Elks and I will retire."

Tilden Smith held out the glass. "May I call you Jack?"

Jack nodded and lit his pipe. "Would it not be better if you and I were there?"

There was a broad smile on Tilden Smith's face as he replied, "You mean hold their hands, Jack? No, if management and men are to join forces they must learn to give respect, listen to others, give and take - they'll not learn that if you or I nanny them."

"It's a brave attempt, Mr. Smith." Jack raised his glass, "Here's to success."

"Let me say this in confidence, Jack. We are losing sixpence on every ton of coal raised. My worry is that if we cannot get costs down and raise production this colliery will close. Within a few weeks those men or their appointees will also know that - how will they react?"

Jack paused for a moment. "It will be a great responsibility for them as well as a new experience -but I will bet you a bottle of whisky they'll rise to the occasion."

Tilden Smith laughed. "Fair enough, but I know I will lose. Treat men like men, it's the only way." He poured out another drink for them.

"Of course if this becomes commonplace I shall be out of a job," said Jack.

"I've always been grateful, Jack, for the fact that you got the men back to work when we opened. There'll always be a job for you in my organisation if the worst were to happen. Now I want to meet now and again to look at progress."

## August 1927

Lizzie put Arthur up to her shoulder and very gently patted his back to bring up any wind. She didn't want him to fret once he was in his cot. It was only three weeks since he was born and she felt very weak and tired. The low back pain troubled her but it generally eased during the day. Since the doctor had spoken to her those four years ago and forbidden her to have more children when May was born, first Irene Doris had come along and then Arthur. Lilian May was always May and Irene Doris was Dot. They had both watched her with great interest as she had fed and changed the baby. There was so much work to do, what with Len and Albert being at the pit and doing shift work. Thank goodness they had a proper bath in the bathroom, at least she was spared the ordeal of the tin bath in front of the kitchen range that had dogged the earlier years. After Arthur was born the doctor had told her that nature had run its course, she would have no more children. That should have come as a relief but somehow it didn't, she was far too conscious of the way time had passed. "Mummy is going to have a rest," she told May and Dot. "I want you to play quietly with your dolls but wake me up if anything happens. Be good now." She gave them a hug and off they went.

She had no idea how long she had been asleep when the insistent ringing of the doorbell woke her into reluctant consciousness. Then May and Dot were skipping into the room. "There's someone at the front door, Mummy!'"

"May, go and open the door and say I am just coming."

Stiff and unrefreshed she made her way to the door and looked out. A young man of about twenty stood there, cap in hand. He seemed vaguely familiar but, no, she couldn't place him.

"My husband's not in. Can I help you?"

She had got used to miners seeking Jack over the years. The young man fiddled with his cap.

"This is the home of Mr. and Mrs. Elks, isn't it? This is the address I was given."

"Yes, I'm Mrs. Elks."

"It's me Ma, Jack. Jack from Bloxwich!"

Lizzie stared, open-mouthed. Now she knew who it was, it was her Jack, as he was from all those years ago in Bloxwich, when he was a young man. Then the realisation dawned on her. It was 'Little Jack'! May and Dot clung to the hem of her dress. "Who is it, Mummy?" "Who is it?"

"Little Jack! How you've grown. May and Dot, this is your brother Jack. Say hello to him."

"I'm sorry I didn't come sooner, Ma. What with working

there never seemed to be the time but I've a few days holiday, so here I am."

"Come in, Jack, there is so much to tell you."

It was towards the end of summer that Bill Haseley, the ageing President of the Association, came to see Jack in his office. He stood upright but needed a stick to help keep his balance and his walk had slowed. When he was in the door, Jack asked him if he would like a drink but the old man declined, he would not break the habits of a lifetime. In his slow voice, Bill explained. "I have come to say it is in my mind to retire, Jack. No longer can I match the young men who surround me, nor have I done these few years past. The words come hard to me after all these years so I ask you to tell the Executive that I am gone to pasture."

"My goodness, Bill! Are you telling me you are resigning as President - there is no need of that, your wise counsel helps us all. Your honesty has been the rock upon which we have built our Association."

"It is the only way I know Jack but that way has been hard – so hard. Sometimes I have gone off to a quiet place to shed a tear at the injustice of it all - to see the children going hungry and watching the brightness die in the eyes of our young ones and there was nought I could do."

"Then stay, Bill, stay!"

"No, you have all done me great honour, more than a man can bear to part with but the time has come to give another the chair. We have taken a fearful drubbing these last few years, so much so I thought we would break and lose everything because we ask for a living wage to live in dignity. I ask that you work here and put your powers to the good of the men and their families. There was never greater need nor harder times. That is why a younger man must take my chair, someone who is young enough to fight hard for the future. The bible gives a man but three score years and ten and in these last years there is a need for peace and contentment. There are the valleys I have not seen these thirty years and I will walk in the Rhondda one last time and say a prayer in the chapel of my youth, the place I got married."

"Are you going back to Wales, Bill?"

"No, my roots are here now and my grandchildren and those to follow will regard it as their home. That is a parting that would be too hard to shoulder. No, a holiday only, as every man should have one holiday in his lifetime. Remember those years ago when I spoke of what we could achieve and we would build the Promised Land? Together we have achieved so much and what do I see? Only that there is more to do."

"We have made progress, Bill. There are fine new houses and playing fields. Our funds enable us to help our men in need. There are communities that bind together and much of it is your doing. Please reconsider."

Bill Haseley slowly shook his head. "My mind is set, not in anger or frustration mark you but in the understanding that I have done all I can and now I want to sit beside the green fields and watch the young play. There is a vigour in youth that I cannot match but I can enjoy and so will be content. Do you remember that meeting at Snowdown when Clarence Pike promised so much I near fell over in astonishment?"

"Aye, I remember," said Jack, "he surprised us all."

"There are some things a man leaves unsaid but my memory tells me there was no surprise on your face. Remember the way I speak and judge what a man says. We all have our way of speaking and I can recognise one man's words spoke by another. Those were your words he used that day, not his own, he had not the wit nor God's gift of humanity to speak them on his own."

Jack chuckled. "Bill, Bill - I assure you I put no pressure on him!"

"Do not consider what I have said a complaint for that was not my direction." Bill smiled at last. "That day was a turning point for our men and what I have said is for no other. In the years to come you will need all your skill to shield our people, all your cleverness. Do not leave them undefended. Take the thanks of a man unschooled in the ways of the world, write my letter for me because my hand shakes, then let me go. If I can take your promise with me that you will do all for our men then I will go untroubled."

"I promise."

"When I have gone, let the bands lead and play a fine tune, a fine Welsh tune. Before then, when you pass me sitting by the fields let you wave to me."

He rose and put out his hand and Jack took it in both of his and squeezed hard.

"Yes, Mr. President."

## 11th November 1928

"What the bloody hell is going on here!" The deputy's bullseye lamp swung along the heading. "I turn my back for two bloody minutes and you knock off! - Get on back to work you bastards."

The hewers and trammers stood, heads bowed, totally silent. As the deputy continued shouting one man looked at him and put his finger to his mouth and went 'Sh-ush'. Twenty seconds later the man with the watch in his hand called out, "Time lads!"

The deputy rounded on him and a finger jabbed out. "Was it you who stopped the shift, Fisher?"

Fisher closed the case of his fob watch and put it in his pocket. "It was me that called out 'it's eleven', if that's what you mean." Several colliers closed around him.

"Don't you have any respect?" one of them asked the deputy.

"'Twas the remembrance," said another.

The bullseye lamp swung around the group. "I've got all your names! You're in the book - there'll be no standing around idle on my shift!"

Fisher looked at him. "Look, you miserable piece of shit, I lost two brothers in the war and when it's the eleventh hour of the eleventh day of November I shall stand still for two minutes and remember - do what you like."

"Get out of the pit, Fisher!"

The call went down the line. "Fisher's being sent out". The call went on. "Rag up, lads, rag up!

Within an hour the pit was at a standstill.


Later in the afternoon Jack entered the Colliery Manager's Office, the first of many visits to Betteshanger that would occur over the years ahead.

"Good afternoon Mr. Kyle, I hope we can get the men back to work quickly."

Kyle scowled, "I'll not take Fisher back, he has no respect for authority!"

Jack was in no mood for diplomacy. "Did you order that the armistice remembrance would be ignored or not allowed?"

"I did not but that wasn't why Fisher was dismissed."

Jack stood his ground. "If Deputy Hay had acted as he did today, anywhere in the country, he'd have been called more than a 'piece of shit'! He'd more than likely been given a severe beating."

"If Fisher apologises he can walk back tomorrow."

"Hell will freeze over first. I can think of nothing more likely to upset the men than this - there's not one that didn't lose a friend or relative in that damn war."

"Fisher called the men out."

"Even your deputy hasn't said that. It's your deputy who should apologise for failing to observe the remembrance."

"Fisher must apologise."

"I'm sorry, Mr. Kyle but in this matter I'm prepared to go over your head to the Directors. I don't think they will take it well, especially as two of them lost sons. If that fails I shall go to every newspaper and have it raised in Parliament. Your attitude is disgraceful! If Hay apologises to the men, Fisher will probably say he's sorry for swearing."

"I'll speak to Hay."

The men returned on the later shift after a letter of apology from Deputy Hay was posted.

## 26th November 1928

Over three hundred angry men waited outside the colliery gates at Snowdown. The four policemen at the gate glanced nervously about, checking that their truncheons and rolled capes were to hand. There was no noise from the men but the silence was more menacing than shouts and jeers. The duty sergeant had already telephoned for reinforcements but he knew the best that could happen was the arrival of another ten men within half an hour. In ten minutes or so the first shift would be coming up to the bank. On the gates were the notices at the centre of the storm. 'Wages will be reduced to the district level with effect from the 16th November 1928. The previous allowance for deep pit working is withdrawn. The revised price list is given below.'

All work had stopped immediately as the men walked out but in an attempt to break the strike the pit had been reopened for the first Monday shift of the 26th November and 96 men had reported for work even though the union had voted for the stoppage.

There was a sudden shuffling amongst the crowd as the pithead wheels turned. The first workers were coming up. Slowly a small group of grimed men assembled at the pithead. The group outside the gates remained quiet.

The police sergeant strode forward to the gate. "I'm taking these workers to the railway station – anyone who interferes will be arrested - don't forget I know each and everyone of you!"

As he marched back he was relieved to see the police van arrive and ten constables pushed through to his side. He motioned them away.

"Back there with the others. Form those men up, constables either side - come up to the gate when you're ready."

As the small column moved forward the crowd split across the road leaving a tight gap and the slow monotonous chant of

'Scabs - Scabs – Scabs' started.

As the two crowds mingled a man shouted. "Thou'll get thy come-uppence when we're back - bloody blacklegs."

A fist came through the crowd and a man went down, then as the crowd surged forward a vast brawl developed. At the head of the column the police sergeant was shouting.

"Run to the station - hold them off lads!" Frantically he laid about with his truncheon and slowly men disengaged and ran toward the station and the safety of the train, leaving men lying on the ground. The shouts of 'Scabs - Scabs – Scabs' followed them down the road.

A week later Jack addressed a meeting of the men, sullen angry men. Despite all their picketing a trickle of men had reported for work every day and they had been unable to prevent this as there were over seventy police on duty at all times. Jack was grateful that no one had been arrested nor further injuries caused, he raised his hands for quiet.

"This stoppage was caused by the management, there is no doubt in my mind on that. Also we have the names of all those who have blacklegged and they'll never be allowed in our union, nor to benefit from it. Those that were members are to be expelled and will lose all benefits - we will pursue them through the Federation wherever they go, should they leave here.

I know that many of you came to Kent and were told of the guaranteed wage and at an arbitrary stroke that guarantee is reduced by one shilling and three pence per day! You will be feeling angry and betrayed - despite our negotiations the owners will not retract. They do not dispute this hot pit deserves a premium - they say you must go down to the district level until times are better – we have that in writing.

Over the years I have asked for your support and you have given it willingly – and suffered for it – aye, and bled for it! You and your families have gone hungry but I will not ask you to do that today. There is a promise that we may negotiate for the premium when times improve.  I promise you I will hold them to that.  Today I ask for your support to return to work.  Soon it will be Christmas and I want no more empty bellies at that time."  He paused as a man shouted a challenge.  "Yes, we all want justice Jimmy Dean.  We can feel noble in a fight but it will not put bread on the table for the kids.  We may win if we fight this battle out to the end but the owners will make us suffer for it.  To retreat is not defeat - we are not defeated, just waiting for a better ground on which to fight."

Next day, after the  ballot, the men returned to work.

## July 1929

The magistrate glared over his glasses at the young man in the dock and the lad stood head down, nervously turning his cap in his hands while the clerk finished reading out the charge.

".  .  .  .  . in that he did take without consent one and half pounds of apples the property of Mr. James Consett with intent to deprive him of their use and gain.  How do you plead?"

From his seat Jack nodded at the lad and he murmured.

"Not guilty."

After Consett had given evidence Jack rose to question him.  "Your Honour, if you please I have some questions for Mr. Consett."

The magistrate gave Jack a look of great distaste.  "If you must, Mr. Elks, but this seems a very clear cut case to me."

Jack dipped his head in respectful acknowledgement.  "Thank you, your Honour," he turned to the witness box, "Mr. Consett, you say that one and half pounds of apples were taken without your consent, is that correct?"

"They were - there were six apples."

"Were these apples ripe?  Is that why they were not shown in evidence."

"Yes, the police sergeant has said they rotted and could not be kept."

"The orchard where these apples grew - how big is it?"

"It is a large orchard with about forty trees."

"Is it overgrown?"

"It's untidy, if that is your meaning.

"What I am getting at, Mr Consett, is whether or not it looks in use, cared for and so on?"

"I know it is in use."

"Is it easy to enter, has it a fence?"

"It has but it is easy to enter."

"Is it not fair to say that most of the local lads 'scrump' apples there? As village lads are prone to do in my experience."

"They do, that is why a stop must be put to it."

"Have you seen the accused, George Kinley, take apples on a previous occasion?"

"No, I have not."

"Mr. Elks," the magistrate intervened, "Kinley was seen taking apples and has been identified. I see no point in these questions."

"I'm sorry, your Honour. I am simply trying to establish that Mr. Consett's orchard, by virtue of its position and appearance, the ease of access and the volume of fruit is occasionally used by young lads of the village, none of whom have been charged, whereas this young man has been."

"Your point is taken, Mr. Elks but I think that is enough."

"I call George Kinley to the stand, your Honour." George was duly sworn in.

"Look up George and answer to the bench. Your name is George Kinley and you live at 3, Church Lane, Eythorne."

"Yes, sir."

"What is your employment?"

"I am a haulage boy at Tilmanstone, sir."

"Did you take the apples?"

"Yes, sir. I had seen others take them and thought the orchard was gone to waste."

"Were there apples on the ground?"

"Thousands, sir."

"When Mr. Consett approached you, did you run away?"

"No, Sir."

"Why was that?"

"I didn't think I had done aught wrong, sir."

"What happened then?"

"Mr. Consett called me a thief and fetched the police sergeant."

"Did you apologise and offer to return the apples?"

"Yes, sir, but Mr. Consett said he would make an example of me - that I was a dirty collier and must be taught a lesson."

When he had returned to the box, Jack made a plea.

"Your Honour. This boy is of good behaviour and is thought well of at work. He has no previous record and this is a first offence. Whilst he had admitted taking the apples, which must be of very small value, he did apologise and has promised that the offence will not be repeated."

The Magistrate turned to George.

"Mr. Elks calls you a boy. Well, you are not, you are turned seventeen. There is considerable evidence that since the miners came to this area, general behaviour has deteriorated and in particular bad behaviour has increased. I will not allow our country villages to be despoiled and criminal behaviour to escalate. I find you guilty as charged and your sentence will be both a deterrent to yourself and others of your kind. You are sentenced to 14 days hard labour."

Armed with a transcript of the proceedings and provoked by a deep sense of anger and injustice Jack took the matter directly to the Home Secretary. The sentence was reduced to 3 days, being the time already served.

## 1st August 1929

The band played, the sun shone and hundreds of men, women and children enjoyed themselves at the Tilmanstone Colliery fete in the grounds of Elvington Court. Laughter echoed around the stalls as balls flew at coconuts and hooplas spun through the air. The ice cream carts did a roaring trade. When the sports were over and prizes had been presented the crowd stayed gathered around the rostrum. Jack waved his arms for quiet.

"Ladies and gentlemen, I'm sure you will all agree that Mr. Tilden Smith has given you a splendid fete and sports day. Not only that but he ordained that we have a sunny day for our pleasure! He will not mind me saying that since he took over as Chairman he has worked hard to make Tilmanstone a better place, to create a family atmosphere. Under his guidance productivity has risen and as a mark of his appreciation he has both moved and agreed that every working man shall have a general wage increase." Jack had to halt as wild cheers echoed all around the grounds. "Yes, costs have been reduced and output per man has increased; so effective from tomorrow, wages for underground men will go up by one shilling and three pence per day and one shilling a day for surface workers. I call on, no, I humbly ask Mr. Tilden Smith to say a few words."

To even louder cheers, Tilden Smith rose.

"Together, you and I, we have transformed this place. Since we set up the Joint Management Committee there has been a perceptible change to the whole atmosphere at our colliery. Men actually smile and wish me good day! There was a time when I could not go there, the feeling of distrust, the anger, the lack of enthusiasm and uncoordinated effort were an affront to us all. But that has been transformed to my very great pleasure and pride, in only a few years. There is a fine future ahead of us. Let me say, we are not on opposite sides - we are on the same side in this venture. You are not my employees, you are my associates. We must work together for harmony and prosperity. Soon we will open the ropeway to take our coal to Dover. Think of that, within a few hours of the coal being dug out it will be entering a ship in Dover Harbour. We have in our coalfield three important ingredients, coal, chalk and clay. I am looking at the ways in which we can exploit this to create a cement manufacturing industry. Then there is gas. The new gas manufacturing process will allow us to provide all the gas that East Kent can consume. When we combine all these manufacturers with a new electricity generating plant we will attract industries from all over the country. That is my vision of the future. Together we will make it happen - by our example we will lead to a new era of expansion to ensure our future is bright and prosperous. Not just for ourselves but for the many out there who will progress from our vision and reap the benefits of joint enterprise, co-operation and harmony."

It was a great loss to the men of Tilmanstone when within four months of the fete, Tilden Smith died at the age of 64. The most harmonious relationship in the Kent coalfield, almost without precedent in the country, came to an end but his legacy in the form of the Joint Management Committee lived on for many years.

## December 1929

Arthur Heron, Chislet Colliery Manager, was waiting when Jack arrived in response to an evening telephone call from the Lodge Chairman.

"I was offered a bet you'd be here in less than an hour, not that I was daft enough to take it. Come into my office."

Jack took off his hat and coat, shaking off the raindrops and scowled at his shoes, dirty from walking through the yard.

"I've only a brief outline, Mr. Heron, perhaps you can fill in the details."

"Have a seat Mr. Elks. At mid-day a collier caller Rogers drew the wages for the 108's men and since then he can't be found and his lodgings are empty."

"How much did he make off with?"

"Nearly two hundred pounds - that's a fortnight's wages.

Very unpleasant this being Christmas week."

Jack checked his watch. "He's been missing over six hours then. Have you informed the police?"

"Yes, they'll be here tomorrow but the local constable is making enquiries in the village. I believe that Rogers was seen heading for the railway station but as yet there is no proof."

"What did you intend to do about this, Mr. Heron?"

"Well, we will give every assistance to the police but other than that I do not think there is anything else. After all, it is your members the money has been stolen from. They must press the charges."

Jack paused to collect his thoughts, a troubled look on his face. "Ben Gallagher, our local chairman, as you know, tells me that Rogers does not normally collect the gang's wages, the gang leader, Ernie Hibbert or his mate Joe Mason do that. If that is the case why was Rogers given the men's money?"

"He has been a member of that gang for nearly a year. The pay clerk thought it was quite proper - that is my opinion also."

"Did Rogers provide any authorisation or did Sturton the Chargeman speak beforehand to the clerk to say it was correct?"

"No, but I repeat, Rogers was a member of that gang so there can be no liability on our behalf."

"Mr. Heron, a lot of men have no wage for Christmas. It would be bad enough at any time but at this time of the year it will come hard! As I see it, it is not the men who have been cheated but the colliery that has been defrauded. I suggest you pay the men and press charges yourself against Rogers. This system you use to pay the gangs is a cause of endless and needless friction and is always open to abuse."

Heron was not moved. "It is the time honoured way and I cannot see how we are to blame."

"You leave me no option, Mr. Heron. I will instruct the men not to make a charge and will issue a summons on their behalf against the colliery for failing to pay their wage, an offence under the Truck Act. If you will not protect them and introduce a fairer system then we must go to the law. I will make the men a loan from union funds until such time as we recover their money. However if you agree to pay the men then I will ensure that they support you in saying that Rogers acted without their permission, so he can be charged with theft."

"I will not, Mr. Elks, we have acted perfectly properly."

"Then I suggest you inform your Directors, Mr. Heron, as it is they who will get the summonses. They, not you, are responsible in law. Good-day to you!"

Three days later the men were paid and the pay system was improved to prevent fraud.

## The Early 1930's

Jack was re-elected to the Executive of the Miners Federation in 1930. The election rules had been modified to ensure that two members were elected to represent the smaller coal-mining districts. Spurred on by conference, the Executive lobbied the newly-formed Labour Government to improve the lot of members and eventually won the seven and half hour day and an amendment to the Unemployment Insurance Act, by which the onus of proving that an applicant was 'genuinely seeking work' no longer fell on the applicant. However as the recession deepened this was often ignored by the civil servants administering the scheme. As the slump continued wages and conditions worsened, with nearly three million men out of work by 1933.

## July 1930

Eddie Lawther, the KMWA President, gazed around the executive. "Well gentlemen, it's been a long session and I'm ready for a drink. Is there any more business before I declare the meeting closed?"

Jack was just finishing the minute notes and he looked up,

catching Eddie's eye.

"Just one small matter, Mr. President - I won't be a minute." He finished off the note.

"Mr. President, I want to ask for a few minutes on a personal matter." Tobacco smoke hung heavy in the small room.

"Speak up, Jack - its only our drinking time!"

Jack was looking forward to that as much as they, as it was now nine in the evening and he had been working continuously since eight o'clock that morning.

"I would like to ask for a committee review of my salary. This is not a demand, just a request. You may not all recall but when I was appointed ten years ago my salary was set at £300 per annum. Then, with all the cutbacks and problems in the early 20's it was cut to £4.1Os per week. That is not a complaint - we had lost a lot of members. Then it was raised to £5 per week in 1927. Membership is improving so I felt I should ask for a review - not a raise necessarily, but a review."

Eddie invited comments. "Would any member wish to speak?"

Wilf Twigger raised his hand. "Mr. President, I feel we are remiss in this - a matter we have overlooked. As Jack has suggested there should at the very least be a periodic review. Jack saves us more than his salary in legal fees alone and he serves us with great devotion, seven days a week."

Bill Gallagher spoke up. "I agree with Wilf. I propose a review every two years and a £1 a week rise with immediate effect. I apologise to Jack for not thinking about it before - to the best of my knowledge he must be the lowest paid Agent in the industry."

"Do I have a proposer and seconder? - I do." Eddie raised his hand. "Those for? - All - passed unanimously." And his hand slapped the table. "Mr. Secretary - put that in the minutes!"

Two minutes later they were off to the pub, to the really serious business of the day.

## March 1931

1926 had seen the introduction of legislation to impose an eight hour day on the miners. The time to get from the bank to the coalface at the start of a shift was not included. This was to last for 5 years and was due for automatic repeal on 8 July 1931. The 1929 Labour Government, due to its minority position, had been unable to fulfil a pledge for an early repeal of the Eight Hour Act. In 1930 a compromise seven and a half hour day had been enacted but subject to a 90 hour fortnight - called the 'spread-over'. This was subject to Federation approval which they had been persuaded to give in the light of other promises, which in the event, came to nothing. In districts where the spread-over was enforced the miners still worked the eight hour day and in other districts wages were reduced.

The Federation met at a special meeting on the 19th March 1931 and voted to cancel the 'spread-over'. The debate then continued on the topic of wages. Jack was called to the stand.

"Fellow delegates, since 1926, in our industry there have been longer working hours, lower wages, higher accident rates and higher output. If you will think hard now, you will be able to answer this question. Which three of those mentioned have affected our men and which one has not? However there is an issue which is at least as iniquitous in its effect on our members as longer hours, lower wages and higher accident rates. It is the total unfairness of the Minimum Wage Act. In the 19 years, since 1912, when this was introduced, our members still get the same minimum now as then. The minimum wage is still judged by unfair rules that make no allowance between the cost of living then and the higher levels prevailing today. Yes, there is a district arrangement for annual review but nowhere does it operate. There is no record that any district has gained an increase in the minimum. What is the point of an annual meeting that refuses any argument for improvement? Time and again I have been told that our men get paid for doing nothing! That if we produce no coal or insufficient coal then the payment is a gift - no matter the hard work involved. This wrong can only be righted by the replacement or review of the existing Act, to consider the specific circumstances whereby improvements made are clear and just in application. Our members lose an average of one shift a week by being turned away and for which there is no pay or redress. With this in mind it is my contention that every contracted man should have not only a daily minimum wage but also one that applies by the week.

I propose that our Executive be instructed to prepare the basis for a new Minimum Wage Bill and be charged to approach the Government with this in all urgency."

Following a lengthy debate this proposal was endorsed and the Miners Federation of Great Britain entered into prolonged discussion with the Government.

## 18th May 1931

Notice of wage reductions had been posted at Tilmanstone two days previous. The Lodge committee had called a meeting of all the men. Jim Evans, as Chairman of the Lodge, rose to loud catcalls and jeers to call the meeting to order. One man at the back was shouting 'traitor' at the top of his voice, another man took exception and a brawl started. Several other men tried to separate them. Jim called in vain for order. Jack sat back quietly on the stand. Slowly the crowd quietened and Jim tried again.

"A proposal had been made to withdraw contracts." He was drowned out by cheers before he could continue. "I have to tell you - I have to tell you that I disagree."

Another brawl broke out and it was several minutes before order was restored. Jim tried again. "If there is more disorder I shall declare this meeting over and those who wish to work can go back and the rest can stay out!"

Against that threat the meeting settled down.

"Now, I call Ron Lye to speak for the proposal."

Quickly, Lye was up and his finger wagging in self-righteous indignation. "We've earned our pay, raised production every year, why should we accept a reduction to make the owners rich?" He sat down to loud cheers but Jim could tell, looking out over the men, that many disagreed. Ron Lye suddenly jumped to his feet and pointed an accusing finger at Jim.

"You're on their management committee - how could you agree to this? You're on their side - getting a backhander I've no doubt!"

Jim reddened at the accusation and was about to answer when Jack lent forward and tapped him on the back. "Let me speak, Jim, this is getting personal!"

"I call on Jack Elks."

Gratefully Jim sat down as Jack rose. He waited for quiet.

"You have the right to strike if you wish, a two thirds majority will bind you - no doubt from the feelings here tonight you are feeling aggrieved - no one wants to accept a wage cut. Before you decide, let me tell you a few truths which Jim Evans cannot because on your behalf he acts under a confidentiality agreement. However I do not. Some here are saying you're to take an unfair pay cut. Yes, that is true, but at the same time the reduction only brings you back to the levels obtaining at the other Kent pits."

He stopped as men started shouting so he waited until the interruptions stopped.

"No, that's not nonsense. If anyone here knows that, it's me. At the moment the country is under severe economic strain and there are three million men out of work. Coal prices have fallen and there is a real possibility this colliery may close because it is losing money – a lot of money. Despite that you work in a place that must be the most harmonious pit in England. Don't throw it away. I am not advising you to strike or not to strike but just remember, two of your members serve on the management committee - you voted for them. Give them the chance to look after your best interests. Times will get better!"

An hour later the meeting voted to continue working.

## June 1931

Ebby Edwards, Vice President of the Miners Federation, made the following report to the June Annual Conference.

*"The industrial recession has for many years enveloped our chief industries and now threatens the entire economic and financial systems of the world. All wages are menaced and we live in an atmosphere of wage cuts. The contradictions of capitalism ever seek to readjust themselves on the bodies and souls of those least able to defend themselves - on those with no other means but the power to labour. For several months we have negotiated with both government and owners to reduce the working day and improve the minimum wage but to little avail. We have gained a reduction of one half hour on the day but that, when judged in comparison with our demand for a seven hour day and a new legal minimum wage, there can be no jubilation. But this I say, when contrasted with the alternative of a national stoppage with all its risks and uncertainties to our men and the trade then we can declare a certain amount of common-sense satisfaction."*

The battle had been lost yet again as the seven and a half hour day would operate for an indefinite period whereas existing wages, including the old minimum wage, were only guaranteed for a further twelve months.

## July 1931

At the Annual Conference of the Miners Federation, Jack tabled a resolution for the formation of a single mineworkers union and addressed the Conference to open the debate.

"Fellow delegates, there will be no apology from me for

raising this issue again - though I have been asked by several of you to withdraw this resolution. Join with me in looking into the future to another day so I can share a vision with you. Not a daydream but a better place to be for all our sakes - our industry thriving under nationalisation and organised for the benefit of the many instead of the few. We have been so close to this vision it almost seemed within our grasp and then it slipped away. But I do not doubt for a moment that the chance will come again if we work toward that end. Why did it slip away? Divided interests, petty-mindedness, self interest and lack of courage on our part all played into the hands of politicians and owners. That is why we must create a single union from our multitude of parts. Could the owners enforce district agreements on us if we presented one single solid face to the world? No, we have fought and lost our battle for the national negotiation of wages, the taste is still bitter in our mouths. Do not doubt that the owners view our Federation as being weak. They steadfastly refuse to discuss wages with us in the full belief that we can do nought about it. I am told we have strong district unions - let me tell you, that strength is an illusion. One area is set against another, a classic case of divide and rule.

The presentation of one face to the world must be to our betterment and advantage. Real strength lies in unity both in our dealings with the owners and the government. There are those who say that only local men can deal with local issues, a truth that cannot be denied. But are wages local issues? Are safety and welfare local issues? Are the reductions in National Insurance benefits local issues? Is the Means Test a local issue? Are the minimum wage, the cost of living and the Mines Act local issues?

Some tell me that all will be well now we have a Labour Government but MacDonald (the Prime Minister) tells us they cannot fulfil their pledges to us. We fight, argue, negotiate and plead for a better wage but we meet with a national refusal on all sides. When we ask the government why the dock-workers earn twice as much as our men they say it arises from their negotiating strength! Wages are low and cannot be increased and we are told there can be no nationalisation. That is the measure of our negotiating strength.

By one act - the creation of a single union - we bind together and grow stronger. Some of you tell me that in 1926 we bound together and broke. Well, let me say, we did not break. There is nothing to lose by binding stronger. Let it be seen that we are one and work as one for a well-regulated single industry. Some say they are concerned that a single union will act so as to make the possibility of a national stoppage more likely. Nothing could be further from my mind or intent. The stoppage itself is evidence of defeat; it is the ultimate weapon that can bring ruin as well as reward. The strength, unity and purpose of a single union will help prevent the stoppage not make it more likely.

A single straw is easily broken but put a bunch together and you create a bond of great strength and resilience. I ask you to put aside the narrow view, approve this resolution. Show the world that we are one body and will not be split asunder. Let our motto be - ONE UNION AND ONE INDUSTRY!"

At the end of the debate the resolution was approved but passed back to the executive to investigate further and to report back to Conference at a later date with detailed proposals. By the end of August the Labour Government had fallen and the Federation had once more to fall back on its own resources and power of persuasion to make progress.

## December 1932

On the 15th of this month, Ebby Edwards the Federation Secretary took a small deputation to meet the Mine Owners Association. Sir Evan Williams was President of the owners association. Jack was one of the Federation representatives. Sir Evan opened the meeting.

"Gentlemen, I am pleased that we meet today to discuss

matters of mutual interest. From the owners point of view those interests concern recruitment, especially of boys, and welfare arrangements as they concern the industry. The welfare levy of one penny a ton is an excessive burden for the industry to bear."

Ebby Edwards responded. "As we are talking on an industry basis we believe there are more important matters to discuss. Particularly we wish to table safety, unemployment, exports, evasions of the Mines Act, national machinery to prevent labour disputes, the employment of boys on night shifts, the wages situation from July next year when the existing agreement expires. Also there is the matter of increasing the production of petrol and oil from coal."

"On behalf of the owners," said Sir Evan, "we welcome your comments on petrol and oil because we believe that it is the most important issue facing our industry."

Ebby felt hope rise and then it was subdued as Sir Evan continued.

"Yes, we urge you to join us in common cause in an approach to the government to tax the imports of oil which damage and threaten our industry. However in the matter of wages after July you must know that the existing agreement is a gentleman's one only and it is quite outside our province to discuss this nationally."

"Sir Evan," Jack intervened, "are you saying to us that a tariff on oil imports, a national matter, can be discussed whilst wages which are of national interest to our members cannot be discussed? Are you to be the sole arbiter of what national interest is to be discussed and only if you approve of a matter will it be allowed on the table?"

Sir Evan responded. "What I am saying, Mr. Elks, is this. The decline in our industry by the reduced consumption of coal, which in our view is caused by high imports of oil, must be arrested by the introduction of an oil tariff. That is the only solution we can foresee and it is in your interests to support us in this."

"If we join you," Jack replied, "then in all fairness we cannot exclude any matter of national interest. That is the issue. If we are to accept responsibility in a matter of national political purposes then you are saying we are partners in the control of this industry. That is clearly untrue because you only wish to discuss matters of which you approve. That is not a partnership."

Evan Williams was unmoved. "The daily wage is agreed by district and the minimum wage by statute. We will not discuss these as they are outside our mandate."

Ebby rejoined, "Are you not prepared to discuss the matter of a national wages machinery without touching on the actual rates? We do not want to put the cart before the horse whatever the outcome."

Evan Williams was stony but polite in response. "Any discussion of national wages in any form is quite unwarranted nor is it acceptable."

"Sir Evan," Jack looked directly at him, "we regard long working hours as a major cause of poor safety and high accident rates. Do you regard discussion on the hours worked to be on the agenda?"

"No!" replied Sir Evan. "The seven and a half hour day, conceded against our best judgement and wishes, is on the statute book. What is the point of discussion? We cannot negotiate for a shorter day if that is your intent."

So the meeting went on and the deputation returned to Conference with nothing gained. They had only one weapon left and that was to get the district unions to agree to give the Federation Executive Committee the power to call on districts to terminate wage agreements simultaneously. At the present time the periods over-lapped. On the 1st March 1933, the delegates' conference voted this power to the Federation. Notwithstanding it would be years before effective action could be taken. By the middle of 1934 the owners had persuaded the government to legislate to halve the Welfare Levy despite the Federation protests.

## December 1932

The Master of Ceremonies rapped his gavel. "Lay-dees and Gentlemen – pray silence for that lady with the golden voice - that melter of the hardest heart, a nightingale of Terpsichorean virtuosity - with you once more - Miss Florrie - FORD!"

There were loud hurrahs and clapping all around the hall. Lizzie put her hands together with the best of them.

Times had got slightly better as 1932 had progressed and Jack had decided to have an evening off to take Lizzie to the Music Hall, the 'Hippodrome' in Snargate Street, in Dover. And not just any old seat but the best seats in the lower circle nearest the stage, with a car from the front door as well. Lizzie was absorbed in the show. Jack was thinking. Perhaps the worst of the recession was over now, so maybe the Federation could be buttressed and the lost ground recovered. He thought back to those heady times of ten years ago, the power-broking and the excitement.

Suddenly he was conscious that Lizzie was shaking his arm. "Jack! Jack! She's going to sing my favourite song. I'm so pleased." She leant forward.

*"When first I saw the lovelight in your eyes,*
*I thought the world had nought but joy for me.*
*And even though we've drifted far apart,*
*I never dream but what I dream of thee."*

Then all the audience joined in the chorus and Lizzie sang along, the pleasure showing on her face.

*"I love you as I've never loved before,*
*Since first I saw you on the village green.*
*Come to me in my dreams of long ago,*

*I love you as I loved you – when you were sweet,*
*When you were sweet – sixteen. "*

As she sang Lizzie squeezed Jack's hand, a tiny tear started in
her eye. "This is a lovely evening - my Dad used to sing that, he
had a fine voice, but......" She was about to say he had gone but
the words would not come. All she had was the blue airmail letter
from her mother saying he had passed on. Then the show was all
over and the curtains closed. Jack helped Lizzie into her coat.

"There's only a few days to Christmas, Jack. I shall be taking
May, Dot and Arthur to see Mr. Benton with the Christmas
parcel."

Jack nodded. "That's good." Benton had been badly injured
in an accident at Tilmanstone three years before and Jack was still
fighting to get compensation on his behalf. "Poor man will never
walk again!"

"It's good for the children to go, Jack. Helps them to
understand the true meaning of Christmas - there's always
someone worse off than yourself."

As they left the Hippodrome, Lizzie was still humming the
refrain. "I love you as I've never loved before . . . . .." Jack was
thinking about the new price list for Snowdown.

## January 1933

Jack made the following report to the Kent Mineworkers
Association Executive Committee:

"Mr. President, the last two months have been particularly
trying as you are well aware and Christmas and New Year
goodwill has been somewhat lacking. With regard to Snowdown,
the thirty men, all members, who were dismissed on the 1st of
January, have not been re-instated. Non-union men working on
the same shifts were retained in clear breach of our agreements
and this violates the seniority rule. The original difficulty arose

due to the arbitrary decision by management to alter the price list when the double conveyor belts were introduced. The ballot was in favour of a strike and two weeks notice was given on the 16th January. I am still in discussion and we are prepared to accept a new price list, which meets our requirements, but they have refused to re-instate all our members. This is a clear indication of victimisation and I ask for your support to my stance that we will not withdraw notices until we are satisfied. If the seniority rule was applied fairly then the issue would be down to two men only. The union pit inspection takes place next week and I propose that I undertake this with the Lodge Secretary. It is my intention to add poor safety and union membership to my discussion with the management so we may address all issues of contention with the notices in. I am confident we will win now that the management has agreed to a fair price list which was their main area of concern.

Last week the entire evening shift at Tilmanstone was laid off and 350 men are idle. The owners tell me that this is due to their failure to renew the contract with the London Power Stations but they are hopeful this will be resolved within four weeks. In an attempt to be fair the losing shift was chosen by drawing numbers. There is nothing to be gained by balloting for strike action, as the present contracts will not sustain even one shift properly. I am in touch with the T.U.C. to see what pressure we can exert on the Power Stations. My main and immediate concern is to meet with the lodge and individuals to ensure that those laid off get the full and correct insurance benefits.

With regard to Chislet I have pleasure in telling you that Sharp, who was dismissed for alleged union activity down the pit, has been re-instated and I have been assured that our officials will in future be called immediately in the event of a disciplinary matter arising. Other matters there concern a demand from the Blean Guardians for the repayment of relief granted in 1926! Some fifteen families are affected and I will be meeting with the Guardians in two weeks time.

At Betteshanger, last week, 150 men lost a day's pay because of a pump failure and I am negotiating for compensation. This is further complicated by the ongoing argument over the introduction of the yardage payment system in place of the previous measurement by weight. Some latitude is needed here because, from my inspection, the men can gain more than they lose and I wish to address any loss via the day rate adjustment. However old habits die hard and I am caught in the middle. May I ask that the Executive review this scheme and issue a statement at a meeting of the men?

On a more personal note I am increasingly being asked by the lodges to do the pit inspection on my own because they do not wish to lose a day's pay. This increases my time down the pit and furthermore I may miss matters of importance already known to our members. It will be helpful if the Lodge responsibilities can be clarified and some directions given.

On a more general note I am in discussion with Dorman Long regarding home deliveries of coal allowances for the men. Up till now this was done by Deal Council but was recently stopped and the present contractor is failing to deliver to everyone. Subject to your approval I will accept nomination for a further three years to the Boards of the Dover Unemployment Exchange and the Education Committee. This takes about one day of my time each month.

Lastly, there have been nine reported incidents of stolen tools in the pits in the last month. Several members have asked me if we can print and issue notices for distribution to all the men and will, if allegations of stealing are proven against members, that they will be dismissed from the association."

## February 1933

The two men might have been tramps, down at heel and with threadbare patched clothes but they each wore caps and had mufflers tied around their necks. Small battered cases, tied with string, lay on the pavement beside them as they sat back on the bench.  It was nearly midnight and they could hear the lap of water on the Embankment wall as the Thames ebbed.  To their left were the Houses of Parliament.  The patrolling policeman had seen them a way off and now moved with slow deliberate steps in their direction.  He had no intention of allowing another Guy Fawkes incident on his beat.

"Bit late to see the sights, lads.  I think you'd better be on your way.  You should be wearing coats on a frosty night like this!"

Ned Bates was the spokesman.  "Just resting our feet for a few minutes, constable."

The accents alerted him.  "You're not from these parts?"

"We're from Yorkshire."

"Where are you staying?"

"We're not staying, just passing through - on our way to Dover."

The constable's suspicions were fully roused.  "Leaving the country are you?"  He felt in his pocket for his briefing sheet.

"No, we're colliers, going for work."

"Well you won't get work sitting idle, so be on your way."

"We only want a short rest, we've walked all the way from Yorkshire!"

The constable fished two pence from his pocket.  "You can get a cup of tea down there -don't be here when I return!"

Three days later Jack walked up to his office door at nine, ready to start the morning's work.  Two worn out men with battered cases sat on the pavement, backs against the wall.  He had known from forty yards away they were pitmen.

"Good morning, lads.  Can I help you?"

Ned Bates spoke up.  "We've come down from Yorkshire.  The Agent gave us this address and said to ask for Jack Elks.  I'm Ned Bates and this is Joe Bide."

"You'd better come in. I'm Jack."

They followed him in the door. "How'd you get here?"

"We walked, took us twenty days. Thought we'd never make it."

"What happened? No, don't tell me, I can guess. When did you last have a square meal? Got any money?"

"We've managed, Mr. Elks."

"Jack. Jack's my name." He felt in his pocket and handed them half a crown. "Go down the High Street, get a good breakfast inside you - leave your bags here. Use the wash and brush up. I'll make a telephone call."

When they had gone he picked up a telephone and asked the telephonist for a number.

"That you, Bert? Good, Jack here. I'm sending two men up on the bus. They need work and digs. Give them a loan to get started, their boots are off their feet – walked all the bloody way from Yorkshire - not that trouble again - see you tomorrow."


## April 1933

Spring had come early and in the Kent countryside the annual blossom had started. Down through the Dover High Street strode Edward Hope, soldier in His Majesty's Army. He had prepared himself carefully for today and his tunic was pressed, his boots shone and belt brasses gleamed. He had taken almost as much care as if it were a general's inspection. It was not that he wanted to impress so much as to please. This was a most important day. In his letter of introduction he had not stated his intention but simply asked for an interview. There had been no reply but he put that down to pressures of work by a busy man rather than rudeness. He turned off the High Street and followed the directions he had been given to St. James Place.

The office was easy to find with its bold brass nameplate. Knocking on the door, he entered, taking off his peaked cap. A clerk looked up as he opened the door.

"Can I help you, sir?"

"I wrote to Mr. Elks asking for an interview."

"I see, sir. Wait here."

A few moments later Edward was in the office, he strode forward and held out his hand. It went unanswered. "Edward Hope, sir. I wrote asking to see you."

Jack sat at his desk, sleeves rolled up, surrounded by a mass of paperwork that seemed to cover the whole of his desk. He stared grumpily over his glasses and sniffed.

"What do you want, young man? A job at the pits?" He stared Edward up and down. "I doubt you'd like it!"

"No Sir, it is a personal and private matter if you will give me a few minutes."

Jack's look turned to distaste. "Go on."

"I have the great pleasure of knowing your daughter Alice, sir. We have been walking out for..."

"You've been what?"

"As I was saying, sir, walking out these last ten months. We are in love and wish to get married. We would like your blessing and approval."

"You'll get no blessing from me. There'll be no approval from me. Marry a bloody soldier! Over my dead body she'll marry the likes of you!"

"But, sir, I ..." Jack cut him short and grated out.

"Now listen to me, lad. She'll not marry you if you're the last man on earth. I've not stood by and seen the likes of you beating union men, to let my daughter take up with you!"

"I've never done that, Sir."

"Heh! Say what you like. If the government orders you out tomorrow and I'm on the picket line what will you do, eh! Bloody kiss me! No, the bloody rifle will be up and I'll be down. No, soldier, no son-in-law of mine is going to be in that position."

"I love Alice, sir. That wouldn't happen these days, I'm sure."

"Don't tell me what can happen! I've seen it first hand,

supporting scabs and blacklegs. I couldn't bear the sight of you."

"I hope you will reconsider, sir."

"You'll not step foot in my house and until Alice is twenty one she will do as I say. If she's fool enough to marry you then, I'll never speak to her again or have her in my house. Am I clear?"

Jack gestured at the door. "Let yourself out, good day."

A forlorn Edward let himself out and made his way back to barracks, his hopes dashed. It would hurt but he had better find another girl.

After a day in conference at Canterbury Jack took time out for a relaxing evening. Passing along the Guildhall he made for the 'Rose and Crown' in North Street. He liked the old pub with its low ceiling and cosy saloon bar; the publican kept a bottle of whisky especially for him. The bar was empty as he entered and he put his coat on the rack. Hearing a noise the publican, Mr. Crisp, put his head around the door.

"Someone will be right with you, Mr. Elks."

A minute later a fine looking woman of about twenty-five appeared. She had long hair, the type that Jack liked. He couldn't stand the modern style of bobbed hair. His interest was aroused.

"My father sent me to look after you, Mr. Elks. He said you like the malt - only the best."

Jack stood at the bar and looked her up and down. "Yes, I'll have a large malt, young lady. There's nothing like a good whisky and a sympathetic lady to warm a man's heart." He put a five pound note on the bar. The large white note looked very impressive.

"Call me Joan, Mr. Elks." She put the glass on the counter. Jack smiled and took a long slow sip of the whisky, savouring the taste.

"Right, Joan, I'm Jack, can't abide being called Mr. Elks by friends."

"Dad tells me you are attending a big conference. It must be so interesting working with all those important people. I hear there are Members of Parliament there!"

Jack looked sad. "You might think - but really it is so lonely. No one to talk to, night after night."

"I don't believe you. A fine looking man like you must have lots of friends."

"I wish it were true. It would be nice to have someone to talk to - bring a bit of comfort to an old man."

"You're not old, Mr. Elks, sorry, Jack. You're in your prime. The ladies will be queuing up to comfort you."

Jack shook his head sorrowfully. "If only that were true. It's so long since I felt the comfort of a good woman."

As Jack emptied the glass, Joan poured another short.

"No, Joan, I sit there each night at dinner thinking that life is passing me by."

"Oh, we can't have that Jack, life is for living."

"I will be here tomorrow, would you do me the honour of having dinner with me at the 'County'. They do a fine meal."

"I've never been there, it's so posh. I'd feel out of place."

"I'd be proud to have you on my arm. Shall we say at eight? I'll send a car for you."

"But it's only a short walk."

"My pleasure," said Jack, "my pleasure. A fine woman like you should be treated with respect."

"Now what shall I wear..." said Joan.

Five weeks after Edward Hope had seen Jack, a distraught Alice returned home from her live-in job in Folkestone where she worked as a maid. Lizzie was aware of Edward Hope's visit. Jack had been so angry that she had scuttled to the kitchen, afraid and upset. He had made it clear, that Lizzie had failed him and let Alice get out of control. If it happened again there would be serious trouble but for the moment the matter was not for discussion, not under any circumstances. Alice sat on a kitchen chair.

"I don't know what I'm going to do, Mum. I do so love him, he's a good man, we would have been so happy."

Lizzie picked up on the word, 'would'.

"You can wait till you're twenty one. That's not so far off, only until the end of the year."

Alice could only whisper. "I know that Mum but Edward has gone. Father said some awful things to him. Edward said we could never get married."

There were more tears. "Edward said it would break up the family. " Lizzie put her arm around her shoulder and gave her a squeeze.

"Don't worry. Things will be alright - you'll see."

It took a while for Alice to screw up her courage. "It won't be alright, Mum. I'm expecting a baby."

Lizzie was stunned. "But you've been working, you never said!" She pulled Alice up and stared at her waistline.

"But you can't be! You may have put on a little weight. I don't believe you."

"Well it's true, Mum. I've been to a doctor. Elsie, the other maid helped me let this dress out a bit so I could keep on working. If Mr. and Mrs. Darcy had known they would have thrown me out long ago."

Alice sat down again. "Mum, I've seen you have children. I know all the signs; there's no mistake. Eddie thought if he went to Dad we could be wed - but it was hopeless!"

Lizzie had reached near panic stage.

"What are we going to do! How do I tell your father!"

She wrung her hands in despair. "Don't say anything - let me think. Go upstairs."


When half past five came Ivy arrived home. Putting her coat on the hallstand, she called into the kitchen.

"I'm home, Mum!"

There was no answer, so Ivy went up the hall and peered in. She could tell immediately that there was something wrong. Any other day Lizzie would have smiled and put the kettle on but not today. She sat at the table, the tea unprepared. Normally the tea would have been on the table and she would have been at the sink preparing vegetables for dinner when father arrived home later.

"What's wrong, Mum? You not well?"

Lizzie put her head in her hands, but not before Ivy could see she had been crying.

"Alice is home."

'That's unusual,' thought Ivy, 'Alice was not due home today and certainly not on a weekday.' Then it dawned on her.

"Lost her job has she. Never mind, there are plenty more."

"I wish that was all it was." Lizzie's voice faltered. "She's - expecting a baby. I'm worried sick, what am I to say to your father - I don't think I can tell him."

Ivy paused, but she was the practical one. "Alice can tell him. Someone has to tell him. That sort of thing can't be hidden for long. How many months?"

"Seven - she thinks seven."

"You must tell Father this evening!"

"I can't. I just can't. He'll be so angry."

"Well, I'll tell him. Now where is Alice?"


As per his usual habit, Jack arrived home about seven thirty. He liked to eat alone in peace and quiet, followed by a whisky as he read the daily paper. Halfway through this pleasure there was a tentative knock at the door. Without looking up he growled, "Come in!" Ivy stepped in and closed the door. "I need to talk to you, Father."

Jack continued reading the paper. "Yes!"

"It's about Alice, Father."

"I've heard enough about Alice for a while – and I've told your mother so."

"It's serious. I'm sorry but you have to be told. Alice is expecting a baby."

Jack threw the newspaper aside and exploded. "LIZZIE!

LIZZIE – come here!"

A frightened Lizzie walked slowly from the kitchen.

"Yes Jack - I'm here."

"Is this true - about Alice?"

Lizzie nodded; her mouth simply would not open.

"Why haven't I been told! How long have you known?"

Ivy answered. "We none of us knew until today when she came home."

Jack's voice thundered out. "YOU MEAN SHE'S HERE - IN MY HOUSE!"

Lizzie found her voice. "She has nowhere else to go - she needs our help. How will the baby fare if she has no one to look after her." That was a long speech for Lizzie and she grasped her hands to stop them shaking.

"When's this baby due?"

"About two months, Jack."

Jack threw his head back and put his arms up.

"I might have known it! That bloody useless soldier! No wonder he stood there saying he had the pleasure of knowing my daughter! If I had known I'd have booted his arse all the way back to barracks."

He glared at them. "And where is this soldier?"

"He's gone."

"She can stay for the time being - but mark you and tell her, I don't want to set eyes on her. She's to keep out of my way. When that baby is due, she's out – d'you hear me, OUT!"

He picked up his paper. "Now let me finish in peace."

Alice's pains started early on the 28th June, before Jack had gone to work. Lizzie woke Jack to tell him, he responded quickly.

"Get her bag packed!" Lizzie hesitated. "Get going. I'm calling a taxi."

"You're not going to send her away, Jack?"

"I meant what I said. So get her ready!"

Tears welled in Lizzie's eyes but she went. Thirty minutes

later the taxi arrived and Jack marched Alice out and threw her case in.

"Here's two shillings - take her to the Workhouse."

Then he slammed the door and walked back to the house. Alice was beyond tears, in abject misery she sat back on the seat willing the pains to slow down. Eddie had gone and she had mourned and grieved for him. There was no future, no hope. She feared the workhouse, everyone knew of its reputation as the place of last resort but she would have given her soul, even gone willingly to the workhouse, for a little love. She closed her eyes and wished for a comforting arm but there was nobody. She was alone and the pain became more urgent.

"You'd better go a bit faster, Cabby. It won't be long now."

Back in the kitchen Lizzie wept and wished she had the strength to prevent all this happening but she could not stand up to Jack, she could not break the habit of the last twenty-five years. There was work to be done, meals to prepare, shopping to organise, beds to be made so she did what she had always done, she pushed her sorrow deep inside herself and got on as best she could.

## August 1933

At the annual conference of the MFGB, Jack made the following plea:

"Fellow delegates, I feel it is my duty to bring to your attention the dangers that grow both here and in Europe by the rise in Fascism. You may ask what does it matter what happens in Europe and Germany? In Germany in particular, the obliteration of Trade Unions, Co-operatives and political organisations represents a real danger to us all. And it is not only there but also in Austria and Spain and other places, such that they can no longer send delegates to the Miners International. Workers rights are being obliterated and their leaders are being arrested and imprisoned and their organisations suppressed. You may consider that it will not happen here but on the evidence of our own history there can be no grounds for complacency. There are many who regard our very existence and organisation as an affront to vested interests - who feel we rise above our station in life. There are many in this country who admire the Nazis and would willingly embrace the right to stamp on us because we will not bow the knee.

I make no bones about it when I say that unless the working class unites to fight Nazi rule and similar regimes then we may face a future assault on us of a nature beyond our experience and to which we will have no answer. There is a danger in our inward concerns regarding unemployment and recession that underpin our present weakness, that we will not raise our eyes and see the approaching danger. Our support of the Miners International must not diminish or waver. We must guard against the rise of Fascism in this country and give it no support or encouragement. Be in no doubt that it does not exist for our betterment nor to aid our future well being. In 1926 the British Fascists were only too willing to destroy us and now the 'Blackshirts' are on our streets and marching again and, mark you, without dispersal by the authorities.

Let us be on our guard and use all our power and intellect to prevent this odious organisation from taking hold of our country and by our support of the Labour Party and right-minded international institutions fight against it in the world around us. Let us be ever watchful of this serious menace to the working class. Bring this development to the notice of our members so that by being forewarned we are forearmed and thereby bolster the efforts of our executive. Ebby Edwards, our Secretary, deserves and needs our support and I am confident that this conference will endorse and support his efforts to obtain the release from prison of the President of the German Miners Federation."

## December 1933

Lizzie had been deeply unhappy for months ever since Alice had gone to the Workhouse but she had drawn back from speaking out in case she incurred Jack's wrath. In the end her unhappiness forced her to speak, that and the nearness of Christmas. One day at breakfast she screwed up her courage.

"It will be Christmas in a few weeks and I don't think I can bear it."

Jack continued eating. "Bear what?"

"Christmas, Jack. It's the one day of the year when we all sit together, meet as a family. I don't think I can bear sitting down knowing Alice is in the Workhouse. I've been there, it's a terrible place, surely no one should be there - not our daughter - not at Christmas."

"She made her own bed!"

"But what about the baby, Jack? Did you know he's called John Frederick? He's such a lovely baby and he's done no wrong. Then there is Albert and Daisy's wedding on Boxing Day - how do we cope with that?"

"I never said you could visit the Workhouse! Besides which I've no time for weddings - can't think what our Albert is up to, getting wed. He's far too young."

Lizzie was about to say that Albert was twenty-three but thought better of it. Dredging up the remains of her courage she returned to the subject of Alice. "I do want her home. Now that 'Little Jack' has moved down from Bloxwich, this will be the first time all twelve of our children can be together for a day. I have never asked for anything for myself before but I am pleading with you - let me bring Alice and the baby home or the shame and hurt will kill me."

Jack relented. "You can fetch her but keep her out of my way!"

So Alice and John Frederick came home and Alice went to Albert and Daisy's wedding. Time passed by, with Jack bad tempered and Lizzie desperately trying to keep the peace, the pain in her side growing, slowing sapping her energy.

## February 1934

The Houses of Parliament loomed up in front of Jack as he made his way across the courtyard to the entrance. He was early for his appointment but he had no idea how long he might be kept waiting. The usher found him an uncomfortable stone bench in a corridor and promised to return when the Minister was ready. "I will inform the Minister you are here, sir!" Then he was gone and all Jack could do was read the paper again and shift his buttocks to prevent paralysis setting in. People scurried about on endless important tasks; well at least Jack hoped they were important.

Two hours later the Minister, or Ernie Brown as he was in a previous life, appeared. As he approached, Jack rose.

"Good morning, Minister."

"Good to see you, Jack. Please call me Ernie, as always, we're not in the Ministry now. Let's retire to the bar."

Gratefully Jack followed.

"I have your letter, Jack and have read it. Perhaps you would like to go through the details and bring me up to date."

"I'll go back to the beginning if you don't mind," said Jack, "it started last November at Chislet Colliery when a new general manager took over. The men were told, without any prior warning or discussion, that as from January all men would use naked lamps underground and the safety lamps were to be withdrawn."

"What sort of naked lamps, Jack?"

"The old acetylene lamps with the open flame. Now these have not been used for many years because of the danger of explosion and naturally the men were up in arms and voted against them. When I met the management they refused to turn over the order."

"What was their reason?"

"The management claim that Chislet is not a gassy mine and that the acetylene lamps are a quarter of the cost of the safety lamps."

"I see. Does the mines inspector agree on the gas situation?"

"He does, but there is no means of knowing if it is liable to change suddenly and it still leaves the problem of dust."

"Do you have reason to believe there will be an explosion?"

"No, and I sincerely hope not, whatever happens; but this puts safety back over thirty years. Did you know that in November last, when 14 men died in an explosion at Grassmoor, it has been established that gas was at fault? In 1932 there were three explosions and in '31 there were three explosions. Hundreds of men have died in explosions since the Senghenydd disaster. Surely there is no place in the mines for naked lights, it is hazardous enough without."

"I wish I could help, Jack but all I can do is try to persuade. Under the Coal Mines Act I cannot force a withdrawal of these lamps. We must assume that no one thought it necessary to specifically prohibit their use after so many years. You have acted correctly in publicly stating and recording your views on the likely hazards. Should any man be injured then the law will back you."

Jack sighed. "You mean, when it's too late, we can get redress. Can you not proceed for an amendment to the Coal Mines Act for naked lights to be prohibited?"

"I regret it is unlikely with the present composition of Parliament. You will of course press it via the Federation, I hope. Ebby Edwards and Tom Smith (Labour Member of Parliament) have already pressed me and will continue to pressure others but it is a slow process."

"I am afraid, Ernie, that the men may force it to a strike but that will put a 1000 men out of work. Then the owners will import men desperate for a job."

"Have you exhausted all discussion, Jack?"

"I have had endless meetings with both management and directors but they are set."

"I will do what I can, Jack. The Mines Inspector has been told to step up his inspection rate and to be particularly thorough but that is all I can offer for the moment."

*The naked lamps were in use for many years despite all protests and subsequent explosions in other mines and the large number of deaths that resulted.*

## September 1934

## THE TIMES

## 261 KILLED IN MINE EXPLOSION

*On the morning of the 22nd of September, 261 men and boys died in an explosion at Gresford Pit in Denbighshire. The exact cause of the disaster is not known but an explosion caused by a build-up of 'firedamp' or gas is suspected. A further three men were killed during rescue operations. Due to dangerous conditions underground the scene of the explosion cannot be investigated for the time being. This is the worst disaster in the coalfields since the explosion at Senghenydd Pit in 1913 when 439 died. The Secretary of Mines has instructed the Chief Inspector of Mines to hold a Court of Inquiry. An appeal fund has been launched by the Lord Mayor of London.*

The report from this enquiry was not published until Feb 1937. Two months later the Manager and Owners were brought to trial and each fined £140 plus costs. The report by the Chief Inspector listed over a dozen serious breaches of law by the

Colliery Manager and wrote that other managers had been similarly guilty of flagrant and persistent breaches of the safety requirements of the Coal Mines Act. During the following five years a further 230 men were to die in underground explosions. Not until 1954 were the improved safety requirements, arising from the Inquiry, enacted by Parliament)

## 31st December 1934

It was 6am and quite dark, there would be no daylight for an hour yet. William Moore looked around the kitchen, pleased that the fire in the grate was well alight and would warm the cold damp air before Dora, his wife, got up to get breakfast for their young daughter. Arthur, his son, was just putting on his jacket and scarf.

"Right, Arthur, we're all ready. You get the bikes ready while I put these plates in the sink."

"Shall I say cheerio to Mum?"

"No, let her rest." He put out the light, while Arthur rushed off. So keen, thought William, so keen to get to work. He smiled to himself, remembering those years ago when he had been fourteen and had been at work only a few weeks.

"Here's your bike, Dad." Arthur was already swinging up onto the saddle and was off down the path to the road.

"Come on, Dad! We'll soon get warm."

There was no sign of frost but there was a sharp nip in the air from a cooling east wind. Then they were off down the road, side by side, to Tilmanstone.

"This is the last day of the old year - must be home in time for the dance. Your Mum's really looking forward to it."

"Can I go, Dad?"

"Who's to look after Brenda if you go?"

"Aw, Dad. I'm grown up now!"

"There'll be plenty of time for that, you'll see."

"Come on, Dad, I'll race you there!"
"Ease up, Son, this job has to last a lifetime!"

Arthur was all alone by the closed ventilation doors waiting for the full tubs to be delivered from the coalface. Eighteen laden tubs, each carrying a ton of coal, backed up the tunnel from the face. "Take 'em up!" The shouted call came from down the passageway. The tunnel leading into the doors and beyond was only just wide enough to let the tubs through with a bare four or five inches of space either side. When the doors were in the open position his job was to 'bell' the engine room to let the convoy be hauled up, then he would follow on behind ready to do the changeover to allow a convoy of empty tubs back down to the tramway leading to the face.

"Keep them tubs moving otherwise the workings will stop - if them doors get bust of damaged that'll be your job gone." The message had been rammed home time and again.

Arthur went forward and opened the doors and rolled a rock into place against each one. The tunnel was clear so he went back to the bell-push. Looking down the track he could see it was all clear so he gave three bells. In the engine room the driver, Cyril, put in the gear and threw the lever forward. The drum turned, took up the slack and then the cable bit and the run started.

As the tubs moved forward Arthur glanced back at the doors. Oh god! One of the doors had swung out, he must open it quick. He rushed forward, tripped then scrabbled to his feet, frantically reaching out to pull the door back. The tubs moved forward remorselessly. It was too late to get back to the bell-push to give the emergency stop and in a panic Arthur pressed himself back hard against the wall. No one heard his scream above the clanking of the tubs and the thumping of the engine.

In the engine room Cyril saw the tubs coming in and stopped hauling. Getting out of the cab he strode back to supervise the unhooking.

"Come on Arthur - let's be moving!" No one answered.

"Arthur, where are you?" He was puzzled, the lad should have followed the run up and now be at the end of the line. Then, in light of his lamp he saw the helmet on the top of the first tub and he ran as fast as he could back down the tunnel. "Arthur, where are you?"

"Come here quick, Cyril." Arthur's voice was rather faint.

"What have you done, lad? What has happened?"

Arthur lay on the trackway, his legs bent and twisted, blood pouring from his head. "HELP! GET HELP! MAN DOWN!" Cyril shouted as loud as he could down the tunnel. "Keep still, Arthur."

Arthur could barely whisper. "Shall I have to go to hospital?"

"You keep still now - we'll have you out soon." A man arrived. "Quick, get on the phone - we need a doctor and a stretcher, fast!"

The doctor had just finished his examination when William Moore arrived, breathless from running. Arthur lay on the stretcher, his dirty clothes and grimed features in strong contrast to the clean white walls of the Ambulance Room.

Dr. Bellemy drew back and shook his head "I'm dreadfully sorry but there is nothing I can do - your son was dead when I arrived."

"May I stay with him?" William's voice was very low.

"Yes, I'll leave you alone for a while. I've got the papers to do. Then we'll get the undertakers here."

William sat down and felt for Arthur's hand, strange he thought, he still feels warm. There was complete silence then, slowly, the tears started. He could not weep but the tears flowed, down his face to his chin and then dropped onto his grimy rags. After a while the words came.

"I'm so sorry, son. So sorry to have brought you to this place - how will I tell your Mum?"

There was no answer and the tears were salty in his mouth. "I cannot let her see you like this - it will break her heart."

He said a silent prayer but it did not help.  Cyril came in, stood beside him and put a hand on his shoulder.

"He asked for you, Bill, but there was no time - we had to get him up as soon as possible."

William did not look up.  "We were so close - T'would be better if it were me, not him.  He had his whole life ahead."

He patted Arthur's hand.  "Do you know Cyril - he raced me here this morning."  Then he cried.

Outside the word spread, down the shaft and along the tramways to the coalface.  Without comment men downed tools and slowly walked out.  Arriving at the surface they filed past the Ambulance Room, very quietly, not wanting to disturb those within.  As always on these occasions, the men of Tilmanstone were showing their respect, there would be no more work today.

## 6 January 1935, THE EAST KENT CORONOR'S COURT

Mr. B. Whitaker, Tilmanstone Colliery Manager under cross-examination by Jack Elks, K.M.W.A., after evidence of the accident had been presented.

JE:    "Do you think it is suitable that a lad of 14 should take such responsibilities?"

BW:    "A suitable as any other job in the pit for his age."

JE:    "How many days training did he have?"

BW:    "Three days with the lad who had done the job previous. Also he had repeated instructions from the Deputy."

JE:    "Would this have happened if he had a more mature judgement?"

BW:    "In such a simple thing, I cannot say."

JE:    "You say you believe the boy made an error of judgement?"

BW:    "I can think of no other possibility."

JE:    "You said the doors are kept open with a piece of rock.

Do you consider that satisfactory?"

BW: "Yes, I tested it myself and found it satisfactory."

JE: "If it is essential to hold the doors open would it not be better to have a proper fastener or automatic lock?"

BE: "It would be possible but I do not believe it would be better."

JE: "Why is that?"

BW: "Because a catch could be easily broken."

JE: "Do you not consider the use of a rock, when better means could be found, an error of judgement?"

BW: "No, the rock has been used for a long time without fault."

JE: "How much would a proper fastener cost?"

BW: "Several pounds - I can only guess - say five pounds."

JE: "Do you not consider that a fair investment in return for a young life?"

BW: "That is an unfair question. In any case there is no evidence that the rock moved."

JE: "When the scene was investigated after the accident, is it not true that the near door had broken at the bottom hinge and had a gash along the side?"

BW: "Yes, but there is no evidence that occurred in this incident."

JE: "Are you suggesting that the door was broke before this?"

BW: "No, I did not mean that, only that we cannot be certain."

JE: "Do you think, at the age of 14, a boy ought to be allowed to go into the pit?"

BW: "That matter is allowed by the regulations."

JE: "How close is the safe place and the bell to the door?"

BW: "About four yards."

JE: "Would it not be better to place them closer together?"

BW: "There has been no problem before at this door."

JE: "Do you intend to make any changes in the light of the evidence given today?"

BW: "I see no reason to do that."

JE: "Would the boy be frightened of losing his job if the door

were not opened fully?"
BW: "No!"
JE: "He had been told he must not let the tubs run into the door, do you think that may have influenced his actions?"
BW: "No, he would have had plenty of time to open the door for the journey. The doors must have been opened otherwise there would have been greater damage."
JE: "Do boys have more accidents than men?"
BW: "Yes, on average but I cannot say that is so at Tilmanstone."
JE: "Will you accept my word that it is also true of Tilmanstone?"
BW: "If you say so, yes."
JE: "Is it your personal opinion that boys of 14 be allowed in the pit."
BW: "Is it necessary for me to express it, Mr. Coroner?"
JE: "I have no more questions."

The Coroner summed up.

"As far as I can see the regulations have been properly observed but I am impressed with the fact that a boy of 14 should have so much responsibility after only a few weeks of experience. I wonder if the regulations might not be revised. It seems possible that his age made him act more impulsively or with less prudence than if he had been of more mature years. This case is an illustration of the hazards these boys face. I shall make a recommendation to the Divisional Inspector that he may consider a revision to the mining regulations. My deep concern is that any possible means to prevent accidents should be taken without delay."

A week after this Coroners Court a boy of fifteen was killed in a haulage accident.

## February 1935, KENT COUNTY COURT

The clerk read out from the order paper. "Item four, Possession Orders in favour of the owners, Dorman Long Limited against John Diffley, Thomas Quinn and John Cook."

Mr. Watts rose. "M'lud, I am acting on behalf of these three men. The amount of rent arrears is not disputed. With your Lordship's permission I have one witness, Mr. Elks, secretary of the Kent Mineworkers Association."

"Granted." Jack entered the box and was sworn in.

"Mr. Elks, John Diffley has been absent from work for nine months. Will you please explain how this arose?"

"He was a hewer at Snowdown Colliery until he was injured by a roof fall nine months ago. He has been unable to work since because of the injuries he sustained."

"How long was he in hospital?"

"Three months."

"Was he in any way responsible for the accident?"

"He was not. Dorman Long have accepted responsibility and I am presently negotiating for compensation on his behalf."

"How long will that take?"

"I cannot be certain but at least six months more is likely."

"Will he be able to return to the pit?"

"The surgeon has said he considers this extremely unlikely but it will be reviewed in twelve months time."

"Thomas Quinn has been off work for six months. How has this arisen?"

"He is suffering from chronic bronchitis and has been signed off by his doctor."

"Does the doctor say this illness is associated with his working in the pit?"

"You have his letter there. He is unable to say it is the sole cause, only that is the likeliest cause in his experience."

"Is any compensation being claimed?"

"This is being considered by the panel doctor but we are at an early stage of the process."

"Has Quinn been absent on previous occasions in the last two years with a similar illness?"

"Yes, on three occasions."

"What happened on those occasions?"

"On the first occasion none, on the second he was given a warning letter and on the third occasion he got a further warning letter so he returned to work immediately."

"On that last occasion you mentioned, was it on the recommendation of his doctor?"

"No, just the opposite to what he said."

"What happened two weeks into his absence for the latest bout of illness?"

"He was sacked."

"With regard to John Cook, what is his situation?"

"He is unable to work because of severe locomotion problems."

"What happened prior to his stopping work?"

"He was hit on the head by a falling rock and a week later he suffered a stroke."

"Are you seeking compensation on his behalf?"

"Yes. Liability has been accepted by Dorman Long but it will be some time before it is concluded."

"What is the marital status of all these men?"

"They are all married with families."

"Why do you consider the applicants have asked for repossession?"

The judge intervened. "That should not be answered unless there is evidence to that effect."

Mr. Watts produced a letter. "M'lud, I have here a letter from Dorman Long to Mr. Elks. If Mr. Elks may answer?"

"Proceed."

"They have stated that the houses are needed for new workers."

"Thank you Mr. Elks. M'lud, through no fault of their own

these three men have fallen on hard times. I ask you in the interests of humanity to put down these orders. Repossessions will only make hard situations worse."

The judge stirred. "In the case of a repossession order there can be no appeal in the interests of humanity. The orders are granted. So that these men can make alternative arrangements the orders will be effective six weeks from today."

## April 1935

Jack decided to move from the house in Temple Ewell, he needed to be closer to work and simply told Lizzie that they were going to Barton Road in Dover.

"When we move back to Dover, we will not take Alice - or the baby. I'll not have her walking about the town shaming me!"

"She has nowhere to go, what will she do?"

"I'll have no argument or discussion on this. Tell her to make arrangements."

On the day of the move Albert arrived home from his morning shift at the colliery to find an agitated Daisy waiting for him. The words tumbled out.

"Your father has left Alice behind. All alone in the old house. I don't know how a man could act this way! Abandon his own daughter! Then there's the baby, what will happen to him? Why, my..."

Albert was tired after his shift at the colliery and the journey home; all he wanted was a wash, a meal and a quick nap by the fire so he wearily interrupted. "Do you know for sure?"

"I'm almost certain, she wasn't in the van when it went past and your Mum looked upset!"

Albert put his jacket back on. "I'll go and see." He knew he would get no peace otherwise.

Albert opened the big front door of the old house and called out.

"Anyone here? - Anyone at home?"

There was no answer and the house looked bare and deserted. He was just about to go back home when he heard a baby cry.

"Are you there, Alice? It's Albert!"

Following the noise he went up the stairs and looked in the bedrooms. There was Alice, sat on a mattress on the floor with baby John Frederick in a small crib beside her. A pathetic small case of belongings lay on the floor. The baby put his arms up to Albert and he picked him up. Alice was beyond tears, she had wept a bucket of tears, she could not even really think. She was unwanted, unloved, there was no future, only the misery of the moment. Albert had to shake her to get her attention. She stared at him with bleak sad eyes.

"You can't stay here, Alice. The landlord will throw you out! Have you any money?" Alice opened her palm and showed him the four shillings she had clasped in her hand. Albert persisted.

"Alice, what are you going to do?"

"There's only one thing I can do - go back to the Workhouse."

Albert looked at her and the baby, then he stooped to pick up her bag.

"You'd better come to me and Daisy. You can't stay here. We can't let you go back to the Workhouse."

Six weeks later Alice ran away leaving the baby behind. After representations from Albert, Jack arranged for John Frederick to be fostered out through the social work of the Board of Guardians; so baby John went to be lost in the mists of time.

Over this period Lizzie's health took a turn for the worst. The worry, the years of hard work, the long years of pregnancy had had their insidious side-effects. She often wished she could speak to her father and mother but father was dead and mother was far away in Australia. Just to feel their love and affection would have been a relief but it could not be. She thought back to those early happy days at the Tavern but they were gone, like life, drifted away.

## November 1935

The Banksman stamped his feet and banged his hands together to keep warm in the cold of the Betteshanger yard. The tub had been lowered to the top of the shaft. Shivering, he stood by the bell-push and called down. "Empty coming down, Toma!"

A shout echoed up the shaft. "All ready - send it down, laddie."

Three presses on the bell-push told the engineman in the engine room to lower the tub. Down below, Toma, the Chargeman, watched the tub descend and stop at the rider block at the top of the scaffolding. The gang was removing old ventilation piping and each time a section had been removed the scaffold had to be lowered six feet, then a tub was dropped down to take away the debris.

"Right, stand aside lads, tub coming in." Toma waved the gang aside then picked up his 'knocker line' and signalled the engine room to lower the tub onto the scaffold. As soon as it was down the old pipes were quickly loaded.

Toma called up to the Banksman. "Take it up, laddie!"

The gang relaxed, no work could be done until the scaffold was lowered to a new position and it would be at least another ten minutes before all was ready.

Toma looked around, feeling pleased. "Well done, lads! We've done forty eight feet so far - we'll get a bonus at this rate." Then he called up the shaft. "Ready to lower scaffold."

Up in the engine room the duty engineman watched the dial reading on the capstan engine and let off six feet of cable, then he locked the lever and went back to the main engine. He checked the dial counter and chalk mark on the tub winding-drum and adjusted that for the extra six feet of drop. Although he only had to operate the engines every half hour he always double checked the markers because otherwise he was working blind and they told him exactly when to stop the descent.

Everything done, he relaxed and went back to his chair. He was still immersed in the football page of the paper when the 'three bells' sounded calling for the tub to be lowered. Pulling back on the lever he slowly lowered the tub down the shaft. Slowly counting off the depth of descent to be extra careful. Behind him the engine room door opened and the fitter walked in. "Got your pools coupon ready, mate?"

The engineman cursed. He had forgotten all about it. He half turned.

"In my jacket pocket - I'll do it now!"

"What jacket? I can see nowt!"

The engineman swung round and pointed. "There! In the corner - plain as daylight!"

Down in the shaft Toma could see the tub approach the riders. "Stand to the side, lads." He waved them aside and just had time to yell a warning as the tub dropped past the riders and plunged into the scaffold, then as it smashed the planking it toppled over and crushed two men against the side.

The house was in darkness with the curtains drawn as Jack knocked on the door of the cottage and waited. The wind whistled down the road made more dismal by the shorn trees and bare ground. Only the box hedges had a green about them. He shivered as he waited, then knocked again. Hesitantly the door opened. A small neat woman hung back in the doorway, pale of face and with darkness around her eyes.

"Good afternoon. Mrs. Newman? I'm Jack Elks from the Mineworkers Association. May I come in?"

She nodded mutely and led him silently into the parlour. Three small children sat quietly on the floor near the fire.

"Please accept my condolences. I knew Henry personally - he was a fine man."

"Please sit down, Mr. Elks - I don't know what to say. A few days ago we sat planning for Christmas and now......" Her voice tailed off.

"I'm sorry to intrude on you so soon but it is important to your future. There are forms to sign for the pension and I need your authority to act on your behalf to pursue a compensation claim."

Mrs. Newman sat very still, only her lower lip tremored and she bit it to keep it still.

"We went to the undertakers this morning - I just hope he didn't suffer."

Jack had never met Henry Newman and he had no way of knowing the answer but he reassured her.

"From what I have been told it was all over in seconds. He would have felt no pain."

Her lower lip quivered again, the only sign of emotion he could see since his arrival.

"Do you need any help with the funeral expenses, Mrs. Newman?"

"No, we have a sixpenny policy with the Co-Op - the collector has already called – the money will be here in a few days." Her lip stopped quivering but she slowly rubbed her wrists together.

"Would you like a cup of tea, Mr. Elks?"

"That is kind of you but no thank you."

She pointed to the children. "They will forget their father - we don't even have a picture or a photograph to remind them."

"Could I get someone from the Welfare Committee to see you - if you need help." Jack volunteered.

"My neighbours have been most kind - they always come around at times like this. Mrs. Grinley, next door, keeps telling me to have a good cry - but - I can't."

Jack passed her the papers and pen. "If you will sign, you will get twelve shillings a week for yourself and three shillings a week for each of the children until they leave school."

"The colliery will want the house back - won't they?"

"I'm afraid so, Mrs. Newman, but not for a while yet."

"It doesn't matter, Mr. Elks - we could not be happy in this house – the memories...... please thank the union for me, it will help keep us together."

She signed the forms and passed them over and Jack rose to leave.

"Mr. Elks, you won't mind if I say that none of these children will ever go to the pit -this will be the end of it."

Jack went on his way. With another man dead and three injured there was more work to do.

## January 1936

To combat the threat of a national strike over wages the coal owners had proposed varying increases in the districts whereas the Federation wanted a flat-rate rise. However in order to overcome objections to the varying rates the owners had proposed a 'Joint Standing Consultative Council' for national issues, provided there were no stoppages and the district rates were accepted. At the end of the month the owners' proposals were hotly debated. Jack had his chance to speak at the MFGB Conference.

"Fellow delegates, there has been some anger at this meeting but I ask you to put it aside. You see before you a happy man and that is how I wish to finish this conference." He peered out over his glasses, looking around the hall. "Let me tell you why. This quote is read directly from the text of the owners' proposals. ' We make this proposal in the earnest hope and belief that it will conduce to the maintenance of good relationship in the industry and to the benefit of all in it!' Join with me to bless this sinner who repents. They use words I had not thought existed in their vocabulary. Co-operation! Common interest! National negotiation! Am I dreaming, perhaps standing at the Pearly Gates?" He paused and looked around the hall.

"No, I am here alive - there are too many present who will not pass that way." He waited till the laughter died.

"Our Kent members have been offered the lowest increase in the district rates but we wish you to accept the owners offers in their entirety for the common good. For over ten years we have fought for a national negotiating machinery - do not turn it away. Embrace this offer and let us use this council to our advantage - let the Federation speak as a national body. The men of Kent are for this proposal, do not let their sacrifice be in vain."

At the end of the debate the owners' proposals were agreed.

## March 1936

The clerk smiled as Jack entered. "Good morning, Mr. Elks. Mr. Kyle is waiting for you." Jack thanked him as he passed through. Percy Kyle, the Betteshanger Colliery Manager was there.

"A good afternoon to you, Mr. Elks. I have read your letter, have a seat, please."

Jack had written the letter a week ago, by hand, as he didn't want the contents to be observed. The background was the fact that the colliers at Betteshanger worked in gangs and their wages were aggregated and paid in a lump sum with one docket and given to the chargeman. The lump sum was calculated after deductions for various stoppages. Sometimes the chargeman would be elected by the men, but many had taken the responsibility by force of character. Also it suited the colliery management to deal with one man so the chargeman gained a position of authority and might not be challenged by the men, even if he abused his position.

"I have a problem, Mr. Kyle - but it is also your problem as well. At this stage I won't mention the man's name except to say he has made a formal complaint to me. He suspected he was being cheated by the chargeman on his gang, so over a few weeks he kept a record of events. Let me take one week as an example, the earnings were calculated at eighteen shillings and nine pence per shift – the chargeman allocated eighteen shillings. With eight men in the gang the chargeman pocketed one pound sixteen shillings he hadn't earned. Take it over a year he's getting about one hundred pounds of the men's money!"

"This is easily solved, Mr. Elks. Why don't the men just speak up?"

"Well, for a start the system has become custom and practice so abuse is possible. By your dealing with the chargeman in this way it implies an authority he does not have but nevertheless an unscrupulous man can exploit it."

"Surely this is easily solved - just one man!"

"I wish it were so but the committee have made quiet enquiries and we believe that at least fifty per cent of the chargemen can be implicated. The main reason we can see for this practice to become commonplace is the fact that your deputies allow the chargemen to move men from gang to gang, the quid pro quo being access to the best faces."

"You're telling me that over twenty of your men are consistently cheating their fellows!"

"Yes."

"Do you believe the management to be implicated?"

"Not as regards the personal allocation of money to the gang. Only that they know it goes on and use their knowledge in creating a chargeman authority he should not have."

"I do not see what I can do about it - this is a union matter - a matter between the men."

"At first sight, I agree," Jack lit his pipe and paused. "That is my reason for seeking a meeting to find a way to end it without splitting the union and having a confrontation with you at the same time. If the man who complained makes it formal I shall have no option but to bring a summons or call the police in. No, what I want is for the pay office to do an individual pay docket for each man so he knows exactly how much he is being paid and why - that way there can be no cheating."

"That will be expensive Mr. Elks. I don't think I can agree to that."

"The present gang docket states total earnings, days off, names of men and so on. All the information for individual dockets is already there - I accept that it means a slight increase in paperwork but nothing too onerous."

"The owners will not accept it just to prevent men cheating men - that is not their concern!"

Jack paused. "I am faced with a situation that must be corrected. If I act only against the man there will be an upheaval in the lodge - probably a damn war! That would lead me to take action against the owners which I do not wish to do."

"How are the owners involved? We pay the correct money to the chargemen."

"You are treating the chargeman as a contractor - which he is not, he is an employee with the same contract as the other men. Under the Truck Act each man is entitled to be paid direct in coin of the realm and it must be clearly stated the reasons for any deductions. My discussions with the tax authorities also confirms this."

"Who will accept the extra cost?"

"I'm afraid, Mr. Kyle, that is the employer responsibility. All I am asking is that you accept that responsibility and follow the law."

"To prevent dishonesty?"

"No, to ensure absolute fairness. In my view a straight changeover would prevent any need to dig up the past. My man will not complain if he knows the situation is corrected. A simple management notice that individual dockets and pay packets will commence on such and such a date is all that is necessary."

"What if the chargemen complain?"

"Just refer them to the committee or myself - they'll be put straight."

"Do you guarantee there'll be no trouble?"

"Absolutely. I'd rather lose twenty men from the association than see a single man cheated. If any chargeman causes trouble I'll expose him to the whole association if necessary."

Four weeks later the new individual pay procedure was introduced and about the same time all the chargemen positions were put to the vote by the men so that in all cases they became union appointees.

## 1936

The second of December was a bright morning, sharp with frost under a cloudless sky. Dimly in the distance to the south the outline of the coast of France could be seen. The car taking Jack to Betteshanger Colliery went at modest speed as he had instructed. He wanted to use the time to plan a strategy before the arranged meeting. Betteshanger had a bad reputation for its treatment of men, a fact that was known throughout all the coalfields in the land. Resentment had simmered away and eventually had exploded into a lightning strike, as short fuses lit and in the resultant explosion of feeling all the men had walked out in a spontaneous gesture. He lit his pipe and ruminated. The strike had taken place without union agreement initially and defied their normal procedures. He would have to be careful on that.

Eventually the car arrived and he made his way to the office of the General Manager, Percy Kyle. The pickets had waved to him as he went through the gates. He knocked on the door

"Jack Elks to see Mr. Kyle." A clerk showed him in.

"Sit down, Jack, please. Have a cup of tea."

Jack drew up a chair and took the proffered cup.

Percy continued. "I know we are at odds, Jack, with this damn dispute but we have known each other long enough to be on first name terms in this office?"

Jack sipped his tea. "Of course, Percy. As long as you're not trying to bribe me with this." He grimaced.

Percy produced a small flask and put a drop in Jack's cup.

"That's better Percy, now we can talk." Jack took an

appreciative sip.

"We must get this dispute settled, Jack, and get back to normal. I thought a private meeting might allow us to make some progress."

"Well, we've got a real problem, Percy. The men are up in arms. A lot of bitter resentment. This is no ordinary upset. My men have put up with bullying and abuse for many years. They claim prolonged victimisation from pit bottom managers and that has been bottled up and then exploded."

"I don't understand it, Jack, very little of this has come my way. Why have they said nowt?"

"Look, Percy, you must have known bullies at school. I bet you didn't run to the headmaster to complain. The men are like that. Scared of losing their jobs if they complain too much."

"Put your allegations on the table, Jack."

"It comes to this. There has been prolonged, unreasonable, improper conduct by your face managers and by two Deputies in particular, Yates and Sylvester. They bully, profane and attempt to short-change the men. It seems the only way they can manage men is to intimidate and profane them, and Mortishead allows it."

He stopped for a sip of tea while Percy waited.

"I know pits can be a rough place but do you know how many Chapel men we have? They don't give profanity and are mortally offended by it. Those men mentioned give no respect, turn men out of the pit in defiance of our agreement, act in anger. I am told they are worse with the boys than the men and that really rankles - most of the boys' fathers work in the pit."

"I'm sorry to hear this, Jack. I've investigated and had statements from my staff, from the pit manager down and I can see none of this mentioned. The event that started all this, the sacking of the boy Percy Gibbs, I deemed unreasonable, as did Mortishead."

Mortishead was the pit manager and was underground when the incident occurred.

"Gibbs was sent back to work in another area after a few

hours and then, bang, they're all out. On the face of it, it seems an over-reaction. I know it was said there had been a lot of cursing, and Yates and Sylvester didn't deny it, but I had no reason to believe it was any worse than general pit talk."

"I find it hard to believe, Percy, that you're unaware of the broader complaints. Don't tell me you don't keep your ear very close to the ground, you even know what's gone on at our meetings before I write the minutes! Let's get down to brass tacks. Suppose the men give in and go back with nothing resolved. Is production going to get back to normal? The boys on the tubs will probably leave in droves to join the forces. God help them, but the army will snap them up quick enough. I know how difficult it is to recruit boys. What's the point of spending money on recruitment when Yates and Sylvester drive men out! Other men want to leave and there's a big recruiting drive starting at Chislet soon."

"What do you propose, Jack?"

"Sack Yates and Sylvester. They defied management instructions in sending men out of the pit. They exceeded their authority under the Mining Act!"

Kyle responded. "From my interviews and the statements made, that includes two of your own men by the way, I think dismissal would be taken as over harsh by my management, though I'm inclined to do that. There we are between the devil and the deep sea. Keep Yates and Sylvester and your men stay out. Sack them and all the deputies come out. Either way the pit stops and all the men lose money!"

"I have a suggestion, Percy."

"Go on."

"What we do is isolate Yates and Sylvester. Put them in a position where the other deputies will stay put and the men go back."

"How the hell do we do that?"

"I make a prima facie case of bullying and intimidation and so on. You suspend Yates and Sylvester, on pay, for failing to follow management instructions. Then we agree to an inquiry into the whole matter. Both their action as deputies and general unsatisfactory behaviour."

"Surely that would put me as piggy in the middle, it would be difficult!"

"No, as I see it," said Jack, "we come to an agreement that in fairness to all we hold a public inquiry before an independent Chairman so that we, not you, put forward the details of the case against these two men. Management can involve if they went to but only to protect the owners interests, I suggest. Also my members will speak up and tell the truth if it's done away from the colliery, out in the open."

"What if Yates and Sylvester won't participate?"

"Then they will stand condemned for all to know. They would have to leave. With a suspension and your guarantee for a fair inquiry, the other deputies won't take issue. With a suspension and a public inquiry I can persuade the men to go back."

Percy pondered on it. "Could be done, Jack. I can take an impartial stance. I would need to be there, of course."

"Independent Chairman, Percy, give him power to adjudicate and make binding recommendations."

"Done!" said Percy. "If they agree we go ahead. If they don't I'll suspend them on short pay and slowly ease them out."

"Agreed."

"And the men will go back immediately?"

"As soon as we've drawn up an agreement and I've spoke to my Executive."

Percy smiled. "Agreed, Jack. Let's draw up the papers!"

"No, Percy. Let's make history!"

## DECEMBER 1936, INQUIRY HELD IN THE TOWN HALL, DEAL

The Commissioner, Mr. W.L. Cook, Industrial Adviser at the

Ministry of Mines, declares that his findings and declaration are given below together with the reasons for them.

*DECLARATION: I direct that the Deputies, Mr. Yates and Mr. Sylvester be suspended and transferred to duties on the surface for a minimum of nine months.*

*Those duties to be supervised by a close management observance of their conduct and actions but they shall not be allowed to have charge of men or boys for the nine month suspension.*

*CONSIDERATIONS: In reaching my finding as declared I am mindful of the fact that although I may rule for dismissal, that Mr. Elks, acting for the Kent Mineworkers Association, specifically did not ask for dismissal, only that they be removed from their existing duties. Also I do not wish to hold responsibility for the loss of a man's livelihood.*

*FINDINGS: I have heard a litany of complaints regarding the conduct of Mr. Yates and Mr. Sylvester, considerable evidence against them was not rebutted and I found them to be evasive and untruthful. They used a personal interpretation of the Mines Act to reinforce authority over their workmen and disobeyed senior management orders when enforcing disciplinary action, which exceeded their authority. I do not accept that authority must be reinforced by the intimidating use of vile and repulsive language.*

*The hazarding of men's lives by sending them down narrow passageways in front of gravity operated vehicles is, to say the least, reprehensible. There is a balance between Statutory Duty and the management of men. Bullying, intimidation and vile language have no part in either. Men working under these conditions may not raise important issues of safety and prevent timely action. Neither are they liable to be productive.*

*CONCLUSION: It is my view that this inquiry, used as a means of resolving an industrial crisis, has proved an effective and open means of promoting harmony. It is my hope that the three parties, the owners, the Federation of Deputies and the*

*Mineworkers Association will together agree and implement procedures and practice to ensure that events as given in evidence cannot happen in future.*

## 1937

Lizzie had not felt well over Christmas but had arranged and organised the family Christmas dinner.  Six months prior to that she had had a slight stoke but the worst effects had gone and she had made a good recovery; except for the left side of her face which still showed signs of paralysis.  The doctor had prescribed lots of rest but that only helped a little and improvements were not sustained.  She did not know it herself but the kidney failure that had started those years ago was insidiously moving on and the poisons in her bloodstream built up.  In early January she collapsed and was taken to hospital where she slowly moved into unconsciousness.

On the 26th January she passed away.  Alice came to the funeral.  It was to be the last time she would see her father alive

After the funeral Jack asked Ivy to come into the parlour to talk.  Ivy was now twenty-two and was planning to marry in a few months time.

"I don't know what to do with your mother gone.  I've relied on her all these years.  It's very lonely knowing she is not there, looking after things.  I'm no good at household matters."

"What about a housekeeper, Dad, you could afford one?"

"I know, but there's May and Dot and Arthur not grown up yet.  Do you think they will take to a housekeeper?"

"No, and there's Herbie, Doug and Jim and Donald - just the washing alone is a mountain. They eat like horses.  I don't know how Mum coped with it."

"I wanted to ask you - will you do it, run the house for me?"

"But I'm getting married in a few months!"

"If you don't do it I shall go to pieces - give me two years,

Ivy. Just two years! Wait for two years."

"I don't know, Dad. It's a lot to take on, I know, I've been doing it for the last two months!"

"I'll get a maid in to help. Florrie Hubbard has said she can do the weekday cleaning."

"I'll speak to Tibby. If he agrees I will but it's two years, then I'm off. Not three or two and a half! Two!"

So Ivy took over the household.

Later in the year Herbie and Douglas joined the airforce and not long after Jim followed them. Donald also left to join the army.

## 26th November 1938

The morning shift at Betteshanger was drawing to a close. On the No. 8 face the hewers were hard at work and the tubs were filling rapidly. Full tubs were mounting up on the tramway and Hugh Cox, the Chargeman, made his way from the face to the line of tubs.

"How's it going Bill?" Bill was William Richardson, the trammer, responsible for getting tubs to and from the coalface.

"We've done a full load, Hugh. No. 8 will get full wage today."

"I've just been in - there's another four tubs coming out."

"Pity they're not for S3."

Bill Morris appeared. "Are these from S3?"

Cox was already walking back to the face and called back. "Get 'em all marked up and away - we're nearly finished."

Ten minutes later Deputy Fells, together with a collier, walked up the road to check the shift out. He noticed 'S3' marks on four tubs in the line. "Cox! Come here!"

Cox walked up with another collier.

"What's this?" Fells pointed at the 'S3' marks.

Cox was puzzled. The marks weren't on the end of the line but in the middle of the line. The end four might have been mistaken marking.

"Must be earlier tubs from S3."

Deputy Fells was annoyed. "There's no coal on S3. There's been none this shift. Get Morris and Richardson." He turned to the collier. "You're witness to those marks."

When Cox, Morris and Richardson were assembled he walked down the line to the tubs. "You three have been marking. Where did these come from?"

When he got no answer he turned away. "You will all come to the Boxhall office at the end of the shift."

## 2nd February 1939, DOVER, COUNTY PETTY SESSIONS

"John Morris, Hugh Cox and William Richardson. You are each charged that at Betteshanger Colliery on the 26th November 1938 you did, with intent to defraud, attempt to cause Messrs Dorman Long Limited to pay money to certain of their servants employed on heading No. S3 by falsely pretending that the contents of four tubs of coal were obtained on heading S3. How do you plead?"

"Not guilty."

Mr. Herbane, the prosecutor rose. "Your Honours, the accused are charged that by the means of false pretence, they tried to get their employer to pay money to men who had not earned it. Not to themselves but to other persons. This is not a matter of petty dishonesty but a serious matter of dereliction of duty and honesty that could not be condoned. I will explain. The men were working on No. 8 face. Nearby is another face called No. S3. On the shift in question there were no men working on No S3. The men on No.8 were paid a minimum wage of eleven shillings a day because output from the face would not allow a higher wage. The situation on S3 is different, where the output allows the men to earn more than the minimum so that each extra tub would earn the gang of men working there an extra three shillings. By the improper allocation of four tubs to S3 the men there would earn an extra twelve shillings while the men on No. 8 would not lose by it."

The Deputy, the collier and the Colliery Manager gave evidence. Cox and Richardson denied the charges, nor was any evidence offered that they had been seen entering the marks. Morris admitted marking the tubs but said he believed the markings were correct. Jack was called as a character witness.

"Mr. Elks, you have known these men for a number of years. Do you consider them honest?"

"I do. I have known Cox for six years and the others for about three years."

"Has there ever been any suggestion that any of them have done anything improper in that time?"

"No, never."

"Would you normally be approached in the event of anything unusual happening with regard to the men?"

"Yes, in my capacity as Secretary to the Mineworkers Association."

"Why is that?"

"We have a written agreement with the management."

"Were you called on this occasion?"

"No!"

"Is that unusual?"

"Yes, our agreement requires that an Association official be present in all disciplinary procedures."

"What are the duties of a 'Chargeman'?"

"He records all output and any agreements with the Deputy regarding special payments and so on."

"Is he a union official?"

"No, but the men vote for him to be appointed."

"Would such a man need to be honest?"

"Scrupulously honest, otherwise he would not be trusted by men or management."

"Would these men have made any gain, personal gain, from the alleged act?"

"Not a penny!"

"Had a mistake been made would the men on face S3 gained by it?"

"No. It was common knowledge that there were no men working on S3. The mistake would have been noted, queried and put right."

Mr Herbane paused for a moment, then he looked directly at Jack in a challenging way, "Are you saying that if Deputy Fells had not noticed these wrong markings that the S3 gang would not have benefited?"

Jack held his ground. "There were no men on S3!"

"Would the accused have known there were no men on S3?"

"Everyone I have questioned knew. I fail to see how these men would not know. In fact in their statements to the manager, which I was shown, the men stated that they knew there were no men on S3. In fact because S3 was closed, Richardson had been transferred to No.8 from S3."

"Is it possible the tubs in question could have come from S3?"

"I cannot say for certain but in the pit, tubs going to and forth from the face to the bank, get mixed up. There are many hundreds of tubs in transit."

When all the evidence had been presented the bench asked if any person wished to speak on behalf of the men and Jack stepped forward.

"I do not want to say anything that I previously gave in evidence but I ask the bench to take into account that prior to this charge these men are of unblemished character and have held a position of trust for many years. Both Richardson and Morris are very young. Cox, who is appointed by the men, has suffered greatly and has been under the doctor for treatment since this charge came up. All these men have been put off without pay for ten weeks. Cox is a family man and his family faces eviction for rent arrears."

The bench retired for ten minutes then returned. "We find

you all guilty as charged. You are each sentenced to three months imprisonment with hard labour. Take them down."

Outside the court Jack spoke to the Colliery Manager.

"That was a hard judgement - to break three men."

"I've no sympathy, dishonesty cannot be allowed. It'll teach them and others a lesson."

"Even so, what do you gain? For the sake of twelve shillings you destroy every chance of co-operation and harmony. Every other man in the pit will take it hard. They never forget!"

"Sorry, Jack, but I'm under orders to call the police in if this type of incident occurs."

"We could have found another way. Now there are six and half thousand men in Kent feeling an injustice has been done. Will you at least hold back on the eviction."

"That I would do if I could but it's out of my hands. Head office are dealing with that."

A week later a hundred men downed tools and walked out as news came through that the eviction was going ahead and, when those men were threatened with summonses, a further two thousand men walked out until they were withdrawn.

## February 1939

The telephone call came through early in the morning from Billy Powell, the lodge secretary at Betteshanger. One hundred men were out on a lightning strike and the company was preparing summonses for breach of contract. Bloody hell, thought Jack, Betteshanger and trouble spelt the same. That bugger Mortishead will be behind this. Were it not for the loss of jobs he could almost wish the place closed down. Billy had responded well and organised a meeting with the men at the Mill Hill welfare club at eleven. Jack ordered a car and got his bag.

Just before eleven Jack arrived at the club and found Billy.

"Get me a drink - I need building up today!"

They went to an empty table and sat down, then Jack started. "Good morning, lads. I have a general picture - would anyone like to speak?"

Geordie Watts spoke up. "Wor canna tek it nae mair - nae coal, only dross and watter. Thee fireman won't deal - jus get on't with thee bluddy wark."

Jack knew enough of 'Geordie' to know that wark meant work and work meant walk. There were shouts of agreement all around. Billy broke in. "There's a fault in the seam. I've been to Mortishead but he won't budge. Sez the lads are being 'ca-canny', playing up for nowt!"

"Aye," another man stood up, "we just meet pigheadedness. I demand a full meeting, vote for a strike!"

The shout went up all around "All out! All out!"

Jack stood up and waved for quiet. "Calm, lads, calm! Taking all the men out will not stop the summonses. The agreement we have requires we follow the agreed procedures - negotiate first and if the vote supports it then we give notice."

Two men got up and starting arguing. Another man got to his feet.

"It's not good enough while we lose money!" Geordie Watts butted in. "We work to wark an gae hame wee empty pockets!"

Jack waited for calm. "If you come out piecemeal there will be no solution - you'll lose wages and get fined. You know how the magistrates view us. Technically you have broken your contracts."

There were more shouts. "Sod 'em, we've taken enough!"

"Lads! Lads! I'm on your side, but how can I negotiate if summonses are issued. It puts us in the wrong before we start. This will be dealt with straight off, I promise, but I want you back tomorrow."

There were more cross arguments and shouting so Billy got up.

"LADS! Come on now! If Jack says straight off, that's a

promise. We must go by the rule book until we all change it."
Billy waited till there was quiet.

"Now, let's have a vote. Those for going back and giving
Jack a chance. Those for? Those against? Most are for going
back." Billy wiped his brow. "Open the bloody bar, steward!"

Later Jack walked into Percy Kyle's office. "Hello Percy.
How do we get this sorted out?"

"The owners have told me, if the men break their contract
then I've to get summonses out."

"Even if the grievance is justified?"

"I don't think it is - I'm assured that the tonnage output is
reasonable compared to other face rates."

"There's only one way of doing this, Percy. Get me a helmet
and we'll go and look together. If I think four tons a man can be
done, I'll say so - if you think you could get a ton out I'll call it
square!"

Jack shone the lamp at the face. "Look at that - half the face
is out. If the men drive in either side you'll not get the conveyor
in and there's not enough face for the whole gang if they go
round." He pointed to the centre area where the coal lay in small
pockets. "There's only two ways - remove it or drive in a new
face further down."

Percy stood in two inches of water. "What if that pocket
peters out in a few yards - that's what I'm led to believe?"

"The men tell me its already gone fifteen yards! I suggest
you put the men on straight yardage plus four shillings a ton.
That'll make them work harder to get it clear. When the pocket is
clear you can reassess. Be a damn sight cheaper than driving in
lower down."

"Straight yardage, Jack. Sixteen shillings a day plus four
shillings a ton. I'll get the Deputy to measure up. Will they come
back for that, till the pocket's clear?"

"The men will be back tomorrow but the summonses will

need to go. Otherwise we have a whole new problem on our hands."

"Agreed, Jack. Let's go get a drink for the comfort of our bones!"

Jack ineffectually tried to dust down his coat. "Look at the state of me. We're getting too old to play silly buggers down here!"

Back in the office Percy poured a couple of drinks. "There are times, Jack, when I think we may be the only two sane men in Kent!"

"Between you and me, Percy, Mortishead is a liability. His stubbornness will sink us all. Thinks that if he gives an inch he loses face. Men respect fairness but bloody mindedness.......no!"

The rest of his thoughts Jack left unsaid.

## 24th May 1939

The Chairman of the District Mines Committee called the meeting to order and checked the agenda.

"There are three items this afternoon. Item one is the general pay increase or award. Item two is the disbursement of the welfare fund - I see that the baths for Chislet reappear! Item three concerns a holidays with pay agreement. Are there any points arising?"

"Yes, Mr. Chairman," said Jack, "I ask that items one and three be considered together."

"I see, do you have any comments,Mr. Mottram?"

"I am happy for them to remain as separate items, perhaps Mr. Elks can explain."

"Yes, Mr. Chairman. There is only so much money in the pot and any increase is based upon the percentage profit division related to the price of coal. For years we have tried to find a means of agreeing paid holidays. From my information today, there is a real chance we can bring these together."

"Your opinion, Mr. Mottram?"

Mottram checked with his adviser. "Yes, we are agreeable but must say we regard the general pay increase to be the more important."

"Good, let us take the pithead baths for Chislet."

"Mr. Chairman," said Jack, "the men have voted for this disbursement. In fact I am under considerable pressure as to why this is not already done. There has been a two year delay in this matter!"

Mottram replied. "I apologise, we have had difficulty in getting the water supply from the board, then we ran into problems with waste disposal. There was concern that waste water would enter the River Stour waterway. This has now been resolved by the preparation of a series of sumps. That is now ready."

The Chairman picked up his pen. "There is no reason why I should not sign the agreement and contract then?"

Mottram and Jack nodded agreement.

"Thank you gentlemen, let us return to the standard wage agreement. Mr. Mottram, will you lead?"

"Yes, Mr. Chairman. The calculation of the percentage profit division gives a figure of two per cent for wage allocation before deduction of permitted direct costs. That leaves one point two per cent for wage variation. The allocation is £64,300 which can be dispersed to the men."

"Mr. Chairman," Jack removed his glasses, "could Mr. Mottram tell us the coal price on which this is based?"

"It represents the average price for the year ending November 1938 of two pounds seventeen shillings per ton."

Jack handed over two documents. "The Ministry states that the average price for the year ending April of this year is three pounds two shillings per ton. The percentage profit figure will rise by four per cent. In simple terms the owners have already pocketed a profit increase of £250,000 without the men getting a penny. Based on the Ministry figures the standard reallocation of variable cost factors as formulated gives an allocation of £120,000 for dispersal."

Mottram interjected. "Mr. Chairman, in all previous years we have taken our average coal price on the basis I stated. That has been our standard practice!"

Jack read from the agreement. "The rule of calculation clearly states for the 'previous twelve months'. Prior to this year the variation has been so small that it would be unlikely to affect our discussion."

Jack carefully avoided mentioning that he had lobbied the Ministry to provide figures three months in advance of normal.

The Chairman checked his notes. "Mr. Mottram, the interpretation is correct. Do you agree with Mr. Elks's calculations?"

"My secretary will check the figures but I am prepared to discuss on that basis. Mr. Elks rarely gets his figures wrong."

"Thank you, Mr. Mottram." Jack was always more gracious when winning. "The allocation works out at eight shillings per week for men and four shillings for boys. Now this is where I wish to deviate from normal practice. As you know we have tried for years to find a means of having paid holidays for the men but without success. I propose that we award half the increase on a weekly wage basis and fund annual holiday pay from the remainder. A holiday year can run from the 1st of July to the following 30th June. For each shift a man works he earns eight pence a day holiday pay, a boy four pence. The accrued entitlement to be paid as a lump sum at the start of the two week annual holiday period. The holiday pay scheme would therefore start this coming 1st July.

The Chairman smiled. "An excellent scheme. It will give the men an incentive both to go to work and stay at work. I understand we are losing men already!"

"Yes," said Jack, "six of my sons have left the pits and have joined the armed forces already. They're convinced it will be a better life though I don't see it myself."

"Mine, too." said the Chairman. "War always draws the adventurous into its fold. Let's hope it doesn't happen."

Mottram coughed. "Mr. Chairman, we have checked the figures and if you will make a formal ruling on the interpretation of the agreement we accept the overall figures of eight and four shillings. The holiday pay scheme is acceptable in principle but I need to check details with Mr. Elks. I have no doubt he has prepared the ground on this."

The Chairman looked around. "I feel we have made real progress today. I approve the four and two shilling rises to be effective from the 1st June. You will bring me a copy of the holiday pay scheme in two weeks, to sign."

"Is that necessary, Mr. Chairman?" Mottram looked concerned.

"Yes. This pay is the men's entitlement so I must be satisfied that the money is allocated correctly and fairly."

Jack had got all he had wanted but added a few more points for good measure.

"Mr. Chairman, there are just a few more things. First accrued holiday pay will earn interest, we must decide what to do with that, then there is the issue of compensation payments..........."

## 26th May 1939

On the morrow Ivy was to be married, everything was ready. Late in the evening she served Jack his dinner.

"I shall be gone tomorrow, Father. Are you coming to my wedding tomorrow?"

"No, I've work to do. You know I don't go to weddings."

"Well, after today, May will look after you but take care. She's only a young girl and you can't tie her down her just to please yourself. She will want a life of her own."

Even Jack seemed affected by the quiet. "This house is still, seems unnatural somehow, what with Don, Herbie, Doug and Jim in the forces. I don't suppose they'll ever come back but they must make their own way."

Ivy took a few steps back towards the door. "I'm off to do my final packing. I've waited long enough and now the time has come for Tib and I to settle down and have a family of our own. He's been a good man to wait."

Jack picked up the newspapers.

"Goodnight, Father."

There was no reply, Jack was buried in the news.

## Chapter 7

## THE WAR YEARS AND AFTER

## 1939

War with Germany was declared on 3$^{rd}$ September.

In the short period after the declaration of war the cost of living rose quickly. In January 1940 alone the index rose 24 points. An employer offer to increase miners' wages by fourpence per day met with derision and flat rejection by the Miners Federation. A slightly better deal put forward by the owners led to deep divisions in the Federation, the first time there had been such a disagreement for over 35 years. In deep disgust Jack resigned from the Federation Executive at the end of 1940.

## Feb 1940

Jack walked up the steps into the Ministry of Fuel and Power ready for his appointment set for 9.30am. He liked to be prompt and a quick glance at his fob watch showed 9.27 as he approached the desk and showed his identity card.

"Jack Elks to see Mr Dutton". The uniformed attendant checked his pass and noted his details in the register before sending him off to room 208.

Jack knew, rather vaguely, that the meeting was about the Kent Coalfield; unusually the meeting was with the Permanent Secretary of the Ministry. All he had to go on was a rather vague telephone call from Dai Grenfell, State Secretary for Mines, warning him to be on his guard. The secrecy of the agenda puzzled him but he put that down to the war and the general air of secrecy it generated.

Anthony Dutton rose to greet him. "So pleased you were able to come, Mr Elks. Let me take your coat and have a seat. A cup of tea will be here shortly."

Jack knew he was being treated with deference but a cup of tea was unlikely to impress him, so as he waited for the next step he carefully filled his pipe and lit up.

"I would rather you didn't do that, Mr Elks. It's so hard to get good tobacco these days and I am trying to give up."

Morosely Jack put his pipe down and thought 'this is going to be a long meeting', he enquired. "Will the Secretary for Mines be attending – or his staff?"

"No, Mr Elks. The Minister is responsible for policy, the matter today is a broader matter, essentially an administrative one related only to the Kent Coalfield."

"Will the owners be represented?"

"Not at this stage, Mr Elks. The War Ministry offered to attend but I felt that as I know their views it was not necessary. No, for the moment our main concern is to consider the best productive use of the 6000 miners in Kent. With the threat of invasion and the build-up of enemy raids on Kent it is the Ministry's view that it would be better to send the men to other coalfields. As you know we are very short of miners and how important it is to raise coal production."

Jack was caught completely unawares. "What has the War Ministry to do with this?"

"In a nutshell Mr Elks, they believe that Kent is one of three areas most likely to be invaded so they want industries moved away if possible. Also they want the railway system clear in case the area needs reinforcing quickly. At a practical level they say that Dover will come under increased shelling from the Calais area. That will push more coal on to the railways. Their assessment is that coal mining will be increasingly disrupted, hence the need to transfer the men."

"Do the owners agree?"

"It will be a Ministry Order, endorsed by the War Cabinet, so they will have no choice in the matter."

"So you intend to go ahead, come what may?"

"I am almost certain, Mr Elks. The purpose of this meeting is to discuss the practical details as how best to achieve the transfer. Provisionally our proposal is to transfer most of the men over the next six months leaving only a skeleton staff at each mine. There are 30,000 vacancies in Wales, Yorkshire, Scotland and the Midlands so we see no problem in sending the men to the area of their choice."

Jack was getting angry and as he spoke it showed. "What about the families, Mr Dutton? Are they all to be herded off. Do you think they are all cowards who will run because of a few guns and aeroplanes? If so, you don't know these people as I do. Do you know why most of them are in Kent? Well, I'll tell you! It's because they weren't wanted in those areas you mentioned, they were treated badly, often abused and often refused work. They suffered for years for lack of work. Some have been in Kent for over 30 years, other places are not home any more. Are there 4000 houses available for their families? Homes are scarce. How many men will you leave to safeguard the pits?"

"It will do no good to get angry, Mr Elks, we must take a rational view!"

Jack growled, "Right, let's be rational then! How many men will stay behind in Kent to look after the mines?"

Dutton considered his notes. I am advised that about two hundred men will be needed for maintenance."

"You only intend the men to be away for a few months then?"

"That cannot be foreseen, Mr Elks. I am advised we must consider a year to eighteen months minimum and possibly longer."

"In that case you are closing the field. I can tell you from my 40 years experience that you cannot mothball a pit. Pressure will subside the pits and all the workings. Floors will move, roadways will collapse and severe flooding follows. You will need to keep

2,000 men back if you wish to keep the pits in proper working order. The whole enterprise in mining is a constant endeavour not just to get the coal out but to keep the pit in working order. To do otherwise will condemn the field never to re-open. The owners would never pay to have them re-established. And it's not just the pits – you are talking about the lives and communities of 20,000 people. Are you prepared to pay 2,000 men to produce virtually nothing?"

"As I said, Mr Elks, I am advised that 200 men will suffice. Whilst I agree it will take time for the men's families to be re-housed there is still the wider benefit to the country to consider with nearly 6,000 men being productively used in safer areas."

"Your minds are made up then? Besides which, who has said the Kent pits are not productive?"

"Kent productivity is not the issue. The men can be better used elsewhere, where there is less liability of disruption. We are hoping for your support and that of your association in creating a climate of acceptance and helping to get the message over to your members."

"Let me tell you, Mr Dutton, not only do I not support you but will use every bit of me to oppose you. Do you expect me to stand by like a trusting fool and see you destroy all we have worked for, for 30 odd years? Don't underestimate our men – if you try to force us you will have another war on your hands."

"Mr Elks, there is the military situation to consider . . . . . ."

"No one will be safe if Kent is invaded. Six thousand men deported against their will, how can they be productive?"

"Will you discuss it with the men?"

"No, I will discuss it with my Executive Committee only and give you a reply but bend your mind to refusal and solid resistance."

## 16 July 1940

The Secretary for Mines, David Grenfell, addressed

Parliament.

"Mr Speaker, I fully endorse the proposal for the introduction of a Coal Trade Policy. We must maintain and maximise coal production despite the loss of export markets. It will be better to stockpile coal reserves than to risk any shortage that may adversely affect our war efforts. To this end we will stock five million tons of coal, the speed with which this is achieved being limited only by rail capacity. I assure the House that no coal mine will be closed, unless it is beyond production capability. I pay tribute to Jack Elks, who is here. He knows what pressure was brought on himself and us to abandon the Kent coalfield. They are still working. All honour to those men. You cannot estimate the amount of moral damage that might have been done to this country even if one coalfield was abandoned because of enemy action. Would the panic spread? The men of Kent have helped to steady us by steadying themselves. We must keep all the pits working because we never know what losses we may face."

This battle went on behind closed doors until 1942 but the men were never moved or the pits closed. Despite the bombing which began in September 1940 and intensified until May 1941 the Kent Coalfield maintained full production.

## May 1941

An MFGB Conference was held this month to discuss the wartime restrictions of the 'Essential Works Order' whereby men classified as, or working as, miners were compelled to stay in mining. Furthermore, under this order men accused of absenteeism could be fined or imprisoned by the local National Services Officer. While the MFGB Executive did not like the proposals they felt compelled by wartime needs to support the measure. Kent was against the order and Jack spoke.

"There is no man here today who will feel stronger than I do regarding the need to work together in this time of war, but the proposals put forward are unfair and greatly to the disadvantage to our men. Despite the considerable increase in the cost of living our men's wages have been held back. The owners say they have promised to hold the price of coal at pre-war levels so we must have pre-war pay. Yet our men pay out wartime prices! Then the government ask why we cannot recruit! Only a year ago this same government said unemployed miners should join the armed forces! When mines are disrupted by enemy action the owners are compensated by the government but our men are not, they get no guaranteed wage. Every proposal our Federation puts to government is rejected. Under this order our men cannot leave, must work every day unless turned away and, cannot strike. That, fellow delegates, is slavery. Is not that what we are fighting about – is that not the purpose of this war to avoid? This proposal should be rejected until there is a balance of fairness, or we go in shackles to any future negotiation."

Although the resolution was passed, the high number of votes against strengthened the arguments of the MFGB Executive and later in the year an agreement was reached that tied wages in greater degree to the cost of living. The 'Essential Works Order' was enacted on 15th May. In August of this year it was said in Parliament that the order 'had been applied as a substitution for a sane wages policy and that all it did was make the men sullen, disappointed and angry!' Later it was said that 'there is greater unrest today in the mining industry than there has been for fifty years!' (Hansard 5/8/41)

## January 1942

Dick Sullivan swung his pick at the coalface and felt it bite deep into the seam, he was crouched low, his knees, shins and boots resting in water. There was no choice as the seam was only thirty inches high. The 2S gang alongside him were in similar straits and there was none of the usual banter. He heaved at the pick and the coal loosened, then he recoiled as a gout of water poured from the face and flooded the floor. In twenty years he had never known conditions like this. Half an hour later the seam once again petered out into a pocket of slag. Along the face he could see the bullseye lamp of the deputy appearing, throwing a beam along the workings.

"Get moving you lazy buggers – get that coal out!" Yates had arrived.

"Mr Yates. There's more water coming in and we've hit a pocket of muck. We'll get no coal from that. We'll need an allowance."

The bullseye probed at the face. "Drop it out and get on! You bloody lot do nothing but complain. You'll get no allowance from me!"

Dick stood his ground. "We're not meeting the target. It's not possible in these conditions! We've had short pay for weeks!"

"There's nowt wrong here a bit of graft won't put right – you'll get nowt from me!"

Out over the English Channel four German Heinkel bombers roared low across the waves towards the white cliffs of Kent. It was to be a quick raid, hit the coastline then around in an arc south to Dover, coming in behind the defences and then back to Calais before the Spitfires from Manston Airfield caught them. As the bombers neared the coast they lifted up and banked south. Betteshanger Colliery was in their path and as they passed over the inside plane dropped a stick of bombs. In the yard a Klaxon was sounding an urgent alarm and the surface men ran for cover as three bombs hit the ground and exploded. The fourth bomb hit the engine room and, by some miracle, failed to explode. The damaged machinery ground to a halt and the cages in the shaft stopped, suspended. Far below the ground the bombs were unheard.

An hour later Dick and the 2S gang trudged back to the Boxhall office, at the bottom of the shaft, glad the shift was over. They were wet, miserable and faced with the prospect of another short pay week. They knew there was trouble because the tubs and transport had come to a halt. Dozens of men milled about the roadway. The message came down the line. 'Trouble up top.' 'Cage not working.'

They reached the bank at ten o'clock the following morning. By the time they reached the top, every man on the shift knew of their plight. Billy Powell, the branch secretary was present and took the brunt of their anger. When the men resumed, their shift conditions got even worse and on pay day everything boiled over. Their pay was almost halved and all the men were up in arms. Billy went to see the manager but was shown the door, so he hurried off to call an executive meeting. Jack attended.

Billy explained, "This is not a new problem. It's been going on for weeks but the management won't listen. They say if there are problems, the makeup pay will take care of it, and there's the rub. Those two, Yates and Sylvester, are on the face. They say the men are making claims for nothing. The men won't take it any longer."

"Yes, I'm sorry", said Jack, "we should have got rid of those two when we had the chance. That bugger Mortishead is behind this."

Tudor Davies, the President, looked pensive. "Mortishead as good as told me we're over a barrel – strikes are illegal. That may be his view, but the men won't take it, I see no option but to back them."

Jack gave them a briefing note. "You say there's a meeting with the men this evening. Make sure you let them know the regulations. I will contact Dorman Long and try to get a meeting – ask the men to hold back for the moment."

Isaac Meuthen, 'Joe', broke in. "If we don't act the men will come out in groups. If we act it must be all or none, otherwise the lodge will break up!"

The following Saturday the Lodge Executive was forced to call another meeting as the complaints and demands of the men reached a peak. Spurred on by events the men forced a motion for a strike, notwithstanding Tudor's emotional call for calm. The men would not be denied. Eventually, Joe Meuthen had to put it to the test.

"A motion has been proposed and seconded that we cease work immediately, despite the wartime regulations banning strikes. Those for? Those against? Motion carried, no dissenters."

Tudor rose. "I will convey the immediate withdrawal of notices to the management."

To loud cheers the men dispersed. Tudor sat with Billy and Joe.

"In my fifty years on this earth I have never broken the law. For the last five years I have been a Justice of the Peace. You will excuse me while I go down to the chapel to say a prayer."

"I hope we don't need your prayers, Tudor!" said Billy.

"It is not for us I am going. After thirty-five years down the pit I will ask for new management. The old 'Mould' should be broken and thrown away."

On Monday morning the pit was idle. Sixteen hundred men were out.

Early on Tuesday, Jack received a call. "Dai Grenfell here, Jack. This is bad news! Can you get the men back quickly?" (Dai, David Grenfell, was the State Secretary for Mines.)

"Sorry, Dai. The management will not agree a meeting. Betteshanger management is probably the worst in the country – the men are furious. Can you help?"

"Sorry, Jack. I'm advised that I mustn't intervene. If you can get the men back it will be overlooked but if they're not back by tomorrow, then I have no choice but to invoke the regulations and the legal side will issue summonses."

January 24<sup>th</sup> was a festive day in Canterbury, there would never be another like it until VE day some three years later. Hundreds of men poured into the West Station, they had been assembling since six in the morning; some men had come from as far afield as Nottingham. Two bands were there and the sound of popular music filled the air. Lodge banners were displayed. At nine o'clock the bands formed up and the procession of over one thousand men marched to the town centre, down along by the city wall, past the old 'Invicta' train and on to the High Street. The city through which they marched had been ravaged by bombs and swathes of houses and shops had been flattened. Local citizens stared in wonder at the display. Over it all the cathedral towered, quiet, serene, untouched and unmoved. In its time it had seen kings and emperors pass by. The men were in festive mood and sang as they went along. The throng halted when it reached the Guildhall. Hurriedly summoned police tried to keep the roads clear. When they tried to move the men on, they showed their summonses.

Inside the court, Lord Hawarden, Chairman of the Magistrates, agreed with the clerk the order of summonses.

"What is that noise outside?"

"The men have arrived en masse – with bands, my Lord."

"They intend to make it a carnival do they?"

"It is just their way, my Lord. I do not think they mean disrespect."

"Tell the senior police officer, there will be no mob rule. Now how do you suggest we proceed?"

"These three men are the leaders. There is only one witness."

"I will see the leaders in court. Keep the remainder of the men outside. This whole matter is outrageous. We cannot have anarchy in wartime. Make ready."

Tudor, Joe and Billy stood in the dock as the clerk read out the charges.

".  .  .  .  ..did, contrary to Defence Regulation 2a, break their contracts of employment and aided and abetted other men in this act."

"How do you plead?"

In turn the three men pleaded, 'Not guilty.'

The prosecutor rose. "I call Mr Mortishead to the stand."

Mortishead sat with two of the owners' representatives; he got up and entered the witness box, then took the oath.

"Mr Mortishead, you are the colliery manager at Betteshanger?"

"I am."

"Please give a brief account of the events around the weekend in question."

"On the 11$^{th}$ January the three accused came to me and Mr Davies handed me a note to the effect that all the men were withdrawing their labour as of that day.  Since that day neither they nor any contracted men have been to work."

"Did Mr Davies say anything?"

"He said the dispute, which came about because of low wages and conditions, had not been resolved and the men had voted to strike until the matter was settled and put right."

"Did you tell them that the breaking of contracts was illegal?"

"I did."

Jack got to his feet.  "I am representing the three men, my Lord.  Mr Mortishead, what were the circumstances leading up to the 11$^{th}$ January?"

"I received a number of complaints about the wages and conditions of the men working on face 2S."

"On how many occasions did you receive complaints?"

"Three."

"What was your response?"

"That the wages had been correctly assessed."

"What was the amount of money in dispute?"

"Very small amounts."

Jack displayed a handful of pay packets. "Is it not true that the men concerned suffered wage reductions of between one third and one half of the target wage?"

"Yes."

"Yet you did not feel that a complaint was justified?"

"I did not."

"What were the conditions that were complained of?"

"Water and poor coal."

"Is it not true that for five weeks men had been working on their knees in a constant flow of water at a thirty inch seam? A seam with little coal in it."

"Yes, but that should not have affected their wages. Conditions were taken into account in setting the target."

"Are you saying that for five weeks they did not work hard enough?"

"Yes."

"Have your face managers, the deputies, made formal complaint of lack of effort."

"Yes."

"In writing as is required by agreed procedures?"

"No."

"After the complaints did you see fit to visit the face and talk to the men of 2S?"

"No."

"Did you speak to the men of 2S at all?"

"No."

"When the three accused spoke to you on the occasions mentioned, how did they approach you?"

"I don't understand."

"Did they swear, were they rude, did they threaten or abuse you?"

"No."

"Is it fair to say that they have acted with courtesy and respect at all times?"

"Yes."

"Would you accept that the wages in dispute over the five weeks amount to about three hundred and fifty pounds?"

"Yes, it would be about that."

"How much production has been lost in this dispute?"

"About sixteen thousand tons to date."

"And what would be its value?"

"About eighty thousand pounds."

"Do you consider that a fair exchange?"

"Yes, management . . . .."

"Thank you, Mr Mortishead, that is all!"

The prosecutor rose. "My Lord, despite all that has been said, these three men have clearly broken their contracts by striking in defiance of the Defence Regulation enacted by Parliament. In addition they have acted on behalf of the men. Tudor Davies is the President, Isaac Meuthen is the Chairman and William Powell is the secretary of the local lodge committee. They have acted in both an irresponsible and an illegal way. They are the leaders in the strike."

Jack was on his feet. "My Lord, I protest . . . .."

"Sit down, Mr Elks!"


Lord Hawarden adjusted his robe, then gave the three men in the dock a withering glare. "You have been found guilty as charged. Do you have anything to say, Davies?"

"Yes, my Lord. As President I am bound to represent the men and follow their democratic wishes. If there is a guilt in this, it is mine alone."

"Meuthen?"

"I accept my responsibility as Chairman of our Lodge Committee."

"Powell?"

"Yes, my Lord. Our members have suffered at the hands of a bullying tyrannical management who take advantage of the men at every opportunity. Time without number I am drawn into disputes. The management of this colliery seems to understand only one thing, the only time they respond is when threatened with a withdrawal of labour. We had no choice in this matter and there was no other way."

Lord Hawarden looked severe. "You are clearly the ringleaders in this widespread offence. As officials of the union I expect a greater sense of responsibility from you, there is also a clear duty to dissuade other men from taking illegal action. Davies and Meuthen, I sentence you both to be imprisoned, with hard labour, for a period of one month. Powell, I sentence you to be imprisoned, with hard labour, for two months. Take them down. Court adjourned."

The men refused to go back to work.

Four days later the smoke from Ebby Edwards' pipe billowed around Jack's office. He could always tell when Ebby was agitated because his pipe puffed like a steam engine. Today Ebby was over-agitated. Ebby was the General Secretary of the Miners Federation.

"Dai, this is getting really serious. I can't turn around without being given another request for action. We'll have every mine in Great Britain out soon if there's not a solution. It will be as bad as the General Strike!"

David Grenfell, the State Secretary for Mines, looked pensive. "Why did those bloody magistrates have to send them to prison?"

Ebby's pipe billowed some more. "You know that the only reason the management have agreed to this meeting is because you are here."

"I'm worried," said Dai, "even if we get agreement to a full reinstatement of wages, are we sure the men will go back?"

"No they won't!" Jack said it in sorrow, "Unless Tudor, Joe and Billy are released they'll stand firm."

"What do you suggest I do?"

"Why not ask the Home Secretary to release them in the cause of unity."

Jack handed over a paper. "I've insisted the meeting is with the Dorman Long directors. No Mortishead. Here's the agenda. Now I want Mortishead out and the wage reinstated, that gives us a lever to call the men together."

"What if they stick by the three in prison?"

"Tell the men, promise I mean, that you'll intervene on their behalf. Use the word promise. They know you, Dai – they'll trust you. If the men have gone back, then getting Tudor, Joe and Billy out of prison will help to mend the wounds. I'm sure the government won't want a festering sore on their hands in wartime."

"Right, if we win I'll do that."

"Now," said Jack, "I have a suggestion; when we arrive you can ask for a few minutes of private discussion – leave me and Ebby outside. In so many words threaten to close the pit down. The only reason it's open is because up to now the men have agreed to that as you well know. Say that it will be of more use to the country if Betteshanger is closed and the miners are put to work in more productive pits. You can tell them that the Federation and our Association are in total support of this. That should frighten the life out of them. And all because of that idiot Mortishead."

Ebby's pipe flared. "I'd be happy with that, I can be back on Friday and hold the other fields off. 'Twill do no good to impugn the loyalty of our men by letting strikes spread."

"Agreed," said Dai, "but no mention of this at the meeting once it's officially underway."

The next day the men returned to work and on the 2$^{nd}$ February, Tudor, Joe and Billy returned to a tumultuous welcome at the Welfare Club while Mortishead was preparing to pack his bags.

## June 1942

During the winter of 1941/2 coal supplies were failing to meet the country's needs and there was a widening gap between consumption and production estimated for the future. There was considerable comment in the newspapers that the shortfall was due to slack working and absenteeism. The average age of working miners was high and there was great wastage due to death, retirement, disablement, industrial diseases and general strain. Men now outside the industry did not want to return to an industry they had grown to dislike and detest, after the years of grinding poverty in the 1920's and 1930's. Working difficulties and conditions of work still caused daily problems and in May, for example, there were 86 strikes lasting only 2 or 3 days each but resulting in the loss of 58,000 days of work. The wartime government proposed steps to take greater control of the industry by taking direct charge of operations, ministry powers to give directions to management, and advisory boards to obtain increased production. The MFGB wanted nationalisation or as near as possible to that aim and put forward proposals themselves, but these were rejected. There arose severe pressure from the mining districts for better wages and as a result a Board of Investigation was set up to allow representations. Jack attended with the MFGB delegation and gave evidence on the second day. When he was called he stood. The Board Chairman, the Master of the Rolls, spoke.

"You are John Elks, Secretary of the Kent Mine Workers Association and a member of the Federation Advisory Committee?"

"I am."

"Do you speak for the Kent Miners or more widely?"

"On a Federation basis, my Lord, however, the points I wish to make could apply to all or a single district."

"Proceed."

"I will not go over the ground covered already by Mr Edwards, but I do wish to make a few explanatory statements to emphasise some of the points made so far. Coal mining is a very labour intensive industry, so if we produce 220 million tons per annum from 700,000 men, we will need 860,000 to get the extra 50,000,000 tons required to reach the target of 270,000,000 tons. While increased mechanisation will assist in meeting the target it cannot be brought to bear quickly enough to be a benefit, except over a number of years.

After many years of poor treatment many of the young men left the mines in the early years of the war and we are left with an ageing population of miners. Now, due to accidents, illness, retirement and so on we are losing 25,000 men each year. The sons of these men are not covered by the Essential Works Order Act. They have seen the treatment of their fathers over the years and want no part of this industry. And why should they when there are better paid and less dangerous jobs available? In the last six months 36,000 men, ex-miners, have been transferred back to the mines and, in the process, had to take a severe pay cut. What good are 36,000 resentful pressed men tied by the Act to work in a pit they detest and despise, most of them left because they were unemployed, not wanted by the industry. Safety has improved slightly over the years but still, even today, 1 man in 7 will suffer serious injury in his working life and this in an industry that pays 25% less in wages than a man in shipbuilding. The comparison is worse with other industries.

Comments have been made that the men are lazy yet the tonnage output per man has increased and the miners are averaging 5.5 shifts per week. All these facts are in the documents we have submitted.

On a purely practical basis let me add the following points. The men have to pay for their own working tools, in some areas they even pay for the dynamite that is used to get at the coal! Many pits still do not have baths and those that do have to be paid for by the men.

There are none here today who would say that coal production is unimportant. Quite the reverse in fact because we know that it is vital to a multitude of industries and domestic users. But how do I answer a man who tells me that it is not true because, if it were, he would be better treated and more fairly paid. While meeting our wage claim on a national basis will not solve all our problems overnight, it is an essential first step in raising morale, making the industry more attractive and reducing grievances. Thank you."

Two weeks later the Board awarded the miners substantial pay rises and, most important, a national minimum weekly wage. This minimum was related to the number of shifts worked but it was a breakthrough from the previous low minimum based on a shift.

## July 1942

Following the success of the June Board of Inquiry the MFGB Executive Committee decided to tackle the issue of a single union. At the July Annual Conference a resolution was put forward to allow the Committee to draft details for a form of change of the organisation. The issue was hotly debated and there was strong pressure against from the Nottingham delegate, George Spencer, the man who had originally set up an employer's union in that district. Jack was the last delegate to speak for the resolution at the end of the debate.

"Fellow delegates, my view on the formation of a single union has been made known to you many times over the years. That view has never wavered. A single union is my fervent desire and is exceeded only by my wish for a nationalised industry. It has been said time and again that only a district can deal with a district matter. Opponents of the single union say it will take over every minutiae of every pit and must therefore fail. It is nonsense to suggest that the districts will shrivel away, for who else will deal with the compensation claims, evictions, unfair dismissals, local welfare arrangements, community affairs, local councils and so forth? The executive of a national union will deal with national issues, national policy and national politics. THE ONLY ISSUE WE HAVE NEED TO CONSIDER IS THE ORGANISATION – NOT THE STRATEGY.

Why do you think the owners have been so successful in their frustration of our just claims for all these years? WHY DID THEY HELP SET UP THE SPENCER UNIONS? They present a solid face and allow dissension to divide our force and arguments. I wish you had all been at the recent Board of Inquiry to see and hear our Secretary, Ebby Edwards, put our case and which was so ably supported by the vast range of facts and figures produced by our Executive Committee and the Labour Research Department. And with what result? The largest increase in pay in our history and the acceptance of a guaranteed weekly wage. Everywhere I go our men say to me 'WHERE IS THE NATIONAL UNION?' Well it is in our grasp, we must not let it slip away. ONE DAY IT WILL BE COUNTED AMONGST OUR GREATEST ACHIEVEMENTS. Let today be a celebration, VOTE FOR THIS PROPOSAL. I SO MOVE."

At the end of the debate there was almost universal support for the proposal, the principle of a single union had been won. Progress, however, came slowly and it was not until July 1944 that the Conference endorsed the single union and the National Union of Mineworkers was formed on 1st January 1945. But Jack did not mind, the 'single union' debate was finally won. Now it was up to the bureaucrats to cross the t's and dot the i's.

## 1944

The great Allied landing in Normandy had started on 6th June and there was great hope that the war in Europe would be over soon. Out of that optimism a large number of government initiatives were set in motion to survey the present industrial position and to make plans for peace.

Early in July, Jack received a telephone call from the Ministry of Fuel and Power. His clerk answered. "It's the Minister for you, Mr Elks. Will you take it?" He held his hand over the mouthpiece. Jack nodded and held his hand out, you did not refuse a call from Gwilym Lloyd George, the Minister.

"Yes, Minister, Jack Elks here, how can I help you?"

"Good morning, Jack, I am issuing instructions for a committee to be set up to do a survey of the Kent Coalfield. I intend to nominate you – I wanted you to nominate two members of your Association so we get a good balance of views."

"What are the terms of reference?"

"Essentially to determine what should be done to make the fullest use of the coal resources of the area after the war."

"Who will be the Chairman?"

"Sir John Dalton, the Regional Controller."

"That's a good choice, he's a far-sighted man. May I make a suggestion?"

"Yes, of course."

"We've battled with the owners for years to improve facilities. Say we find we need more men then we'll need more homes. More homes means more children. If the terms of reference do not specify we look at housing and services then the survey will be limited to owners' matters, not the wider picture."

"I will put that to Sir John and let you see the terms before we proceed."

Sir John Dalton called the meeting to order. "Gentlemen, you have all got a copy of the geological survey in front of you. I ask Mr Dines, the district Geologist, to give us a summary."

Dines got to his feet. "I have a few charts to show you. Coal deposits are proved within the boundaries shown. Coal reserves

261

in the field, which are economically viable to produce at today's costings, amount to 2000 million tons. Present output is under two million tons per annum. A peacetime market is extrapolated to reach four million tons and that is possible from existing mines. At that level of production there are reserves for five hundred years."

Mr Magee, Owners' Representative, raised his hand. "Mr Chairman, on behalf of the owners I must state that it is not our intention to raise output above the pre-war level of two point two million tons. The owners have made a careful assessment of both production and sales potential."

The Chairman peered over his glasses. "Can the secretary to the owners explain why?"

Mr Bandgett responded. "Yes, Mr Chairman, we have made detailed costings and must say that it is not possible to raise capital to allow expansion beyond that point."

The Chairman made a note. "Have you assessed the capital requirements for, say, four million tons?"

"We have."

Jack was pleased, if the owners could not find the capital it reinforced the argument for nationalisation. "Mr Chairman, on a point of order, do not our terms of reference state we can ignore financial limitations in considering how to get greater output. We may look at the finance to meet a higher level, but do not have to consider how it may be raised."

"That is how I see it – does anyone have any comment?"

Jack continued "It may help the meeting if Mr Dines can state categorically that four million tons per annum is achievable and that is the potential market."

"Mr Dines?"

Dines explained that four million was the output achievable by existing mines, beyond that new shafts might be necessary. Coal demand after the war would not be met unless all mines increased capacity by at least one hundred per cent. The potential market for Kent coal in the south east was ten times existing output but it was considered impossible to reach that level in less than ten to fifteen years.

"Is everyone satisfied?" The Chairman looked around the meeting. "Mr Harley, you are the consulting engineer for the owners. Do you agree with Mr Dines?"

"Yes, I cannot answer if the market can absorb the four million tons but the field is capable of doubling output if mechanised."

"Good!" said the Chairman. "We will proceed on the basis that the target output is four million tons."

Jack stepped in. "Mr Chairman, Mr Magee said that an assessment whereby that level might be reached had already been concluded. Cannot that information be given to this committee to save time. The Minister is pressing us to report early."

"Mr Magee, will you help us in this matter?"

"Yes, Mr Chairman. I could make our report available but that will make open our commercial secrets. This is a matter for the owners. This question of doubling output is not a matter for workers' representatives. I ask that they withdraw when that is discussed."

The Chairman sighed. Jack responded. "Mr Chairman, I was assured that this committee was a broad church. It will have no meaning unless all members participate equally. Perhaps the owners have something to hide but I do not see what that could possibly be."

Magee returned to the fray. "We must retain commercial secrets, not open them up to any Tom, Dick or Harry!"

By Jack's side, Billy Powell spoke up. "Mr Chairman, I do resent the implication that we cannot, or will not, maintain secrets. There may be a need for confidentiality but I am sure the Chair will direct on that."

Magee put the boot in. "I do not see how a man convicted of a criminal offence and imprisoned can be trusted!"

Jack was quick off the mark. "It is true that Mr Powell has been in prison but he was appointed here by the Minister, and approved, as a man with a deep knowledge of mining and the community that serves it. He has been a Lodge Secretary for ten years and is implicitly trusted by all our members. Furthermore, he was convicted for a breach of a wartime regulation arising from a strike precipitated by men like Magee who were convinced the men could be abused safely, because of that regulation."

Magee was standing, red in the face, wagging hand raised. The Chairman intervened. "There will be calm. Sit down!"

He looked at Magee. "Mr Magee, you will apologise otherwise I shall ask the Minister to remove your name."

"I regret what I said to Mr Powell, it was not meant to be personal!"

Jack sniffed,. "It sounded bloody personal from my seat."

"Gentlemen please. Let us get on with the meeting. We will proceed as follows, one, how to increase capacity? Two, what services will we need to meet it? Three infrastructure needs such as housing? Four, Welfare. Any comments?"

Billy responded. "After the events of this meeting I do not see how we can omit better industrial relations. I ask that it be included under item 3."

The Chairman glared at Magee. "Yes, I will make time for that! Will you or will you not make your reports available to us?"

Mr Bandgett spoke up. "Mr Chairman. I will make them available for the next meeting."

Jack was pleased. The owners' representatives had upset the Chairman and that had almost certainly biased him in their favour. The results would almost certainly assist the case for nationalisation; and thanks to Billy they had got industrial relations on the agenda. Old Dai Powell would have been proud of his son if he had lived to see the day. Jobs would be safe for a long time with 500 years of reserves under the ground.

When the committee report was produced two months later, every single one of the Association's suggestions for improvements had been accepted. A commitment to the coalfield, a sustained target for increased growth, more housing and better welfare, including hospital facilities and rehabilitation measures for injured men and so on. He decided it had been a master stroke putting Billy Powell's name on the list. The Committee had been so polite to him after that first day,. Billy had taken every advantage of it. As Jack considered, 'If that silly bugger Magee hadn't reacted I would have had to provoke him!'

After the first meeting Jack argued that additional housing stock should not be increased significantly in the villages adjacent to the collieries as this created isolated communities; miners should be more dispersed, particularly in and around Canterbury, Ramsgate, Dover and Deal. The true value of that would not be realised for another forty years. He wanted the miners to become a part of Kent.

## 8 May 1945

The Welfare Club was packed to the doors but the greatest danger was the real possibility that the bar would run out of beer. Jack had an honoured place at the corner table near the bar, attended by the Lodge Committee.

"Another drink, Jack?"

"Aye, I'll have a scotch, thanks."

On the stage the President, Tudor Davies, tapped the microphone and it 'clinked' in response.

"Ladies and Gentlemen."

"Get on with it, Tudor!"

"I will – I will – as soon as there is a moment's quiet."

Slowly a sort of quiet prevailed.

"As you all know – the Germans are beaten. Today is 'Victory in Europe' day. Thanks to God it is nearly over – our men, our families and our country are safe once more. Soon the lights will go on. God bless you all."

*'I'm going to get lit up*
*When the lights go on in London.*
*I'm going to get lit up*
*As I've never been before.*
*You will find me on the tiles,*
*You will find me wreathed in smiles.*
*I'm going to get so lit up*
*I'll be visible for miles! . . . . . .'*

## 1946

On a glorious fine day in May, Jack made his way to Deal to meet three old friends for a drink at the miners Welfare Club at Mill Hill. The three were waiting when he arrived, Tudor Davies, Billy Powell and Joe Meuthen. Billy ordered a round of drinks and they retired to a corner table. Billy raised his glass. "Cheers! Now Jack, have you come to tell us we're all to go back to prison to finish our sentence, now the war is over."

Jack savoured his whisky before replying. "No – nothing like that lads. I've a letter from the Ministry. There's to be a special Victory Parade in London on 8th June and they want us to send some men to take part in the march. Now, the men must be underground workers. I will read from the letter, - 'to be clad in smart overalls, new pit helmets complete with head lamps – to represent the hard working miners who worked on the home front.' I thought it would be nice for you three to go."

Billy could barely conceal his mirth. "Is this the same Ministry that summonsed us and had us sent to prison." Tudor shook his head in wonderment.

"It is," said Jack, "further, you have to be at the assembly at 6 am, must take your own snap and won't disperse until 6 pm. It will be a long shift. I thought it might show that everything is forgiven and forgotten."

Billy and Tudor were about to burst out when Joe Meuthen

spoke quickly.

"Thank you, Jack. I would take it as a great honour to go and represent our district. Someone has to show that we are as loyal and as patriotic as any other and we love our country. Think of all those men in our pits, many pressed into service like the 'Bevin Boys', who have died and been injured at work in the last six years. Those who will suffer the silicosis and the hardships to come. I will march for all who did not make it through as well as those here today and with proper respect. Put you my name down, Jack."

So Isaac 'Joe' Meuthen marched in the great parade.

## 1 January 1947

Cold biting wind swept in from the North Sea. Overnight the temperature had dropped to well under zero and all the puddles were frozen. There was every sign of more snow and the wind cut through any clothing. Jack was well muffled with overcoat, scarf, gloves and hat. Next to him stood Billy Powell, both were staring at the large noticeboard, placed at the entrance to Betteshanger Colliery.

'THIS COLLIERY IS NOW MANAGED BY THE NATIONAL COAL BOARD ON BEHALF OF THE PEOPLE'

Billy banged his hands together. "That's a fine notice, Jack, I never thought we would see the day."

"Aye, I've been waiting over forty years. I lost hope in the thirties – there seemed no possibility."

"Have you heard who's to be on the Area Board?"

"Well for a start there's no one from the industry – it looks like jobs for the boys. Lots of Generals, Admirals and so forth." Jack shook his head in sadness.

"The men will not be best pleased," Billy sounded as

disappointed as Jack, "do you think it will make things better?"

Jack walked back to the car. "Only time will tell, Billy. In the meantime, we had best be on our guard – that's the same ground management in there."

"We're getting the coal out but there are no wagons to take it away!"

"Are we organised for Sunday, Billy. Is the band ready?"

Billy nodded.

## 5 January 1947

Jack stood by the Bandmaster. "Are you ready, Mr Cotterel?"

"All ready, Jack."

A column of over 1,000 men, women and children, well wrapped up against the cold, snaked back down the road in Betteshanger village.

"Will you do me a favour, Mr Cotterel? Step off with 'Blaze Away'. You won't remember '26 but then we marched to defeat – this time we've won."

Jack walked back to the head of the column where an elderly man stood waiting. George Walker was 72, the oldest man working underground.

"Are you ready to raise the flag, George?"

Pride was keeping George warm. "Too right, Jack. I've waited over sixty years for this day. It will be a fitting year to retire."

"Take them off, Billy." He waved down the line. "Heads up, plenty of pride, lads – lots of pride."

Jack tried not to flinch as the band struck up, he had been to the Snowdown celebrations the night before and the whisky had flowed. Later there would be more celebrations at Tilmanstone. There must be no holding back, Jack decided, a weekend like this did not come to many men in their lifetime.

The winter of 1946/47 was to be the coldest for 53 years.

## 1950

Jack was ill for several months in the period before May of this year but he stubbornly resisted any attempt to reduce his work hours or drinking. The doctor told him time and time again to cut down or face an uncertain future. It did no good, he could not, and would not, change the habits of a lifetime. Though he retired officially on 30th April, he could not give up and had negotiated several advisory jobs, both with the union and the National Coal Board. On 1st May he went to Sandwich, in Kent, to attend a meeting. During that meeting he collapsed and had to go to bed. The next morning he was so bad that an ambulance was called and he was taken to the Buckland Hospital in Dover. At noon on that day, 2nd May, he died. His death and the date of his funeral were widely publicised. The newspaper had a picture of him wearing his grey 'Homburg' hat, he would have been pleased with that.

On the day of his funeral all the Kent Colliery Bands led the cortege. Fifty six bandsmen in full uniform marched slowly from the Union Offices in Maison Dieu Road followed by over twenty official cars decked with hundreds of wreaths. They slow marched to the High Street, then up and on towards the cemetery at St James. The miners were seeing to their own, there would be no holding back. As the procession made its way up the High Street a passing Army Officer stepped to the kerbside and saluted till it had passed. It seemed to be an offering of peace as well as respect.

When the cortege reached the cemetery the already large crowd of mourners was joined by larger numbers of miners who had come to pay their final respects. Quiet, sombre men of serious face wearing black armbands. There were so many they overflowed into the road along the boundary wall. The band played Handel's 'Deep Harmony' and this was followed by the last post. Then the official mourners went back to the Union Offices in Maison Dieu Road where many fine words were said in Jack's memory. All of these things were said. 'He was a great man!' 'Devoted to the welfare of others.' 'His loss will be immense, he was a wise counsellor.' 'He realised how harmony and true charity will bring peace and prosperity not only to our industry, but to all mankind.'

Back at the graveside, after the official cars had gone, large numbers of simple working men queued at his graveside to stand in silence for a few moments and some laid small bundles of flowers. They hung about talking quietly amongst themselves, sorrowful at the passing of a man they considered a friend. There were no fine words or orations. Jack was with his own, the miners.

Late in the afternoon a lone woman entered the cemetery and stood looking at the flowers. There were no tears in her eyes but she was sad and dignified. She placed a small wreath with the others, the card was simply marked 'F'. She had wanted to write 'In loving memory, Florrie' but had felt it might cause offence. Silently she said goodbye and promised Jack she would care for their son's grave, the boy who had lived such a few years. Then she walked away.

On the morning he died, Jack might have thought it ironic that he was where he was, but he was unconscious through the morning. The hospital to which they had taken him was the Buckland Hospital. Before the war it had been the Workhouse. The place to which he had sent Alice and her son all those years ago.

## EPILOGUE

This story was not written to condemn or condone. Rather it is to show how people lived and how the circumstances of the time affected lives years ago. We are not only the product of our childhood but also the times in which we live. In the period written about, mainly from 1890 to 1945, working class people, whatever their ability or aspirations were expected to settle for their lot in life. Education was rudimentary and secondary education beyond many people's pockets. Not until about 1945 was secondary education made free for all. Throughout Jack's lifetime housing, working and living conditions were uniformly poor, even disgraceful. Men organised themselves because of the exploitation and conditions of work enforced by the entrepreneurs of the day. These matters were often an affront to people's senses, safety and wellbeing. Malnutrition among the poor was commonplace and, as a result, they suffered poor health. This occurred in the 20$^{th}$ Century, not vaguely in 'times gone by'. From 1920 until 1950 Jack put great political and personal effort into his fight for the miners. Many men in his position sold out but, to his credit, he never did; if so he might have died a rich man.

From about 1920 the local newspapers made constant weekly reports of events in the Kent Coalfield. Accident, injuries and death to miners were commonplace. Almost monthly there were court battles over evictions, industrial diseases, bad employment practices and compensation payments. Safety, or lack of it, was always an issue. Throughout it all the fortitude and hope of simple men shines through. The miners even had to subscribe to the building of pithead baths so they could go home clean! And then pay to use them!! History shows that vested interests, such as the great landowners and monied classes, gave nothing willingly. All was given grudgingly and with the utmost reluctance over scores of years. Looking back, I can only wonder that men did not revolt and sweep it all aside; brushed off all that hindered progress toward the creation of a more just and humanitarian society. It is to the credit of our forebears that they achieved great progress through the ballot box and often the only weapon they had – dignified and intelligent argument.

Today there are many things we take for granted. The National Health Service, non means tested National Insurance, free Secondary education, a national bank in the form of the Bank of England, the National Assistance Act, legal aid for the poor, the Citizens Advice Bureau and so on were ultimately achieved through the socialist ambitions of men like Jack and the many, many others with like-minded ideals.

Jack Elks was my Grandfather, my father was Albert, the third son. Because Jack was on his own during part of World War Two he lived with my mother and father from 1943 to 1946, but he rarely spoke to me; we had no real grandfather/grandson relationship. His life seemed to exist outside the family. It was through the writing of this book that I have come to know him and, so perhaps to an understanding that he did not want my love – nor did he get it! So we both lost, though I am sure he did not know it. I have no personal memory of my grandmother, Lizzie, who died when I was two years old, but in tribute to her memory I thank her for the gift of a loving father.

Looking back, be grateful for the courage, endurance, fortitude and faith of those men and women long ago. They would be pleased to know they had not been forgotten. I can think of no greater tribute to a life than that men weep at our passing, as they did for Jack in May 1950.

BRIAN A F ELKS